CHAUCER STUDIES VII

CHAUCER'S DREAM POETRY:
SOURCES AND ANALOGUES

CHAUCER STUDIES

I

MUSIC IN THE AGE OF CHAUCER

Nigel Wilkins

II

CHAUCER'S LANGUAGE AND THE PHILOSOPHERS'
TRADITION

J. D. Burnley

III

ESSAYS ON TROILUS AND CRISEYDE

Edited by Mary Salu

IV

CHAUCER SONGS

Nigel Wilkins

V

CHAUCER'S BOCCACCIO

Sources of Troilus *and the* Knight's
and Franklin's Tales

Edited and translated by N. R. Havely

VI

STYLE AND SYNTAX IN CHAUCER'S POETRY

G. H. Roscow

CHAUCER'S DREAM POETRY: SOURCES AND ANALOGUES

Edited and translated by
B. A. WINDEATT

D. S. BREWER · ROWMAN & LITTLEFIELD

First published 1982 by D. S. Brewer
240 Hills Road, Cambridge
an imprint of Boydell & Brewer Ltd, PO Box 9,
Woodbridge, Suffolk IP12 3DF
and Rowman & Littlefield Inc, 81 Adams Drive,
Totowa, New Jersey N.J. 07512, USA

British Library Cataloguing in Publication Data
Windeatt, B. A.
    Chaucer's Dream Poetry: Sources and
    Analogues.—(Chaucer studies; 7)
    1.   Chaucer, Geoffrey—Sources
    I.   Title   II. Series
    821'.1   PR1912

ISBN 0-85991-072-5

Photoset in Great Britain by
Rowland Phototypesetting Ltd, Bury St Edmunds, Suffolk
and printed by St Edmundsbury Press,
Bury St Edmunds, Suffolk

Contents

Abbreviations

BD	*The Book of the Duchess*
HF	*The House of Fame*
LGW	*The Legend of Good Women*
PF	*The Parliament of Fowls*

BJRL	*Bulletin of the John Rylands Library*
CFMA	*Classiques français du moyen âge*
ChauR	*The Chaucer Review*
HLF	*Histoire littéraire de la France*
JEGP	*Journal of English and Germanic Philology*
MLN	*Modern Language Notes*
MLR	*Modern Language Review*
MP	*Modern Philology*
MS	*Mediaeval Studies*
PMLA	*Publications of the Modern Language Association of America*
PQ	*Philological Quarterly*
SATF	*Société des anciens textes français*
SP	*Studies in Philology*

All reference to Chaucer is to *The Works of Geoffrey Chaucer*, ed. F. N. Robinson, 2nd edn (London, 1957).

Preface

The very variety of the sources and analogues that lie behind Chaucer's dream poetry – which will prevent detailed individual consideration here of those sources – emphasizes how Chaucer's dream poems represent the outcome of a poetic process that has distilled a whole range of influences, models and allusions. While some pieces in the present volume are best considered as analogues, many others were themselves evidently very much part of Chaucer's reading, for his own poems both recall their diction and often embody, yet reformulate, some of their distinctive scenes and moments. In this way, Chaucer's relation to the sources and background of his dream poems can reveal something of the poet at work, and suggest how a process of re-creative translation and refashioning produces poems that breathe traditions yet speak with originality.

Chaucer's approach to the sources of inspiration for the dream poems is thus a 'translation' which involves a number of different types of poetic interaction with his own reading. In his dream poems Chaucer is not generally found following a received narrative source, as he may be broadly characterized as doing in some *Canterbury Tales* or in the *Troilus:* in such works the narrative original offers a line around which Chaucer's own elaborating and adapting imagination works in 'translation'. But in the dream poems – as will appear from comparison with the sources translated in this volume – Chaucer's imagination is not drawn to extended imitation or translation of the whole narrative line of any single source. Instead, Chaucer's mind has evidently seized on some of the more expressive, more striking, and more strongly visualized component scenes or sections of his sources, and then puts them together within his own distinctive forms. Thus, in *The Book of the Duchess*, echoes are clearly heard of scenes and elements in four poems by Machaut (*Le Jugement dou Roy de Behaingne, Le Dit de la Fonteinne Amoureuse, Remede de Fortune*, and *Le Dit dou Lyon*), and one by Froissart (*Le Paradys d'Amours*), not to mention other influences. In this way, Chaucer's 'translation' can range from an imaginatively selective response to the larger movement of his sources down to specifically focussed 'spot' quotations. It is a type of creative translation that distinguishes itself from its sources by its power both to co-ordinate and to crystallize.

It is through this characteristically selective power that Chaucer's mind grasps what is best in his French sources, and avoids what seem to us their weaknesses in narrative and structure. Although Machaut is now recognized as an important composer, and Froissart has justly been celebrated for his *Chronicles*, their poetry and that of their period is less accessible to general modern appreciation. Yet for Chaucer the works of Machaut will have been a major part of contemporary courtly poetry.[1] Although modern taste has been

ix

sophisticated into different directions and expectations, it is still possible to feel the courtly sophistication of Machaut's work: its great technical accomplishment and poise, to be expected from such a musicianly poet, is the formal expression of preoccupations and material that gracefully celebrate, as they delicately explore, a world of courtly feeling.[2] In such a poetry the parts may tend to be more memorable and expressive to us than the whole: the continuity of the whole as the narrator's experience exists, but not forcefully. And if the extant pattern of his borrowing suggests Chaucer's own assessment of these poems, then this is also the effect they have had on him. In a musical sense, he has borrowed from the French poems not their idea of the whole work so much as certain movements and motifs, introductions, transitions and developments, which have been subjected to the essentially combinative power of Chaucer's poetic imagination, and emerge in contexts which can release further meaning in them.

That a significant part of Chaucer's power to innovate-through-borrowing lies in his ability to co-ordinate what he has borrowed and absorbed can be seen in his structuring of the *Book of the Duchess*. The framework of the narrator's dream and his sleeplessness stem from Froissart's *Paradys*, and his reading of the affecting story of Ceyx and Alcyone recalls the use of that story in the young lord's overheard lament in the *Fonteinne Amoureuse*. Here, in establishing the setting of his own poem, Chaucer's imagination has seized on relatively small but arresting parts of lengthy poems by Machaut and Froissart, and brings them together, co-ordinating them to set a scene which in its emphases becomes very much Chaucer's own. This power of co-ordinating his sources into something individual emerges in the conceit of an insomniac bribing the God of Sleep with promises of a sumptuous bed (*BD*, 240ff.). The idea of a plea to Morpheus is rather fleetingly present near the start of Froissart's *Paradys* (p. 42) and the notion of giving a feather bed is more specifically but still briefly mentioned by the lord in *Fonteinne Amoureuse* (p. 33). The joke about the bed in *BD* may seem a piece of distinctively 'Chaucerian' humour, yet to feel a tinge of disappointment in discovering that Chaucer has not written these lines without suggestion from other men's writing is to underestimate how in his dream poems Chaucer can repeatedly make something personal and distinctive by realizing the potential of what he found in his reading. Both Machaut and Froissart had thrown away the idea of bribing Morpheus: they do not use it in a way that makes anything of it. By contrast, Chaucer's imagination has seized on this promising item. It is he who has expanded it with characteristic relish for the details of the bedding, so as to realize its comic potential.

Although Chaucer's mind may well have retained the germ of the idea from the French poems, through the new emphasis with which he handles it the idea is given much greater effectiveness. At such a moment Chaucer the 'translator' is both borrowing and originating. Knowledge of the French poems that were in Chaucer's mind should not diminish admiration for Chaucer's originality simply understood, but can focus attention on the sphere in which his originality really operates, by laying bare to us some of the process of co-ordinating, extending, crystallizing, by which Chaucer's imagination sees how much more he can do with the materials left by the French poets.

This co-ordinating and re-creating process can further be seen in the way that Chaucer's imagination has absorbed and then made his own use of the two Machaut poems most extensively drawn upon for the *Book of the Duchess*: the *Behaingne* and the *Remede de Fortune*. The *Behaingne* is one of Machaut's poems in which the narrative context is realized not only with exceptional effectiveness, but is also very well united with the thematic, emotional preoccupations of the poem. The chance meeting in a forest of the lady, absent-minded with grief, and the sorrowing, jilted knight allows them to move into their recollections in a way that gives the poem a shape in the reader's mind. Behind the chance meeting in the forest with the preoccupied Man in Black, there lies Chaucer's familiarity – proved by close verbal echoes – with the whole dramatic setting of *Behaingne*. Thus, the knight's drawing out of information from the lady in her grief is the influential 'shape' of a scene that lies behind the narrator's first moments of meeting with Chaucer's Man in Black (p. 5). And many details of expression of feeling in Machaut's speeches for knight and lady are taken over into *BD*: the Man in Black is given lines from both Machaut's knight and lady, for the French knight's recollections of his lady in a retrospect of affection are combined in Chaucer with the lady's devotion to a lover separated in death (see pp. 5, 6, 7ff.).

Again – at first sight – it might seem that an arresting, immediate quality of a memorable personal experience in Chaucer's account of the encounter with the knight is diminished in force of originality when we discover that a quite complex tissue of recollected scenes and settings from Chaucer's French reading lies behind this part of *BD*. For indeed, there are other allusions than to the *Behaingne*: some aspects of the meeting with a young knight and hearing his complaint of separation recall the position of the narrator in the *Fonteinne Amoureuse*, while the setting recalls the *Roman de la Rose*. A number of literary accounts of meetings, natural settings, and overheard complaints evidently lies behind the meeting with the Black Knight. Yet this does not diminish the essential originality with which Chaucer has coordinated what he has absorbed from his French reading. Chaucer's account of the meeting with the Man in Black remains more striking than its French parallels because of the way Chaucer has distilled and concentrated into a relatively briefer space some of the most powerful aspects of the situations in the French poems.

Chaucer's ability so fluently to seize on important features of his sources and to recombine them suggests an easy familiarity with the French poems.[3] That familiarity is borne out not only by the frequency of direct verbal echoes in English of French lines and diction, but also by the way these echoes are scatteringly woven into Chaucer's writing, by no means in their original sequence and order in the French works. This is particularly clear from the instances of Chaucer's borrowings cited as footnotes to their original contexts within the translations of the *Behaingne* and *Remede*. Machaut's graceful style offered some model expressions of courtly feeling and experience, which Chaucer evidently knew familiarly and did not feel the need to improve on in themselves, although he makes free to use them in his own contexts. As he composes relevant speeches in *BD*, appropriate phrases and lines from the *Behaingne* and *Remede* bubble up to the surface of his writing. In Chaucer's use of the close verbal texture of both these French poems the poet's imagination can be observed playing over the familiar verbal surface of

Machaut's works and recycling their resources by sorting and recombining their lines and phrases within the English poem.[4]

The thoroughness with which Chaucer adapts what he takes over is shown in his use of the opening of the *Remede de Fortune*. The original passage offers some analysis of courtly experience and feeling, and the majority of significant points are found recombined and re-sorted into the Man in Black's recollection of his own experience in love (p. 58ff.). Yet while the very words and phrases of the French original may re-emerge as translated particles carried over and embodied within the English poem, this very closeness to Chaucer's sources exists in terms that show how Chaucer controls his closest verbal borrowings by his control of the context in which those 'borrowings' are deployed. Little could be more intrinsically conventional than the Black Knight's description of his lady and his courtship, and his reproaches of Fortune. These sentiments – in many cases a patchwork of Machaut's phrases – are revivified by context. It is the 'voicing' of such phrases by the persona of the Man in Black in an elegiac context that allows what he says to seem both universal yet tinged and edged with a particular and individual suffering.

Chaucer's reformulating of his 'borrowings' through the contexts he gives them is part of that way in his dream poems – as comparison with the sources shows – that some of his most creative adaptation of the original materials lies in the co-ordinating of new structures.[5] Most of Chaucer's other writing involves a stronger narrative line than the dream poetry. By contrast, at the opening of the dream poems there is no familiar story or tale to be heard anew. Instead, the experience of the 'I' of the poem is to unfold, and the structure of the poem will embody his progress, and perhaps his confusions. Structure may consequently be a very real and immediate reflection of the dreamer's progress, when the way ahead is not necessarily clear either to him or the reader. Comparison with Chaucer's sources and analogues does provide some point of contrast for the effectiveness of Chaucer's way of thematically co-ordinating structure. While the structure of Machaut's long poems is often a graceful and understated thematic progression which may easily nowadays be underestimated or overlooked, the inevitable use in this present volume of selections and extracts from some of them is actually quite true to the more discernible use that Chaucer makes of the French poems.

For the sources and analogues – however many scenes and sequences they may have suggested – will not provide an analogue for that reinterpreting which is expressed through the structure of Chaucer's poems, where juxtaposition and contrast form part of the cumulative meaning of poems like *The Parliament of Fowls* and *The House of Fame*. Such concern for structure is evidently reflected in the devices that Chaucer does choose to use from his French reading, especially in those moments of transition and connection that evidently caught his interest in his sources.

The interlude with the little dog in *BD* is a good instance of how Chaucer draws on his reading as he shows his own concern for an effective moment of transition in his poems.[6] Comparison with Chaucer's sources once again reveals how what may seem at first sight a vividly, personally observed experience, actually has its analogues in earlier poems. Yet to register how much more Chaucer makes of what he receives is to credit Chaucer with the power to promote a sense of vivid personal observation which is in itself poetic originality. The episode with the little dog represents a crystallizing in Chaucer's mind of possibly as many as three separate incidents in two Machaut poems. For the dog itself, there is of course the moment with the lady's *chiennet* in the *Behaingne* (p. 17), but on to that Chaucer has evidently grafted aspects of other scenes. Chaucer retains the idea of the dog as a means of contact and transition between the poet and his superiors, but the yapping and snapping little dog is instead endowed with some of the friendly behaviour of the lion who guides the poet from one setting to another in the *Dit dou Lyon* (pp.67–8). Yet since the lion deliberately offers to lead the poet, a more general resemblance to the way Chaucer's whelp draws on the poet after it by fleeing from him can perhaps be seen in the way the narrator follows the song-bird at the opening of the *Behaingne*. Machaut's scenes with the dog and the lion have great liveliness and charm – it is no surprise that they should evidently have lodged in Chaucer's mind – and it is no disparagement of Machaut to see how Chaucer, by fusing together what were separate moments in Machaut and superimposing the one on to the other, shows an imagination which can be fresh and original even where its component raw material is 'borrowed'.

The two Machaut scenes here are the means by which important new departures are effected in the narratives, just as the little dog in *BD* leads the poet to the central scene with the Man in Black. In both the *Fonteinne Amoureuse* and Chaucer's *BD* the story of Ceyx and Alcyone is not the central concern of the poem, yet expresses an important idea in relation to it, the theme of separation and the difficulty of communication and understanding. For the young duke, unable to declare his feelings to his lady, thinks of getting Morpheus to cause his lady to dream of his love (p. 32), just as the God intimated to Alcyone the fact of her husband's death. The rather disproportionate space that Chaucer spends in his version of the story in describing the mechanics of how messages are transferred (*BD*, 131ff.) is part of that wider concern with processes of communication and understanding (rather explicit in *HF*) which seems to underlie Chaucer's poems.

But whereas the story of Ceyx and Alcyone has this clearly drawn application in the *Fonteinne Amoureuse* to the duke's circumstances, in *BD* the parallelism, the juxtapositive relationship between the bereavement and unaccepting grief of Alcyone and the Black Knight emerges cumulatively as the structure of the poem can be seen as a whole. This structuring by juxtaposition is a feature running through Chaucer's dream poems, and is all the more marked when comparison with their sources shows how this has been achieved. In the *Parliament* the scenes observed by the narrator are contrived to follow each other in a thematic and allusive series which accumulates into a very inclusive consideration of the types and nature of love. The narrator is, as usual, a bookish poet, and the unfolding of the poem is thus set in a context of rather self-conscious literary activity.[7] And fittingly, the sources at first are specific literary texts: the celestial vision of Scipio is contrived by Chaucer into his opening phase to establish as one touchstone the cosmic dimension to human life and love. With his unerring sense for the parts of another work that he wants, Chaucer adroitly echoes key phrases of the *Somnium* in his *Parliament*. Once the dream begins properly, Chaucer moves to a closer type of translation, in his close following of the description of

Venus's temple from Boccaccio's *Teseida*, which he takes over into his own poem. And after this rather particular and textual relationship to other poems, in the tableau of Nature and the parliament of birds Chaucer evidently moves into much freer innovative writing, more his own in its range and variety of writing. Yet also – as the translated analogues indicate – in the general setting of a debate and assembly of birds, and the representation of exchanges of argument and abuse between them, Chaucer is writing within a very well-established literary tradition.[8]

With this very considerable range and diversity of sources and analogues for the *Parliament* the distinctive power of Chaucer emerges in his ability to co-ordinate all these materials into the sequence observed and recorded in the experience of the narrator poet. For although the narrator seems little the wiser for what he has seen, it is open to the reflective reader to notice ('only connect') how the juxtaposition of the reading of the *Somnium*, the vision of Venus, and the parliament of Nature, holds together a comprehensive range of the ways that love is to be known and expressed. The juxtaposition of his various sources is co-ordinated by Chaucer with an economy that allows the component parts of the vision to exist in themselves and relative to the other parts of the work, without authorial connections, comparisons, or interpretations being pressed. Even the narrator's movement from Venus's garden to Nature's parliament is quite briefly passed over, without diminishing the emphasis on the two scenes (*PF*, 295ff.).

In this, the co-ordinating of source elements into a new whole in the *Parliament* compares rather markedly with Chaucer's procedure in the *House of Fame*. In contrast to the *Parliament*, the whole 'connective' process through which the *House of Fame* as a poem is held together through the remarkable physical travellings of its dreamer attracts more attention to itself. The relationship of *HF* to its sources and analogues is in many ways a more fragmented one as a result. While the poem has many echoes and snatches of other works and draws on varied traditions, it is not so sustainedly comparable with extended narrative sources in other works as are the *Book of the Duchess* and the *Parliament*, although some analogues for the House of Fame itself have been included in the present collection from Froissart and the *Panthère d'Amours*.[9]

Comparison with poems of this type can bring out the ways in which Chaucer in his dream poems shares the tendency of the authors of many analogous poems to convey meaning through setting. Indeed, by comparison with most of his other writing, Chaucer in his dream poetry gives much more emphasis to the background and setting of events for its own sake, because this contributes to their meaning.[10] The remarkably decorated and glazed bedroom in which the dreamer 'awakes' into his dream in *BD* (321–34), with its stained glass windows of the Troy-story and its walls decorated with the *Roman de la Rose*, forms a room-interior itself expressive of the dreamer's inner disposition and cast of mind through the influences upon him. The settings of *PF* and *HF* are similarly distinctive in the way that they crystallize into the forms of structures and settings some of the main preoccupations of the poems. It is Chaucer's imagination which has brought together the intimidating gate from Dante and the garden of Venus from Boccaccio to which it gives entry. It is Chaucer's imagination which brings within one poem the painted representation of the *Aeneid* and the architectural conception of the house of Fame, linked by a journey so remarkable it can only open up a sense of space, distance and proportion. And although the elements of Chaucer's description of natural setting in *BD* may be taken from the *Roman*, the sense of space which then focusses down on the Man in Black with his back to the huge oak tree is distinctively Chaucer's touch, expressing how the Black Knight and the grief that preoccupies him are apart from the hunt and the general life of the court at 'a long castel with walles white,/Be seynt Johan! on a ryche hil' to which the knight rides home at the end of the poem.

If such moments of natural description in the dream poems as the woodland in *BD* where the Black Knight sits – or the morning walk to the daisy in the Prologue to *LGW* – are expressed within conventional formulations, then this is because the forest or the daisy plays a role within a larger literary framework of conceptions associated with certain natural things, as can be seen in the poems involved with the daisy by Machaut, Froissart and Deschamps which are translated in this collection.[11]

A comparison with the sources and analogues offers a further significant instance of the ways in which Chaucer's poems can be seen to exist in their own distinctive fashion within tradition. This is their association with the long line of poems concerned with the presenting of cases and complaints for consideration, arbitration and judgement, for a poem like Machaut's *Jugement dou Roy de Behaingne* is itself linked back to the earlier poems of *débat*. Appraisal of presented arguments, and careful discrimination between described states of feeling and experiences, are often at the heart of the poems that Chaucer either draws upon or seems more distantly to echo in his dream poems. In such poems of debate and judgement a certain formality and balance – in style and in set-pieces of procedure – lend authority and a sense of completeness. With this in mind, the comparison between Chaucer's poems and their sources and analogues suggests how much he has given vigour and movement to those parts of his poems which draw on this tradition of formal plaint, debate and judgement (such as in the assemblies presided over by Nature and Fame). Yet the comparison shows how Chaucer has preserved in his own work – for all its animatedness – some of that underlying formality, that sense of procedure and of grouping of figures found in the poems that formed part of the English poet's French reading and background.

The characterization of the poet-figure in his own works also involves some interesting parallels between the role of the first person in Machaut's poems and Chaucer's. For in poems often concerned with judgement the author presents himself as unjudging. A more prestigious and decisive figure than the writer is cast as the judge, and the poet is presented as a bookish character, meek and humble, uncertain and unassertive. A tentative role and subordinate station are especially seen where Machaut projects himself in his poems as the servant of his patrons, who themselves play a role within his works, as with the Kings of Bohemia and Navarre, and the Duke de Berry. And similarly, Deschamps in the *Lay de Franchise* writes a poem in which a King of France, together with allegorical figures, plays a role on centre-stage, while the self-effacing poet observes – as in the *Behaingne* – from a bush.

Such poems offer intriguing sources or analogues for the persona of the poet in Chaucer's works and the way he presents a relationship with his patrons, especially in the *Book of the Duchess* and the Prologue to the *Legend*. Again, the comparison with Chaucer's French reading may at first seem to qualify the distinctiveness of Chaucer's achievements in sketching the anxious character of his narrator and in the skilful play on that bookish, inexperienced figure as the observer of the poem. Yet the comparison with another fourteenth-century poet like Machaut – a courtly poet, but not of noble birth – helps focus more sharply what Chaucer himself has done. The resemblances between Machaut's and Chaucer's positions as poets in their times are significant, as also are the ways they develop the potential in the role of the poet-figure. But in the end the English poet can be seen to have gone much further in the uses he makes of the first person in the dream poems, because – despite the persona of the nervous narrator – Chaucer is so much bolder an artist than Machaut or Froissart.

It is singularly appropriate that Chaucer should have been described by Deschamps as *Grant translateur* in a balade accompanying a present to Chaucer of some of his own works.[12] Deschamps addresses Chaucer as the translator of the *Romaunt of the Rose* who has 'sown the flowers and planted the rose tree [in England] for those who are ignorant of French' (*qu'i as/ Semé les fleurs et planté le rosier/ Aux ignorans de la langue Pandras,/Grant translateur, noble Geoffrey Chaucier. . . .).*[13] And although modern readers may well feel that it is to some of Chaucer's 'translations' from Italian that greatness attaches, Deschamps in his balade (*c.*1385) is evidently thinking of Chaucer as a translator from French especially, who has carried across into English some of the works of French poetry. It is the purpose of this present collection of translations – largely of Chaucer's sources in French – to draw together the main materials from which he 'translated', and also some analogous works that are part of the French literary background of Chaucer's 'minor' or 'dream' poems. The ways in which Chaucer transforms as he translates these French poems reveals his greatness as a re-creating translator, and makes it indeed particularly fitting that he should be hailed in French by a contemporary French poet as *Grant translateur.*[14]

NOTES

[1] For a survey, cf. J. I. Wimsatt, *Chaucer and the French Love Poets* (Chapel Hill, 1968), and also his 'Chaucer and French Poetry,' in *Geoffrey Chaucer (Writers and their Background)*, ed. D. Brewer (London, 1974), pp. 109–36. For the background of literary dreams and visions, cf. A. C. Spearing, *Medieval Dream-Poetry* (Cambridge, 1976), ch. 1.

[2] Cf. D. Kelly, *Medieval Imagination: Rhetoric and the Poetry of Courtly Love* (Madison, 1978), esp. ch. 6 'Guillaume de Machaut and the Sublimation of Courtly Love in Imagination'.

[3] Cf. also Chaucer's recollection of Froissart's brief allusion to Enclimpostair as a son of the God of Sleep (p. 42). The graceful ease with which Machaut and Froissart use Classical allusion in their poems probably offered an interesting model and example to Chaucer.

[4] This close knowledge and power to sort and combine phrases from French poems is shown in the way that in *BD* Chaucer echoes some diction from Machaut's lyric poetry. The reproach of Fortune thus echoes the diction of Machaut's Eighth Motet (ed. Chichmaref, Vol. II, pp. 497–8): 'The trayteresse fals and ful of gyle' (620) . . . The false trayteresse pervers' (813) [cf. *La desloyal renoïe, parjure,/ Fausse, traître, perverse!* (16–17)]; 'An ydole

of fals portraiture' (626) [cf. *Une ydole est de fausse pourtraiture* (9)]; 'She is
the monstres heed ywryen,/ As filth over ystrawed with floures' (628–9) [cf.
C'est fiens couvers de riche couverture,/ Qui dehors luist et dedans est ordure
(7–8)]; 'Withoute feyth, lawe, or mesure,/ She is fals . . .' (632–3) [cf. *Elle est
non seüre,/ Sans foy, sans loy, sans droit, et sans mesure* (5–6)]; 'I lykne hyr to
the scorpioun' (636) [cf. *Oint et puis point de si mortel pointure* (18)]. Again, in
the Black Knight's conceit 'For there nys planete in firmament,/Ne in ayr ne
in erthe noon element,/ That they ne yive me a yifte echone/ Of wepynge
. . .' (693–6) there seems a reminiscence of Machaut's *Lay de Confort: Qu'en
terre n'a element,/ Ne planette en firmament/ Qui de pleur don/ Ne me face* (ed.
Chichmaref, Vol. II, p. 415, 10–13). Moreover, the Black Knight's outburst
on death ('Allas, deth, what ayleth the,/ That thou noldest have taken me,/
Whan thou toke my lady swete . . . etc. (481ff.) has resemblances to
Machaut's Third Motet: *Hé! Mors, com tu es haïe/De moy, quant tu as
ravie/Ma joie, ma druerie* . . . (ed. Chichmaref, Vol. II, p. 487, 1–8).

⁵ Cf. R. M. Jordan, *Chaucer and the Shape of Creation* (Cambridge, Mass.,
1967) and R. O. Payne, *The Key of Remembrance* (New Haven, 1963), ch. 4.

⁶ Cf. J. B. Friedman, 'The Dreamer, the Whelp and Consolation in the *Book
of the Duchess*,' *ChauR*, 3 (1968–9), 145–62.

⁷ Cf. A. C. Spearing, *Medieval Dream-Poetry* (Cambridge, 1976), ch. 2.

⁸ On the background to *PF*, cf. D. S. Brewer (ed.), *The Parlement of Foulys*
(London, 1960), 'Introduction', and also J. A. W. Bennett, *The Parlement of
Foules* (Oxford, 1957).

⁹ For the complex range of analogues to *HF*, cf. J. A. W. Bennett, *Chaucer's
Book of Fame* (Oxford, 1968). Cf. also The Triumph of Fame in *The Triumphs
of Petrarch*, transl. E. H. Wilkins (Chicago, 1962).

¹⁰ Cf. V. A. Kolve, 'Chaucer and the Visual Arts,' in *Geoffrey Chaucer (Writers
and their Background)*, ed. D. Brewer (London, 1974), pp. 290–320.

¹¹ For the background, see especially J. L. Lowes, 'The Prologue to the *Legend
of Good Women* as Related to the French *Marguerite* Poems, and the
Filostrato,' *PMLA*, 19 (1904), 593–683; and also J. I. Wimsatt, *The
Marguerite Poetry of Guillaume de Machaut* (Chapel Hill, 1970).

¹² Cf. T. A. Jenkins, 'Deschamps' Balade to Chaucer,' *MLN*, 33 (1918),
268–78.

¹³ *Œuvres*, ed. le marquis de Queux de Saint-Hilaire and G. Raynaud, SATF,
11 vols. (Paris 1878–1903), II, 138–9.

¹⁴ This is discussed more fully in my book *Chaucer as Translator* (forthcoming).

Selection and arrangement

The collection of material in this volume has been selected with the aim of drawing together conveniently in one place the more important narrative sources and analogues for Chaucer's dream poetry which are otherwise difficult of access for the English reader. Such important sources and influences as the *Roman de la Rose* or various of the Classical poets – which are quite readily available in translations – are accordingly not included here for reasons of space. Nor has the type of very brief and isolated allusion or resemblance been gathered here which can be cited adequately in the annotation to editions of Chaucer's works. The aim has been to enable the reader to gain an impression for himself of the intrinsic nature of the works that formed some of the most influential reading behind Chaucer's dream poems, and thus to enable assessment of what Chaucer has achieved creatively in his absorption of the French influences upon him. The choice of most of these more extended sources and analogues is a fairly obvious one, although considerations of space have prevented the inclusion of some works which may offer only tangential or very approximate analogues to Chaucer's work, and of others which may well not precede in date Chaucer's own writing. With some of the longer works translated here it has been necessary to give extracts, although this does not seem untrue to the nature of Chaucer's judiciously selective interest in them. Although the volume has for convenience been organized into sections, so that the especially significant sources or analogues for particular Chaucer poems are grouped together, this is not meant to imply that some of these poems were not more generally influential on more than one of Chaucer's poems and his work as a whole. The unity of the collection is that it attempts to present a poet's reading.

I

Sources and Analogues of
'The Book of the Duchess'

Le Jugement dou Roy de Behaingne
Guillaume de Machaut

Machaut was born *c.*1300 in the village of Machaut in the Ardennes He studied theology, but it is not known where, and became master of arts and a cleric. From *c.*1323 he was in the service of Jean of Luxembourg, King of Bohemia (son of the Holy Roman Emperor Henry VII, and father of the illustrious Charles IV of Bohemia). Machaut served the 'Roy de Behaingne' as secretary, accompanying him on his various campaigns in Poland, Silesia, Lithuania. Through the king's influence he became canon of Rheims cathedral in 1337, and *c.*1340 retired to Rheims until his death in 1377. Nowadays acknowledged as a composer, Machaut was also author of ten long narrative *dits* (*Le Dit dou Vergier, Le Jugement dou Roy de Behaingne, Remede de Fortune, Le Dit dou Lyon, Le Dit de l'Alerion, Le Jugement dou Roy de Navarre, Le Comfort d'Ami, La Fonteinne Amoureuse, Le Voir-Dit, La Prise d'Alexandrie*), and also of four shorter *dits* (*Le Dit de la Harpe, Le Dit de la Marguerite, Le Dit de la Fleur de Lis et de la Marguerite, Le Dit de la Rose*), as well as much lyric poetry. A prolific poet, Machaut was also a much imitated one. The *Navarre* and *Confort d'Ami* bear witness to his later links with Charles II (le Mauvais), King of Navarre, and the *Fonteinne Amoureuse* stems from his relations with Jean II (le Bon), King of France, and his sons, including Jean, duc de Berry, while his last long poem, the *Prise d'Alexandrie*, celebrates the career of Pierre de Lusignan, King of Cyprus (Chaucer's 'worthy Petro, kyng of Cipre,' *MkT*, VII, 2391).

The *Jugement dou Roy de Behaingne* is probably the second of Machaut's long poems, and it has exerted a most important influence on Chaucer's conception in the *Book of the Duchess*, while providing the model of many Chaucer lines. The text is translated from the *Œuvres*, ed. E. Hoepffner, SATF (Paris, 1908–21), and some of Chaucer's more significant borrowings are indicated by footnotes.

At Easter time when everything is full of cheerfulness, when the earth decks itself with many gay colours, when good love pierces without wound beneath the breast of many beautiful ladies, many lovers and many maidens, causing them many new joys and many sorrows – at this sweet time, towards the month of May, I dressed myself handsomely like one who loved very perfectly, with a constant love.

The day was perfectly mild and temperate (*attemprez*), fair, shining, clear, fresh and pure, without chill.★ The dew shone so brightly on the grass, that I

★Cf. *Book of the Duchess*: *And eke the welken was so fair, – / Blew, bryght, clere was the ayr, / And ful attempre for sothe hyt was; / For nother to cold nor hoot yt nas, / Ne in al the welken was no clowde,* 339–43.

3

was completely dazzled when I turned my look that way, because of the sunlight. The birds, because of the delightful sweetness of the new season, all sang so joyously that I walked along to the call of their sweet song. One bird went fluttering over all of them crying 'Oci, oci!' And I followed it until it perched in a place by a stream and near a fine tower, where there were many trees and many sweet-smelling flowers of various colours.★

[33] Then I lay down with delight, and concealed myself as well as I could beneath the trees so that I could not be seen, in order to listen to the very sweet sound of the pretty singing. I was so delighted in listening to the sweet song that I could never describe it.

But as I was enjoying in this way the very sweet bird-song that I listened to, I saw coming along a narrow green path a lady deep in thought, and all alone except for a little dog and a young girl. Her simple manner certainly seemed full of grief.

And on the other side, a little way off from me, a knight, very nobly arrayed, came alone towards her along the road. I thought that they were lovers. I then pressed myself so deep within the leafy branches that they did not see me at all. But when the lover, whom Nature had endowed with many of her gifts, came near the noble lady he greeted her like a gracious, prudent, well-educated man.† And the lady, preoccupied with her thoughts, passed him by without answering him at all. And he straightway went back, took her by the edge of her gown and gently said to her, 'Most sweet lady, do you despise my greeting?'‡

And when she saw him she replied with a sigh like somebody who had no hope of anything, 'Certainly, my lord, I didn't hear you, I was prevented by my thoughts. But if I have done anything wrong or discourteous, please pardon me for it.' Without more ado, the knight said gently, 'My lady, no pardon is necessary, for no wrong-doing nor ill will was involved. But I beg you, please, to tell me what you are thinking about.'§

The lady sighed deeply and said, 'For God's sake, leave me in peace, fair sir, for I do not need you to cause me more grief and vexation than I already receive.' And he drew closer to her to draw out her thoughts and said to her, 'Sweet, gracious lady, I see you in sadness. But I swear to you and promise by

---

★Cf. . . . . And I hym folwed, and hyt forth wente/ Doun by a floury grene wente/ Ful thikke of gras, ful softe and swete./ With floures fele, faire under fete,/ And litel used, hyt semed thus . . . 397–401.

†Cf. A wonder wel-farynge knyght – / By the maner me thoghte so – /Of good mochel . . . 452–4.

‡Cf. I went and stood ryght at his fet,/ And grette hym, but he spak noght,/ But argued with his owne thoght. . . ./ So, throgh hys sorwe and hevy thoght,/ Made hym that he herde me noght. . . ./ But at the last, to sayn ryght soth,/ He was war of me, how y stood/ Before hym, and did of myn hood,/ And had ygret hym as I best koude,/ Debonayrly, and nothyng lowde./ He sayde, 'I prey the, be not wroth./ I herde the not, to seyn the soth,/ Ne I sawgh the not, syr, trewely' 502ff..

§Cf. 'I am ryght sory yif I have ought/ Destroubled yow out of your thought./ Foryive me, yif I have mystake.'/ 'Yis, th'amendes is lyght to make,'/ Quod he, 'for ther lyeth noon therto;/ There ys nothyng myssayd nor do' . . . 523–8.

my faith, that if you will reveal your grief to me, I will do all in my power to redress it.'*

The lady thanked him for this and said, 'My lord, nobody can help me and nobody except God could alleviate the heavy sorrow which makes me grow pale, keeps my heart in sadness and weeping, and places me in such languishing sorrow that, to tell the truth, no heart could have any more.'†

[102] 'My lady, what wrong makes you sorrow so much? Tell me what it is, for I think I myself experience such grievous suffering, so sad, so harsh, so severe, so bitter, that you may be certain that there is no lady, no human being, nor ever was, that ever endured such suffering.'

'Indeed, sir, I well believe that such sorrow does not inflict on your heart what I endure. Because of this, you shall know my thoughts, which you have wanted to know. But before everything else, you will promise me that, without any lies, you will tell me your own sorrow.'

'My lady, I promise you, by my faith and my soul, that I will confess to you everything of the thoughts which kindle and burn me, and often wound and slay my heart. I shall not lie about any of it.'

'Indeed, sir, and I shall also tell you.' 'Now tell me then; I shall very gladly hear you.'

[124] 'Sir, for seven or eight whole years now my heart has been a servant and tenant of Bonne Amour, and I have spent my youth in her paths. For from the very first I knew her, I have with pleasure placed in her service, heart, body, ability, life, possessions and power and all that I have.‡ She retained me in homage to her and gave me in my lover a very loyal heart, fine and good, sweet, gracious and wise, the flower of courtesy, of perfect honour and pleasant manner, and the very best of the very good. And he had a fine, handsome body, young, noble, graceful in manner, full of all that is needful in a true lover. And he was above all thought worthy to be loved, for he was true, loyal, and discreet in all matters of love, and I loved him so loyally that I surrendered my whole heart to loving him and had no other wish. In him was my hope, my joy, and my pleasure, my heart, my love, my thought, my desire.§ My heart rejoiced

*Cf. *And I saw that, and gan me aqueynte/ With hym, and fond hym so tretable. . . ./ Anoon ryght I gan fynde a tale/ To hym, to loke wher I myght ought/ Have more knowynge of hys thought. . . ./ 'But, sir, oo thyng wol ye here?/ Me thynketh in gret sorowe I yow see./ But certes, sire, yif that yee/ Wolde ought discure me youre woo,/ I wolde, as wys God helpe me soo,/ Amende hyt, yif I kan or may./ Ye mowe preve hyt be assay;/ For, by my trouthe, to make yow hool,/ I wol do al my power hool./ And telleth me of your sorwes smerte . . .'* 532ff..

†Cf. *'Graunt mercy, goode frend,' quod he,/ 'I thanke thee that thow woldest soo,/ But hyt may never the rather be doo./ No man may my sorwe glade,/ That maketh my hewe to falle and fade,/ And hath myn understondynge lorn,/ That me ys wo that I was born!'* 560–6.

‡Cf. *'Dredeles, I have ever yit/ Be tributarye and yiven rente/ To Love, hooly with good entente,/ And throgh plesaunce become his thral/ With good wille, body, hert, and al./ Al this I putte in his servage,/ As to my lord, and dide homage,'* 764–70.

§Cf. *'Ryght on thys same, as I have seyd,/ Was hooly al my love leyd;/ For certes she was, that swete wif,/ My suffisaunce, my lust, my lyf,/ Myn hap, myn hele, and al my blesse,/ My worldes welfare, and my goddesse,/ And I hooly hires and everydel,'* 1035–41.

simply to see him and hear him. All my comfort was in him: he was all my delight, all my solace, my pleasure, my treasure. He was to me a wall, a fortress, a resort. And he loved me, and above all he served and feared me. He called me his heart, his love, his lady; all was mine, and my heart well knew it; nothing could displease him which pleased me. Our two hearts were so well paired that the one was never contrary to the other: thus both were of one accord; they had one thought and were alike in will and desire. They felt good or ill, and happiness always conjointly, and it was never otherwise between the two of them, but there was always such loyalty that there was never any unworthy thought in our love.*

[177] 'Alas! unhappy me! now everything is changed for the worse, for all my sweetness is now sorrowful toil, and my joys are bitter sorrows, and my thoughts – in which my heart used to delight and sweetly solace all ills – are become and will remain sorrowful, sad and bitter. My days will be in darkness, full of unhappiness, my hopes without any certainty, and my sweetness will be cruel harshness.† For I should tremble, change colour, and shiver, lament, weep, sigh and groan, and shake in fear of despair. To my weary heart no good will ever come, nor will my heart attain to any comfort or joy before death takes me – that death which wrongs me greatly in not slaying me when it has slain and taken away from me my sweet friend, whom I loved with a pure heart, and he me. But wretched me! alas, I am left behind him. I have no wish to live for a day or half a day in such heavy grief, but would rather die from the pain that grieves me.'‡

[206] And I who had pressed myself in among the leaves saw that with these words the sweet-mannered lady fell down as if dead.§ However, the knight – who was very worthy and noble – often begged and urged her very gently that she should take heart. But it was all to no avail, for the lady, whom heavy grief assailed for her lover, felt such cruel pangs that all strength and breath failed in her. And when he saw that the lady neither heard nor understood him, he was more sorrowful than could be, but nonetheless, when he saw that she had fainted he did as much as he could. In his hand he collected the dew on the green grass, and with it he so softly bedewed all over her tear-stained face that the lady, who had for a long while lost all consciousness and strength, opened her eyes and began to sigh deeply, mourning for him who made her desire death through true love. But the knight with his generous heart said, 'Dear lady, for love of God, calm yourself; you are killing yourself with such

---

*Cf. 'Oure hertes wern so evene a payre,/ That never nas that oon contrayre/ To that other, for no woo./ For sothe, ylyche they suffred thoo/ Oo blysse, and eke oo sorwe bothe;/ Ylyche they were bothe glad and wrothe;/ Al was us oon, withoute were./ And thus we lyved ful many a yere/ So wel, I kan nat telle how . . .' 1289–97.

†Cf. 'My song ys turned to pleynynge,/ And al my laughtre to wepynge,/ My glade thoghtes to hevynesse . . ./ To derke ys turned al my lyght,/ My wyt ys foly, my day ys nyght . . .' etc. 599ff..

‡Cf. 'I have of sorwe so gret won/ That joye gete I never non,/ Now that I see my lady bryght . . ./ Is fro me ded and ys agoon./ Allas, deth, what ayleth the,/ That thou noldest have taken me,/ Whan thou toke my lady swete . . .' 475ff..

§Cf. Whan he had mad thus his complaynte,/ Hys sorwful hert gan faste faynte,/ And his spirites wexen dede . . . 487ff.

behaviour, for I see very well that you are grieving very much for love of him. Do not show such weakness of heart like this, for it is not worthy or honourable either.'

[239] 'You speak truly, sir. But it is a grief to me to see the daylight, who loved with so perfect a love, for I cannot escape from it by any means. And thus I see my death is near indeed.'

'My lady, now listen to what I shall say and do not take it ill. It is no surprise if you are miserable, for it is certainly right that you should be sad. But truly, it would be easier to relieve your sorrow than mine.'

'But how, sir? Tell me how, and deliver your speech.'

'Very gladly, if you will listen to me, and cast out sadness from your heart, so that you give all your attention to hearing me.'⋆

'Indeed, sir, I cannot be very happy, but I will do all in my power, without word of a lie.'

'I shall tell you without more delay of some of the pains I have to suffer. My lady, since the time that I had understanding and that my heart could feel and comprehend what it is to love, I did not cease to wish to be in love.† For a long time, in order to be a lover, before my heart was given to any lady, I made devout entreaty to Bonne Amour, that she would place my heart to the honour of her in whom it would make its stay, and praise and renown should come of this.‡ And if my heart could do anything that should be remembered or deserve reward from the lady through service, then at some time she should deign to remember me who wish to be hers, without ever leaving, for the whole of my life.

[281] 'Through Fortune who is all too common in lying to everybody, it so happened that I came upon a company of many lovely ladies, young, noble, joyous and gay.§ I was struck by one among all the others, who, just as the sun outshines the moon in brightness, so she surpassed the rest in worth, in honour, grace and beauty.⋆⋆ And she also pleased me by being so humble and simple for, to tell you the truth, one could not find her equal in the whole world, and the whole world would not be enough to describe her beauty

---

⋆Cf. 'Blythely,' quod he; 'com sytte adoun!/ I telle the upon a condicioun/ That thou shalt hooly, with al thy wyt,/ Doo thyn entent to herkene hit,' 749–52.

†Cf. 'Syr,' quod he, 'sith first I kouthe/ Have any maner wyt fro youthe,/ Or kyndely understondyng/ To comprehende, in any thyng,/ What love was, in myn owne wyt . . .' 759–63.

‡Cf. 'And ful devoutly I prayed hym to,/ He shulde besette myn herte so/ That hyt plesance to hym were,/ And worship to my lady dere./ And this was longe, and many a yer,/ Or that myn herte was set owher . . .' 771–6.

§Cf. 'Hit happed that I cam on a day/ Into a place ther that I say,/ Trewly, the fayrest companye/ Of ladyes that evere man with yë/ Had seen togedres in oo place./ Shal I clepe hyt hap other grace/ That broght me there? Nay, but Fortune,/ That ys to lyen ful comune,/ The false trayteresse pervers!' 805–13.

⋆⋆Cf. 'Among these ladyes thus echon,/ Soth to seyen y sawgh oon/ That was lyk noon of the route;/ For I dar swere, withoute doute,/ That as the someres sonne bryght/ Ys fairer, clerer, and hath more lyght/ Than any other planete in heven,/ The moone, or the sterres seven,/ For al the world so hadde she/ Surmounted hem alle of beaute,/ Of maner, and of comlynesse . . ./ Of goodlyhede . . .' 817ff.

completely.* For I saw her dancing there so daintily, and singing so very prettily, laughing and playing so gracefully, that never was a more gracious treasure seen.† Her hair resembled thread of gold, yet was not excessively blonde.‡ Her forehead was white and smooth and unlined, and so well-formed that it was neither too broad nor too narrow, and her brows, which were of a very fine shape, seemed like a black thread on the white skin and were much esteemed.

'But her two eyes – which wished to cross the threshold of my heart through their power and their fair welcome, in order to give me the pain I suffer – her eyes were laughing, and changed very little, in order to be more piercing and sharp, sweet, humble and attractive, all full of bonds to bind a lover in pure love. Her eyelids were fluttering and her eyes were not too wide open, winning everything through their sweet piercing. There was no way of preventing that they went to strike my heart within me as they pleased and kept it for their own. But their gaze, giving mercy in a gracious manner, was not lightly given to fools.§

'For when they wished to let fly one of their darts, her eyes knew how to do it so prudently and subtly that nobody could know except he on whom the arrow fell. Pure, fragrant, long and well-shaped, she had a nose perfectly proportioned to her face, for it was neither too small nor too large. But her little mouth, properly small, red, plump, always laughing, delightful, sweet, makes me languish, when my heart longs. For whoever sees her mouth speaking, and sees it laughing and tastes its sweetness, esteems and declares it above all others. When she smiled her cheeks made two dimples, which were pink and white and a little plump and made her more beautiful.

[352] 'And there is still more: she had white, small, regular teeth, and her chin was a little dimpled, rounded underneath and above. But her complexion was amazing and unlike any other, for it was full of life, fresh and pinker than the rose in May before it is gathered.** And briefly, her throat was white as snow, smooth, beautifully proportioned – there was not a line in it, nor any sign

---

*Cf. 'But which a visage had she thertoo!/ Allas! myn herte ys wonder woo/ That I ne kan discryven hyt!/ . . . I have no wit that kan suffise/ To comprehenden hir beaute . . .' 895ff.

†Cf. 'I sawgh hyr daunce so comlily,/ Carole and synge so swetely,/ Laughe and pleye so womanly,/ And loke so debonairly,/ So goodly speke and so frendly,/ That, certes, y trowe that evermor/ Nas seyn so blysful a tresor . . .' 848–54.

‡Cf. '. . . For every heer on hir hed,/ Soth to seyne, hyt was not red,/ Ne nouther yelowe, ne broun hyt nas,/ Me thoghte most lyk gold hyt was . . .' 855–8.

§Cf. 'And whiche eyen my lady hadde!/ Debonaire, goode, glade, and sadde,/ Symple, of good mochel, noght to wyde./ Therto hir look nas not asyde,/ Ne overthwert, but beset so wel/ Hyt drew and took up, everydel,/ Al that on hir gan beholde./ Hir eyen semed anoon she wolde/ Have mercy; fooles wenden soo;/ But hyt was never the rather doo./ Hyt nas no countrefeted thyng;/ Hyt was hir owne pure lokyng/ That the goddesse, dame Nature,/ Had mad hem opene by mesure,/ And close; for, were she never so glad,/ Hyr lokynge was not foly sprad . . .' 859–74.

**Cf. 'But thus moche dar I sayn, that she/ Was whit, rody, fressh, and lyvely hewed . . .' 904–5.

of a bone, and she also had a lovely neck that I praise and value.* It is also right that I speak of her long, straight arms, which were beautifully made in every part, for she had white hands and long fingers. To my liking were her white, firm and high breasts, pointed and rounded, graceful and beautifully shaped, and little, in proportion with her body. Her body was certainly beautifully proportioned, pretty, compact, young, refined, dimpled, tall, straight, well-made, graceful, poised and slender. She had very well shaped hips, thighs and legs, and she had arched, rounded and beautifully jointed feet, beautifully shod. Of the remainder that I did not see, my lady, I can tell you that everything was in accordance with nature, beautifully fashioned and formed.† And this that is left undescribed, of which I do not wish to say anymore, must be considered without comparison as more sweet and beautiful than any other. She had delicate skin, white and soft, gleaming more than anything if one examined it well, and quite without spot. Her skin was gentle and firm, fresh as dew, but she was graced with a humble and assured manner and a very fine bearing. Truly, she was so beautiful that I firmly believe that if Nature, who makes everything in her subtle way, wished to make another like my lady, she would never know how to succeed, if there were not the model of this lady who surpasses all others in beauty.‡ And I tell you that never yet in my life did I see a lady so completely beautiful in body. As to her age, she was fourteen and a half, or thereabouts.

[409] 'And so, my lady, when I saw her figure, which was so flawlessly beautiful, the sweet impression of that figure was so imprinted in my heart that it remains there and can never leave, through which I endure great sorrow and great suffering.§ And without doubt, before I had left her presence, Plaisance established herself within my heart as I gazed at her sweet face, so that indeed, if I had the possessions of Octavian, and knew the knowledge of Galen, and all these benefits were mine, I would have given up everything so that I could see her at will or knew what to do that she wanted and would be pleased by.

'But Fine Amour, who saw that I was taken prisoner by Plaisance, caused a sweet laughing look to be shot through my heart and so bind me that he made me quite unrepentantly subject to her very sweet *Dangier* or Standoffishness. It pleased me so much to feel this reserve when she did not deign to allow her look to fall on me, that, without word of a lie, I did not know what was happening to me or where I was. For I lost all sense, strength, and confidence, so powerfully did I feel myself subject to love through her eyes. Then the desire to be loved by

---

*Cf. '*But swich a fairnesse of a nekke/ Had that swete that boon nor brekke/ Nas ther non sene that myssat./ Hyt was whit, smothe, streght, and pure flat,/ Wythouten hole; or canel-boon,/ As be semynge, had she noon./ Hyr throte, as I have now memoyre,/ Semed a round tour of yvoyre,/ Of good gretnesse, and noght to gret,*' 939–47.

†Cf. '*Ryght faire shuldres and body long/ She had, and armes, every lyth/ Fattyssh, flesshy, not gret therwith;/ Ryght white handes, and nayles rede,/ Rounde brestes; and of good brede/ Hyr hippes were, a streight flat bak./ I knew on hir noon other lak/ That al hir lymmes nere pure sewynge/ In as fer as I had knowynge,*' 952–60.

‡Cf. '*For certes, Nature had swich lest/ To make that fair, that trewly she/ Was hir chef patron of beaute/ And chef ensample of al hir werk,/ And moustre . . .*' 908–12.

§Cf. '*. . . for be hyt never so derk,/ Me thynketh I se hir ever moo,*' 912–3.

her was so strongly kindled in my heart that in my sighing I am a hundred times called wretched because of it. For in my longing I felt such sorrow that my strength ebbed away, and all my thoughts were on gazíng at her sweet face.

[453] 'For I would have very gladly told her how much I loved her from my heart. But the fear of refusal held me back from this.* But on the other hand, Bel Acueil called me, laughing Dous Regart assured me, and Dous Espoirs sweetly and loyally affirmed to me that such great beauty could never exist if it did not possess pity.† These three have exhorted me and said so much to me, that I decided anyway that I would tell her of my love. Alas, thus I debated with myself all alone!‡ But when I thought to tell her of my woes, my heart was so fearful, so feeble, so weak, so wretched, so anguished, so discomfited, so tremulous, so ashamed, and so strongly enflamed with the sickness of love, that there was no sense, confidence or consideration in it, but it was as if my heart was frozen and seized when I was able to see face to face her perfect beauty.§ Then my heart was bitten by the pangs of love, and pricked by the joyful pricking of love, and filled with sweet nourishment by Dous Penser, who caused all my sorrow to end and made me hope for my cure.

'Thus I often had both joy and torment in loving. I stayed in this condition for a long while, one hour happy and another hour unhappy, and I never dared to ask for the relief of my sorrow. But nevertheless, the great distress of love, burning desire, the cruel languishing in which I had remained for many days, her courteously welcoming manner, the hope of ending my grief, her great beauty, her sweet and lovely, laughing eyes, and the fact that there was not a drop of pride in her – all these things gave me a boldness to ask her mercy, in a very cowardly manner. I said to her humbly, fearfully and with a much altered manner, "My dear lady, your beauty burns and enflames my heart so that, without any blameworthy thought, I love you above all, with heart and body, from true desire and from my soul. I beg you, sweet lady, to have mercy upon me, for truly, I shall die of this love if I do not have some relief from your heart which has so afflicted mine."**

[509] 'And when I had thus told her my grief, I saw her sweet face change a

---

*Cf. '*I bethoghte me what woo/ And sorwe that I suffred thoo/ For hir, and yet she wyste hyt noght,/ Ne telle hir durste I nat my thoght./ "Allas!" thoghte I, "y kan no red;/ And but I telle hir, I nam but ded;/ And yif I telle hyr, to seye ryght soth,/ I am adred she wol be wroth./ Allas! what shal I thanne do?"* ' 1183–91.

†Cf. '. . . *I bethoghte me that Nature/ Ne formed never in creature/ So moche beaute, trewely,/ And bounte, wythoute mercy,*' 1195–8.

‡Cf. '. . . *In this debat I was so wo,/ Me thoghte myn herte braste atweyne!*' 1192–3.

§Cf. '*I not wel how that I began,/ Ful evel rehersen hyt I kan;/* . . . *For many a word I over-skipte/ In my tale, for pure fere/ Lest my wordes mysset were./ With sorweful herte, and woundes dede,/ Softe and quakynge for pure drede/ And shame, and styntynge in my tale/ For ferde, and myn hewe al pale,/ Ful ofte I wex bothe pale and red./ Bowynge to hir, I heng the hed;/ I durste nat ones loke hir on,/ For wit, maner, and al was goon,*' 1203ff.

**Cf. '. . . *I seyde "mercy!" and no more./ Hyt nas no game, hyt sat me sore,*' 1219–20.

little, as it seemed to me, and because of this I was in fear of being refused.* But her look, her gentleness, and her graceful laugh always assured me, so that by them I was emboldened to say, "Alas! noble lady, for love of God, do not kill your loyal lover, who is so bound in your bonds that he loses all consolation and all happiness."

'Then that simple, quiet lady, for whom Love constrained and ruled me, turned to me and said, "Indeed, my friend, I would not want to cause grief or harm to anybody. One should do as one would be done by. And, fair friend, there is no good that will not be rewarded, nor no evil that will not be punished. If Love, then, has kindled you to love, she will give you her reward for it in time and in season, if you love without having treasonous thoughts. And if Love finds you to be other than good, do not doubt for a minute that she will be your mortal enemy and you will never be given cure nor assistance, nor any concession for your sorrow. Go then, fair sir, towards Love and make your laments and your complaints to her. In her lies your death and your help, not in me, and I do not think I am the cause of your suffering. By my faith, I do not know what more to say to you. I bid you good-bye."†

[549] 'Then the beautiful lady left me, she who bestowed on me such great sorrow that my heart came very near to leaving when she left. But the sweetness of her pleasant look caused by its sweet art that I looked at her. As God preserve me, when she left me she looked at me so sweetly that it seemed to me that her looks said to me truly, "My friend, I love you very lovingly." Then I was completely comforted by the noble power of this look, which was then worth so much to me that it has always nourished and sustained me in good hope. And if it had not been for that, I truly suspect that I would have fallen into despair, but nothing could make me sorrowful when her smiling gaze was upon me, so that in this way, my lady, her look comforted and helped me in my sorrow.

'I stayed there all alone in great nervousness, and in my thoughts began to picture to myself again her splendour, her great gentleness, her colour, her worthiness, her fine bearing, her manner of coming and going, her fine figure, her gracious way of speaking, her noble deportment, her pleasant look, and her face which was so sweet, meek and gentle, that it was the model of all beauty.‡ And when I had gone over everything in my mind's eye, I indeed had great delight and perfect happiness and considered myself a very happy man in that I faithfully loved her. Then since I am so given over to her service that all my pleasure is in serving her, I cannot do any other work. I served her, loved, concealed, feared and obeyed so very long that nothing recompensed me. But in the end, I loved and cherished her so much that she recognized that I acted for her honour and her good, and that my heart loved her above anything else.§

---

*Cf. *'And whan I had my tale y-doo,/ God wot, she acounted nat a stree/ Of al my tale, so thoghte me . . .'* 1236–8.

†Cf. *'I kan not now wel counterfete/ Hir wordes, but this was the grete/ Of hir answere: she sayde "nay"/ Al outerly . . .'* 1241–4.

‡Cf. *'. . . For hit* [her face] *was sad, symple, and benygne,'* 918.

§Cf. *'So hit befel, another yere,/ I thoughte ones I wolde fonde/ To do hir knowe and understonde/ My woo; and she wel understod/ That I ne wilned thyng but god,/ And worship, and to kepe hir name/ Over alle thyng, and drede hir shame,/ And was so besy hyr to serve;/ And pitee were I shulde sterve,/ Syth that I wilned noon harm, ywis . . .'* 1258–67.

I did so much that she considered me hers, in such a way that with a laughing heart and a happy face she said to me, "Friend, here is your dear beloved, who doesn't wish to be proud towards you any more. Love wishes it, who with a good heart moves me to do this. And truly, it cannot be otherwise, for a very great thing is necessary for it to be done. Because of this, I give you my love with my heart, without any going back. I beg you to protect my honour, for I love and honour you above all."

[612] 'And when I saw that my lady called me her lover so sweetly, and had given me the sweet granting of her love without any holding back, you will not be surprised, dear lady, if I was happy. For previously I was distressed, wretched, lost, scorned and isolated, without any hope, when I was without her very sweet encouragement. But I was recovered, brought back from death, rich above all, full of great encouragement and removed from sorrow, when she said to me, "Friend, I grant myself to you with a very good heart."* And this very sweet granting was a hundred thousand times greater to me than a king's, so that nobody would be able to describe the happiness I felt. For I was so happy that I could not thank her for it, nor knew how to speak.

'But in the end, as a true lover, with a pure heart kindled with love, and without any thought of unworthy contrivance, I very humbly said to her, with head bowed and without fear, "Lady, whom I love more than any other or than myself – for whom I employ my wits, time, heart, life and love, as much as I can, but not as much as I ought – I thank you for the noble gift of your sweet mercy.† For so much have you enriched me, so filled me with joy, so cured and rewarded me that truly, if all that is beneath the heavens, and all that was and will be, were freely given to me to do with as I wished, I should consider your grace a hundred times greater. I pray to God that I never do anything wrong towards you which might destroy our love, and that I may be able to fulfil your wishes as I wish to do, humbly, without haughtiness or pride. For if I can, I will serve you better than I used to, with a very loyal heart, and I will protect your honour in every way, and I will not do anything in word, in deed, or in thought towards you or others over which you might be angy.‡ But you will be my lady and my sweet heart, my earthly god, adored above all. And without doubt, if I do anything against your will, or anything that might anger or displease you, then indeed you may be sure that it is done through carelessness."

[668] 'My lady, in this way, as you have heard, I thanked her for the noble gift of her sweet mercy. And she also swore and assured me very firmly that she would always love me loyally, without abandoning and leaving me. Thus I reigned in joy for a long while without having anything that was contrary to happiness, but was extremely happy and lighthearted, much more cheerful than I used to be. And it was right that, as much as I could, I was gracious and elegant, for I was everywhere taken for the king and the most loved of lovers.

'But when faithless and changeable Fortune had placed me up so high, just

---

*Cf. 'But if myn herte was ywaxe/ Glad, that is no nede to axe!/ As helpe me God, I was as blyve/ Reysed, as fro deth to lyve . . .' 1275–8.

†Cf. '. . . My lady yaf me al hooly/ The noble yifte of hir mercy . . .' 1269–70.

‡Cf. 'And swor, and hertely gan hir hete,/ Ever to be stedfast and trewe,/ And love hir alwey fresshly newe,/ And never other lady have,/ And al hir worship for to save . . .' 1226–30.

like the evil, mean-spirited creature she is, she did not care a plum for me and my good. Thus she changed her expression, and deserted me, and turned her face away from me when she had set me up on her wheel. Then she turned the wheel, and I fell into the mud. But this she did, the traitress, always quick to betray those she puts under her wing, because God and fair Nature – when they formed her whom I love – took such great delight in the very great beauty they gave her that they forgot to put loyalty there as well. For I know very well and see quite openly that my lady, who has such a graceful figure and whom my heart fears, loves, obeys, and serves, has without cause taken another lover than me. So that, my lady, if I weep and groan deeply, and often say "alas", it is no wonder, when her fine beauty, which has no equal, and her blooming, fresh, rosy colour, and her very sweet look which torments me, are all gone away from me, and she dismisses me from everything, and deprives and cuts me off from all good. Alas! how shall I ever have a happy heart? And very wrongly has she taken back from me my joy and comfort, and put me in such great distress that I well know that I will die of it. Nothing can prevent me from this nor offer a single consolation.

[722] 'But what makes my heart shatter is that I do not know whom to blame for my unhappiness. For it seems to me that if I am thrown down by Fortune from the high degree where I had previously mounted up through her whom, to tell the truth, I did not trust or lean upon, then I ought not to begrudge it her, for she was doing her duty and has no other calling except to betray those she sees rising and growing wealthy, and to cause those who are down below to rise up. She cannot hold anybody so dear as to give him security in his good fortune, and whether in joy or in unhappiness she has very soon whirled him up or down. It is her nature: it is only a vain and unreal form of thing; it is a happiness which is worth little and lasts little time. He is a fool who trusts her! Everybody is deceived and nobody defies her.

'And if I blame the death that embitters me on my lovely lady, with what reason and with what instance would I do so? She has put herself in subjection and wholly given herself to Love, and wishes that Love should have sovereign dominion over her, so that she cannot do other than Love's pleasure and must obey in all cases. It follows that if my lady is pleased to leave me in order to cherish somebody else, then Love does that and not my lady, in whom all worthiness is, for she follows her duty and her honour in obeying her sovereign. So it seems to me that when I was enflamed to love by Love, in doing this Love did me more wrong than my worthy lady – if Love could do me wrong, I mean. But I cannot understand this at all, because for a long time Love like a sweet and tender mother has nourished me as best she could with her sweet goods. And I have not yet noticed, in any misfortune that I have suffered, that she has not always been near to me like a friend and served me with all my courses, with tears before and afterwards with sighs. It is my food, but there is no more appetite or demand. By my soul, there is nothing to which I am drawn except only that which breaks my heart.

[784] 'Thus Love grows in my heart with my sorrow, and does not go away whether by night or day, in this way accompanying me in my sorrowful weeping, out of her goodness. I declare this to be great friendship in one who has been mother to me in prosperity, and still is in my adversity. Thus I cannot complain on her rightly, for always I find her with me. And I am not destroyed by her at all, for she cannot change hearts, since God does not wish it. For when

God created my lady who used to call me her lover, over whom my heart sorrows too much, if He and Nature, when they made her fine, pure beauty – delightful above all other creatures to everybody – had then put loyalty into her gentle shape, I would still be called her lover; and her heart, which promised me so much good, would never have been my enemy. For this reason I declare that in this Nature and God – saving their honours and reverences – acted ignorantly when they made so very beautiful an appearance without faithfulness. For if she had a hundred times less beauty and she was loyal, the great goodness of loyalty would have done her more honour than if she were a hundred thousand times more beautiful.

'So I think I ought not to reproach Bonne Amour, or Fortune, or my lady for my sorrows. And what about myself? Indeed, yes! For I am put from abundance into exile, from security into mortal danger, from happiness into grief, through her subtle look, and from freedom into servitude where nobody loves nor values me, and my honour, my love, my service, and my life are not worth a cherry. Nonetheless, it seems to me that I did not make a mistake when I fell in love with her, for there was not in this mortal world any woman who was so excellent, as it was said. I became hers then with a good intent and never thought about it, because of the greatness of the very good name of she who has destroyed me. But all that glisters is not gold, and one should not love his pleasure so much that he cannot draw back from it if he thinks to. If I had been the best man in the world, I would not have chosen other than her, nor could I have chosen a better, if I had found loyalty in her.

'So I do not know what to blame, nor whom to reproach, for the grievous sorrow and unhappiness that I have. If I am asked about all this, I reply to everybody that God and Nature have done this. It is misfortune and sorrow, in that they made her body in every way so beautiful, so noble, so sweet that there could not be a better, if only she were faithful. Shall I blame these divinities? I shall not do so, for they are very much greater than I am. Thus I shall bear things from now on – it is my best course.

[861] 'Now I have told you how Love caused me to be a faithful lover, and everything that happened to me: how I was taken and how I was kept, how my lady did not remember me, the good and ill that I have had to endure until this day, how I have help from no one, how I cannot avenge the heavy sorrow that has slain and destroyed me.

'And so I say, if you have listened to me well, that the sorrow for which I am languishing to death, and which has stained my face and made it grow pale by its force, is a hundred thousand times greater than your woes. For pure joy and perfect sweetness are your pain compared with the sorrow which is martyring me.'

[881] 'Indeed, sir, I would not wish to deny that you have much sorrow and vexation, and you lose what your heart desires. But nevertheless, it is my opinion, and I would dare to express it, that, when your sorrow and mine are compared, there is less sorrow and more joy in you than there is in me. I wish to tell you the reason for this: you have told me that you faithfully love this lady who has caused you such pain, and you will love with a loyal heart as long as you live. And since you love her in this way, truly, I believe that you desire her love. For I see it happen very rarely that there is love without desire, or that desire can do without love and hope. And sometimes you have memories of her. When your heart is overwhelmed by desire, you recall the fair-haired beauty of

whom you have so many memories. You must have some thought which causes some joy to be born in you, which sets back the sorrow which dominates you, so that through memory you have happy thoughts which scatter and forget your sorrow.

'But my suffering multiplies night and day without ceasing, and the stream of my tears is always growing. I cannot have any thought or hope of bringing back my love. But by serving, by honouring, by concealing, by fearing, by cheerfully enduring and suffering, by loving well and obeying very humbly, you are still able to have relief, joy, and the love of her to whom your heart is inclined. And so I declare that I have greater torment. It seems to me the reason is very evident and palpable: for it is possible for you to have your lady again, but according to Nature it is impossible for me to have my lover again.'

[929] 'My lady, there is more honour, intelligence and tact in you than in any other creature, for I would soon be discomfited by your intelligence if I could not reply to your arguments. For truly, I would not know how to do it as wisely as I needed. But I want to repeat your arguments if I can. You claim that I love without deception, and will love for as long as I can endure, without repenting of it. And since I love, I must have desire, which can never be without hope, and I also have memory, which often moves me to have many thoughts. Indeed, my lady, I grant you all this to be true, with the only exception that I have no hope at all. But you know very well, my lady, that it is just as well that your understanding and mine do not meet or agree in anything, but rather, are opposed to each other. I don't wish to leave unmentioned that you say that I can still do so much by honouring, by serving well, by suffering, by fearing, by obeying, by loyally loving, that I can recover my lady in joy. But it would be a very great feat to keep her, for her heart would not stop in one place any more than a ball in a game. And your love, which is so worthy and laudable, you can never recover by any means, and for this reason you look so weak and pale. Accordingly, you say that my sorrows are much smaller than yours. I will reply to these arguments as best I can, and I will pause a little over each one and say what I feel and know about it from the personal experience of feeling.

[977] 'My lady, it is true that I love very loyally she who hates me, my beautiful lady, who is my death and my destruction when I see her love somebody else and care nothing for me whom she should love faithfully – and I am scarcely surprised at this love. For if she loved my life and my honour, she would not for anything let me languish for a single hour in the sorrow in which I live and remain. But it is Love first, and secondly my lady, which cause to grow in power that wave of sorrow that floods my heart. For this reason, I have desire. But what is it? It is desire to die soon, for nothing can come to me through which I could hope to be cured. And if I had the love of the best of women as I used to, I do not know if I would trust in it. No, indeed! Why? I would not dare. For as is said, nature overcomes nurture, and unless he loses his own nature the wolf always returns to the wood. This is pure truth. And for this reason there is no hope in my desire. Therein lies despair so acute that I would be overcome by the memory you tell of, which causes the thought to enter me which makes me happy. Truly I can never take pleasure in this, nor do I see, feel, nor hear, since my lady has taken a new lover.

'I want to prove that there is nothing which can give me more pain, and which makes my heart despair more than to remember. You know, and it is obvious – everybody sees it – that if I were never reminded of my lady who keeps me in such anguish, then my sorrow would be forgotten. And if it were forgotten, forgetfulness would see to it that sorrow would cease or completely die away, and this could cure me of all my ills. But what happens? Memory, by its subtle craft, brings back to my mind the gentle face and noble figure for which my heart is in exile, but my sorrow still goes on. Why? Because I thought myself to be loved, when I was very sweetly called her beloved. Alas! wretched me! now it is indeed otherwise, when my lady newly loves another. And can one think of anything worse, my lady? Indeed no! For this is to bring a lover to ruin, and not one among five hundred thousand would escape from such a mortal danger. Thus it many times happens, when I remember this, that my exhausted heart becomes so sorrowful within my body that I must faint.

[1048] 'And if thought is engendered in me by memory, what is it? It is discomfited, sad, mournful, weary and desperate. And by my faith, I have no thought which is not against me, to put it at its worst. Do you know why? Because I see my lady's changeableness. And if the joy that I had when I was in her grace were not greater than I could say, I could not think or imagine the heavy sorrow which grips me were any the less. But in that I had so much the greater happiness, my wretchedness is so much the more cruel. And when I have no hope, I cannot imagine or see that I might have my lady back again.

'And I will tell you what makes me grieve. My lady, it seems to me that something which divides itself between many places, and is always as alive with ceaseless movement as the trembling leaf, and is not all stable, is thus always changing and variable, now here, now there, by the fireside or at the table. And this is a very anxious thing, for in no way can one have her securely. It is indeed a game of enchantment, where what one thinks to have for sure, one has not at all.* Thus it is, my lady, although nobody says so, that with my lady – who changes and varies, gives and takes back, now hates, now is a lover – there is no one place that has all of her heart, and if someone shares it, truly, I believe he has a poor share of it, and that share soon goes away. In truth, a lover cannot hold any man so dear that he would want him to have a share in his love-affairs. And for this reason, I cannot fully have her heart, at which I lament. For with a heart that passes thus from hand to hand, if one has it today, one does not have it tomorrow. And anyway, the true lover is a real bird of prey, for he wants nothing for his complete happiness, except the whole heart of her to whom he gives himself. So I say that you would have back your lover as quickly as the nature would change of her whose heart was once wholly and irrevocably set on me. For one cannot draw the wolf from his skin without flaying him, and one cannot make a sparrow-hawk out of a cow, or the other way around.

[1108] 'And, sweet lady, it is the custom everywhere, of both men and women, that when the soul has left the body, and the body is in the earth beneath its stone, then very soon it is forgotten, although there may be weeping for it. For I see nobody who so remains in his grief that he is not seeking for happiness before the year is out, however loyal a lover he be, and I would not want to except great or small. And indeed, I think this is sensible. So you will follow this custom: you will not break it, for you will be reproached by nobody

*Cf. '. . . for hyt ys nothyng stable,/ Now by the fire, now at table;/ For many oon hath she thus yblent./ She ys pley of enchauntement,/ That semeth oon and ys not soo . . .' 645–9.

16

for it, and you will pray sincerely for his soul. But I cannot put behind me the lady that I cannot forget. For Memory keeps her very close to me, so that she does not leave for a day, an hour, a half-an-hour. And I see her quite often, which completely throws me. For a long time I follow her with my eyes, and I have no happiness, nor benefit, but instead I see somebody else who does have joy. It is this which destroys me. For if she did not wish to love either me or him, then I would not be lamenting to anybody of the sorrows that I have, but rather I would have carried them humbly in my heart and been discreet and stayed in hope of joy, fearing neither unhappiness nor sorrow.

'I do not wish to take away my heart for fear of the parting, and – to tell the truth – I would not know how to repent of loving. I should be a false lover if I took myself off, for I gave to her my love, and I will love her, whatever happens to me. By my faith, I love her so faithfully that I have a hundred times more grief for her than I have for myself when I see her honour being diminished. For those who know of this deed will point her out, and think less of her, and always consider her a deceiving woman. It is so base and ugly a transgression that whoever commits it, however much power he may have, will be quite undone. Because of this, my lady, I conclude that I have more sorrow, and that your ills will sooner be brought to a cure than those with which I am seized. And indeed I would dare to submit my case to judgement, if we could have a judge who wished to adjudicate faithfully and truly.'

[1168] 'By my soul, sir, I wish for my part, and dare to say, that I desire judgement from my heart. Now let us see who we want to choose, who without delay may know how to judge which of us is wrong. For I think that the woe I bear is so cruel that I must soon die.' 'My lady, I wish that the judge be chosen at your will.' 'But fair sir, I beg that he must be chosen by nobody but you, for you asked for it first, and because of that you ought to say.' 'Indeed, my lady, now do not wash your hands of the matter but say, for your part, for you know more than I do.'

And when I saw that they wished that judgement should be made of their sorrowful lots, my heart was as if new with happiness at it. I did not know which of two things I would do, whether to go towards them or stay where I was. For I would very gladly have helped them to choose such a judge as could understand how to judge between their hardships, a judge so completely appropriate that he would be absolutely experienced and make a convincing judgement. For a very long time I thought it over to myself and decided that I would go over to them. Then without delay I got up and went towards them over the thick, green grass. And when I came so close to them that I could see them quite openly, the little dog – which did not know me at all – began to yap, at which I noticed the lady started and called to it. But the little dog took very little notice of her call and came up to me barking and clung on to my clothes by its teeth.* I seized hold of it, and it left off barking in fright. I was inwardly very pleased, because in carrying it back to the lady I had an excuse and purpose to take me where I wanted to go, and so I smoothed the dog's fur.

[1219] When I arrived where I wanted to be, I was not at all disturbed or frightened, but greeted the company with a cheerful expression, as for my part I well knew how to do. The knight, who was wise, courteous and well-spoken,

---

*Cf. '. . . And as I wente, ther cam by mee/ A whelp . . .' 388–9.

17

tall and straight, handsome, agile, and well-schooled and accustomed to acting with honour, courteously came to me without delay to return my greeting. And the lady, in whom Nature had had such a hand that her great beauty surpassed comprehension, drew towards me very meekly and sweetly. For she had a very gracious manner, and a perfectly humble and sweet manner, golden hair, laughing eyes brighter than any falcon's, and her figure was beautiful, neat, fine and tall, and as elegant as a merlin's. Her eyes were set at just the right distance apart, and her expression was very sweetly appealing, but her bearing and her fine yet simple apparel were without parallel. And she was as white as snow when it lies on the branch, wise, loyal, courteous, and with a noble heart, and so perfect in everything that she was more beautiful in her faithfulness than in her beauty. There was no pride or cruelty in her, nor anything contrary to friendliness. Her face was marked very much by being drenched with tears, but nonetheless possessed a rather refined colour and pure gentleness.

The lady called me and then asked me very sensibly what brought me there. And I who very much wanted to hear her, related the whole story to her: how I had come there, and whence I had come, while they recounted their unhappiness. Then the knight said pleasantly in a low voice, 'I believe he has heard all our discussions.'

[1267] And I said to him, 'Sir, you can be sure of it. I have indeed listened to them most attentively and gladly, but do not think that I have anything other than good intentions in this. For truly, Venus was by a stream on a grassy path in this orchard, where I was delighting in listening to the bird's song. And when I came here, sir, I noticed you, and also my lady coming from the other side. I will tell you what I resolved to do: I looked for the leafiest part of the copse and thrust myself into it, for I was very afraid of causing you annoyance, and I listened all through to your joys and sorrows. Now it seems to me that you and my lady, whose head is bowed with her grief, would very much like to know through a judgement which of your sorrows is the heavier. And you do not wish to be the first to select a judge, nor my lady either.

'For this reason I have come advisedly, to name to you a knight very skilled in matters of love. For neither in this country or beyond the sea is there a nobler, more courteous heart. He surpasses Alexander in largess and Hector in prowess. He is the root and branch of all nobility, and he does not live like a servant in his wealth. He wishes for nothing but the honour of all earthly good, and he is happier when he can say "you keep it" than a covetous man is when he can take his property. God and the Church, and faithfulness, he loves, and also justice, to such an extent that he is called the Sword of Justice. He is humble and gentle and full of generosity to his friends, fierce and unrelenting to his enemies. In brief, wherever he goes, he is always given by good people the highest praise for his wisdom and honour. And if he happens to have his enemy at an advantage, Nature and his own good heart instruct him to have pity. He is a very noble man, for Prowess everywhere carries his sword, Boldness leads and urges him on, and Largess opens for him the door to all hearts. He treats good people like brothers and sisters, the great, the less great, and the humble. And of Love, sir, he knows all the attacks and onsets, the joys and ills, the complaints and the tears, better than Ovid, who knew all its ways. And if you want to know his name which is good and of noble renown, then tell me or not.'

[1331] 'Indeed, my friend, we beg you to know, for I think there never was or will be a man who was in every way as perfect as he is in word and deed.'

'Sir, he is the King of Bohemia, of the name of Luxembourg, son of Henry, the good King of Germany, who through force of arms was crowned Emperor at Rome, with his mother. For this reason it is right and proper that he is a good man, for he should be from both his father's and his mother's side. Accordingly, fair sir, it would be very good to choose such a judge, who would well know how to point out to you which of you suffers most pain. I urge you then to choose him.'

The knight replied wisely, 'I believe God has brought us here,' and he said, 'My lady, if you take him for judge, I accept that.' And the lady replied calmly, 'Sir, I hear so much good said of the King, and he is so wise, worthy and splendid, that I agree to this.'

'Many thanks, my lady. Now we are agreed on that. I pray God that the good king lead us soon into a fair haven, if we may speak to him at the place to which we must go.'

I replied, 'If you like, I know very well how to lead you to the place where he is. I am sure of it, for indeed, I ate and drank yesterday with his people in the castle of Durbuy. He is still there; he will not leave there today. And it isn't at all far away, only a stone's throw.'

[1371] The knight urged the lady to go without further delay, and the lady said, 'I have no wish to object, but I don't know which way to take.' I said, 'My lady, I will very gladly show you. Please come. I will go on in front and you will come along after.' And so, eager to go, I set off on the way.

And when they saw Durbuy from nearby, they stopped and marvelled at the sight, for never in their lives, they said, had they seen so beautiful and noble a castle. And without doubt it is very strong and exceedingly delightful, beautiful, and also very hospitably open. For if the kings of Germany and France were before the castle, they would not leave before they went in and out of it, if they wished, every time they needed to be in that district. It is set on a rock in the middle of a valley, entirely surrounded by water which laps, deep and broad, around it. There are gardens all around, so beautiful that one could not wish for any lovelier, and there are so many birds that the valley echoes with their song. The water, too, makes a very tranquil sound, so that one could not find any greater delight in anything, and there are craggy rocks all around, yet at some distance from the castle. But the house on the rock is so fine that nobody ever saw another more beautiful, for there is not a single flaw in it. There is an excellent fountain in the courtyard, with bright, clear, pure water from the rock, cold as ice and sweeter than the Seine. The vessel into which the water falls is chiselled from pure marble of light and dark hues, and so beautiful that there was none such since the time of Abel. By the river bank there is a broad, expansive meadow, with many types of trees.

[1423] But I must come back to my subject. When they had seen the house I tackled them and said, 'It is time to go. Let us enter, for we are not doing anything here.' So we went along the way, crossed the bridge, and did not stop anywhere until we knocked at the door. But the porter opened the door very willingly. As it was myself who had knocked, and I was first and quite used to being there, I said, 'This knight, and this lady as well, come to talk to the king, if he is here.' And the porter immediately replied that he was there. I said, 'My friend, please find out if it is possible to speak with him.' He said that he would go, but just as he was leaving us to go up, a fine, noble knight, handsome and gay, came to us. He was called Honour, and was more knowledgeable than anybody. He certainly did not come to us alone, but a lovely lady, beautiful and gay, kept him company, and she was called Lady Courtesy. As soon as she saw us she greeted us and then received us very handsomely, and so did Honour, as he ought to do. Then courteously, laughingly, calmly, they both took each of the pair by the finger. But I ought to say that Courtesy accompanied the knight, with joy and without reserve, and Honour wished to accompany the lady. Then together they began to explain their thoughts. They went along whilst talking to where they were led, mounting the marble steps until they entered the good king's chamber.

The good king – he who was always wise, loyal, valiant, liberal and graceful, and gentle, humble and courteous towards everybody – was seated in very great joy on a silken carpet, and a clerk whose name I could not tell you was reading to him about the siege of Troy. Boldness was there with him – and her daughter Prowess – gently holding by the hand Largess, a lady of very great nobility. There were also there: Richesse, Amour, Biauté, Loiauté, and Leësse, Desirs, Pensers, Volenté and Noblesse, Franchise, Honneur, Courtoisie, and Juenesse. These sixteen were with the king and never left him. God and Nature had granted them to him since he was born, and so they all served him. This is a great favour. And if any one there commits some undeniable wrong, Raison is there to rub out the wrong. In this fashion the noble king was sitting. When he saw the lady he rose and took her by the hand, for Courtesy taught him to do so. Afterwards he greeted the knight, approving of him very much, and then asked them very wisely what brought them there. He asked them about themselves, for they pleased him. The knight asked the lady if she would tell the king, and she said that she would not, that it was more fitting that the knight should do so first. He then replied that he would tell everything thoroughly from beginning to end just as it was.

[1509] 'Sire,' he said, 'there is near here a green and flowery garden where there is a great noise of nightingales singing. I came there this morning to listen to their fine service and their beautiful singing, although my inconsolable heart could take little joy in it. But nonetheless, I had come there in this way by chance, pensive with all the cares that Love sent me. I saw coming along a narrow, green and grassy way this lady that has come here with me. She seemed to me to have a bewildered expression, and so I immediately made my way towards her over the thick grass. And when I was near I greeted her, but she did not say a word – at which I was very surprised – nor showed any sign of acknowledging me by her look or her manner. And I, wondering why this was, said very politely, "Most sweet and dear lady, why do you not wish to listen to what I say?" And I drew her by part of her gown. At this she trembled, and her lovely face changed colour. She replied that she could not stop any longer, but she apologized very profusely to me for being so wrapped up in the thoughts on which she was musing. And I asked her why her heart was so pensive. In the end I said and did so much that she told me everything that I asked her. I swore and pledged by my faith that when she had finished what she had to say, I would tell her my own thoughts.

'And thus she said that she used to have a loyal lover who loyally loved her and she him. But death had taken him away from this earth. And the worthiness, the intelligence, the value, the prowess, the honour, of which he was, as she said, the flower, made him to be utterly the best of good men. For this reason she was deep in thought and always would be, and – as she thought –

she wept and lamented for him, so that her face was bathed in tears. And because of this, she held that the sorrow she felt for her lover was heavier than that which had me in its grip.

[1563] 'And, sir, I had to say quite the opposite. I love faithfully from my heart, and without any going back, the most beautiful and sweetest face that Nature could ever create, who formerly abandoned all of her heart to me. She called me her heart, her love, her lover, and, according to what she said, loved me above all others. Now, sir, she has no more concern for me – thus she has abandoned me and taken a new lover. And by my soul, I have not deserved it. And now she gives and distributes elsewhere my own reward: I have no part or scrap of it. And this, sir, is why my heart is breaking. Considering my case, it seems to me that I have a worse fate than the lady, although her love be dead – may God have his soul in paradise!

'And this clerk, sir, who seems to me gay, handsome and capable, was hidden in the garden and covered by the thickest of the green foliage. He popped out when he had heard all of our disagreement. He advised us that the rights and wrongs of the case should be put to you, and we agreed on this. For our debate had lasted a long time, and we had put forward many arguments, as it is written down more fully above. Now we have come here to you, so that the right may be adjudged and known, and that what you have to say may be held to by both of us. You can immediately end this debate if you wish, because we have made you our judge. Sir, you have now heard completely our whole position. Please be kind enough to give your judgement for we have wanted it for a long time, and this lady and myself most devoutly beg you to do it.'

[1609] When the knight had presented their arguments to him who well knew how to act wisely, the noble king, who was a very worthy man, replied, 'As God protect me, you have chosen in me a judge ignorant and ill-provided with sense, nor did I ever hear or see of such a judgement. I would have very little idea of how to adjudicate it. But nonetheless, I wish to have the advice of my company about it, for I have a fine and noble company.' Then smiling, he called Loyalty, who was there, Love, Youth, and Raison, who spoke first. The noble king then asked them, 'What would those of you say, who know all rights? This knight, who is noble and able, and this golden-haired lady too, have come to me here – for which I thank them – and wish to hear judgement from me as to which of them has most pain and care. The lady had a faithful lover who loved and served her and she him, as much as she could. Now it has happened that Death, who receives all, has taken him away. Her heart is grief-stricken over this, for in his time he had such great excellence that there was nobody better, nor anybody more handsome.

'The knight, without repenting of it, loves with his whole heart a lady who is in his opinion the most beautiful alive. And she promised him an unchanging faithfulness, and she regarded him as a dearly loved lover – he was sure of it. Now the lady has set her heart on another and utterly thrown him over, and has no care for him. And before his eyes he sees the beautiful lady and the new lover who has the sweet goods that he has deserved.

[1652] 'Now I have told you why they have come to hear what I have to say. And doubtless, a heart which languishes in this way destroys itself and lives in great misery. You ought then to give me advice about it, as best you can, for each of you is my dear and intimate friend, and I trust in you very greatly, as you well know. Speak then, Raison. I want to hear your opinion first for you have given me much good advice.'

Raison, which was beautiful and of good renown, replied as follows, 'Sire, I declare that both these two lovers are in great distress when they have lost in this way the objects of their love, and their hearts are breaking just as wax melts and diminishes in front of the fire. But that they are altogether equal in suffering and misfortune, I would not wish to say. I will tell you what I feel, since it must be done. This lady can never see her true lover, and since she will not see him anymore it will come to pass that she will forget him. For the heart will never love something so much that it will not forget it through distance. Indeed, I am not saying that for a while she will not have pain and anguish over it. But Youth, which is so gay and joyous, would not for anything allow that it should not be forgotten. For Youth, sire, very soon forgets what is not seen. I declare, then, that Love does not have so much power in itself that it could last for an hour of the day without the lover, or without the lady too. And if one of the three is lacking, the other two will fall short: it is necessary that Love, the lover, and the lady be all three together, otherwise the love is worthless. And since the lady and Love have lost the company of the lover, truly, I would not give a rotten apple for their love – that is to say, the love that is of this world. It is very good to do one's duty, and that the soul can perceive it. But there is not a soul or a living man who loves without blame and who does not, if he is caught by the amorous flame, love the body rather better than the soul. Why is this? Love comes from carnal affection, and its desire and condition are completely inclined towards the delight of the flesh. No man or woman who wants to love can ensure that he or she does not commit vice or sin through it. This must be so, and it is contrary to the soul. On the other hand, as soon as the soul leaves the body, love goes away and scatters, and this I see everywhere, as God preserve me. Thus the love of this lady, which is so worthy, is always diminishing day by day.

[1724] 'But as for this lover, who has rashly started to love without my advice, and has so got himself into it, the wretch, that he is completely undone by it, the woes of loving are in his heart and are extremely bitter to him. Love makes him burn both night and day, so that he would not, nor could not, forget his enemy. Do you know why? Because Company, Love, Beauty, Joyful Youth, and Loyalty – which should in no way be forgotten – make him languish in great folly, in rage, in grief, in frenzy, in great jealousy, and in peril of his soul and of his life. For his sorrowful heart never leaves his lady, but accompanies her everywhere – and he who is nearest the fire, burns most. And Loyalty prohibits him to do anything false. But if he had worked by my advice, he would not have continued his love when his lady took a new lover. For in such a case, the lady sets the pace and calls the tune. Then Beauty tells him that he does better if he languishes for love of her than if he takes pleasure in another, and so does Love. Youth nurtures him with folly in this misfortune, in this mad mistake, for in it he loses his wits and his strength. Thus the wretch languishes in sorrow, for when he sees that in his presence somebody else rejoices in the lady who used to call him her lover, his heart becomes so jealous, so anguished, that it is a marvel that he does not kill himself, or prepare to kill the cause of his torment. And Jealousy puts this into him at his ear. And if he had her love, just as he used to, what would he do? Indeed, he would do nothing, for he would never trust in it. And for this reason, he never has any hope of any other solace, since he can never be nonchalant about this lady who makes him sorrow so much. Accordingly, I say that he has more woe than this lady here, and that his heart is in greater care for the reasons that you have heard. And, according to my wish, this knight has spoken very well – for I have found it written out above – and has proved his point through reason, as it seems to me.'

[1785] When Raison had recited all of her opinion, Love spoke. She was delightfully beautiful, and graceful in manner and countenance. She said, 'Raison, you have set out your argument very well. I accept it, except that it would be wrong to take his heart out of the prison of that very beautiful woman for whom he feels the spark of love. I wish that he love and serve her as the one in whom he has had much happiness. For if he could live a thousand years and always serve her, he would never deserve through service the great sweetness that she used to show him. And if Plaisance, who causes many strange changes, causes him to be uncertain of his lady, should he for that reason be in despair? Indeed no! There are still a hundred thousand in my service who love very nearly as strongly as he, and they have precious little reward for it. I have the power to cure him and to rid him of sorrow, but he has no trust nor hope in me, and this is what makes him sorrow more.'

[1812] 'How is this, Love?' said Raison. 'Is it through your tricks that he will love, without having any help, she who has given her heart elsewhere? And does he who serves you not receive the reward that he deserves? Truly, he is foolish to serve when he loses his reward.'

After this Loyalty went up to Love and said, 'It is not right, if he is true, loyal and upright, that he should be among those who beat the bushes while other people take the birds. For if the lady, whom I sternly reprove and blame – and quite rightly, for she deserves great blame for changing about unfaithfully – if she had not first removed her heart from this lover who was always hers to command, oh! Love, Love, I would have spoken differently! But without doubt, when he loves her with all his might, and she forgets him without cause, then he must dance just as she dances, not that he should do anything through which he might lose my favour. For if he left her, and looked out for himself elsewhere, I do not consider that he would be doing something wrong against me. And so I thoroughly agree with Raison (for she made a very good and true statement) that the knight is right and the lady is wrong.'

[1848] And when Youth (who was very gay and full of happiness and who takes no account of any gift or promise except only what suits her will) had heard what Raison and Loyalty had said, she thought very little of it, for she was very full of her own will and said aloud, 'Indeed, Raison, your knowledge is deficient, and you must know, Loyalty, that you are worthless. For this lover, with whatever woe or pang that Love may curse him, will never leave the beautiful woman, who surpasses all others in beauty, in gentleness and in fine colour. May it never please God for it to happen that he ever refrain from loving that beautiful creature! For if at the moment he is not wanted or thought worthy, at least he loves her and follows her with his heart. Is this not a great deal? Must he cease to love her? Certainly not! For undoubtedly, one is not always loved, or made welcome, or called lover. He is a foolish lover who listens to you, Raison, or follows your words, or your company. And I declare that whoever does so does not see anything. And by my faith, we will do so much, Amours, my lady and I, that his heart will be so caught, and in such bondage,

23

that he will never leave, night or day. And your efforts, don't worry, will never be strong enough that the pure heart of this lover will be away from the very beautiful lady where it finds very little consolation. My lady Love, who burns, tinges and enflames his heart, and I who am still all aflame, will keep him to this love; for by my soul, he should stay with it. And may he bear and sustain any further sorrowful woes which are caused him by his lady.'

Then the noble king considered, and laughed amiably at what Youth had just proposed. But not for a moment did he think any the less of her for it, because she was doing what she had to do in speaking as she had, and he esteemed her more than any material gain. He said, 'Youth, fair lady, you are great sovereigns, you and Love, who keep this lover in great distress, poverty, misery and sadness. See how the wretch has lost all help, and his heart has no refuge or recourse except to death, which is hastening to him. For you wish to torture him too much and ruin him utterly. Now, if you please, he has found an adviser good and true, and if you let him receive some advice, you would do well. For he is caught in such tight bonds that he knows no means or device to escape.'

'Indeed, sir, that is of no account. But rather, he will love the very fair creature for whom he has so much love. And if he dies of it, everybody will call him a martyr for love and it will be to his honour.'

[1921] When Youth had finished speaking, the king spoke to them and said, 'We are not assembled here to argue over whether he should or should not love his lady, but to find out which has the greater love, and who feels more keenly the woes of love, as it seems to me. Now you are all agreed that there is a greater concentration of pain in this lover than in the lady. I do not dissent from this agreement. On the contrary, I completely agree that this lover is further from consolation than the lady is, who is consoled by God. I would give judgement accordingly, although I am not accustomed to such things, and I well know indeed, that somebody else would have done it better. However, I will say this: I have considered the opinion of Raison to be correct, and the arguments of you who wish for justice. I have also taken heed of Loyalty, who has spoken pure truth on the matter and pursues no trickery or falseness, as also of Love, who has spoken well on the subject as well, and of Youth. All feel that this lover suffers more sadness, and is wounded more severely by the woes of love, than the very noble lady – that he is further removed from the comfort that he needs. For this reason, I give and declare my judgement that he has the greater evil than she has, and more care and grief.'

When the good king had given his verdict, enacted by Raison, the knight thanked him there in his presence, while the lady was so lost in her thoughts that she uttered no word. But nonetheless, in the end she granted that she accepted the judgement that the king had made. For he was so wise and loyal that he would never do anything but justice to anybody.

[1968] Then the king with a smile took them by their fingertips and seated them on a Nordic carpet far away from the others, so that there was nobody there but the three of them. He urged and implored each of them to take comfort, for if their hearts bore such woe for a long time then both he and she could be dead from it – and this should never happen, but each of them should take heart once more. For the heart that drenches itself in such weeping and sorrow destroys itself and makes itself ill. And one often sees it said that one should forget everything that one perfectly well sees cannot be amended or brought back by complaints and tears. If they did this, he said, they would not err against Loyalty. But if they injured themselves in this weeping for love they were murdering their souls and their lives. Afterwards, the king called his household: there came Franchise, Honneur, and Courtoisie, Biauté, Desir, Leëse the joyful, and Hardiesse, Prouesse, Amour, Loiauté and Largesse, Voloir, Penser, Richesse with Juenesse, and then Raison, who was mistress of all. The king commanded them that each of them should seek to honour these two lovers, and that Love should keep them from Melancholy. Then the meal was prepared, for it was already near evening. And they did his will without hesitation, as good and well-instructed people. Then they approached the lovers without more ado, and each of them did all he could which he thought would please them, as folk who were full of ardour and good will.

[2010] Then the lovers asked leave to depart, but they were pleasantly refused, for Courtoisie, Franchise, Honneur and her friend Largesse, the noble king, and all who were there very pressingly begged them to stay. It was near the hour of supper, and at this horns were sounded through the castle. Then they rose and went in pairs, two by two, to the hall, and afterwards in courtesy they washed their hands. Then they sat and ate and drank, as was right, for there was a very great abundance of good things. After they had eaten, the noble king drew them by the edge of their gowns and said, 'You will not leave me, for I do wish at this time to rid you of the thoughts that cause you pain.' The knight began to thank him very humbly, as did the lady, who said she could not put off her departure for very long. And in the end the king kept them for eight days with great joy, and at their departure gave them very generous gifts of horses, harnesses, jewels and silver. At the end of eight days they departed and asked leave of the king, in whom they had found so much honour that they said they had never before seen so good and noble a king. But Honour kept them company, as also did Courtoisie, Juenesse, Amour and happy Richesse, and many others whose names I don't know. For they mounted their horses and conveyed them on their way, until they brought both of the lovers to their homes, and then they returned to the king at Durbuy.

[2052] Here I will bring my subject to an end, and will rhyme no more about it, for I have enough rhymes to write elsewhere. But at the end of this little book I will ensure that whoever would like to know truly my name and surname will clearly be able to perceive and see it in the last line of the book, provided that he separates the first seven syllables and puts the letters together again in a different way without forgetting or leaving out any. In this way, whoever wants to know my name will be able to know it. He will not esteem me any more for that, yet nonetheless it will make no difference. And I shall be a true lover, fine and full of joy, for if I did not have anything more in this world than that I love my lady, simple and quiet, against her will, I have enough. For love has honoured me and richly rewarded my pain when I gave my heart to my lady in this way for always. And in its sorrows my heart is comforted that when the sorrows of love were first felt, humble succour was thought of for gentle woe.

Le Dit de la Fonteinne Amoureuse
Guillaume de Machaut

In the *Fonteinne Amoureuse* Machaut reveals in an anagram that he composed the poem for Jean, duc de Berry. It appears from the theme of the *dit* that Machaut wrote it to mark the Duke's departure in 1360 for England, where he was to stay as a hostage under the terms of the Treaty of Brétigny. The lady would consequently be the Duke's recently wedded wife, Jeanne d'Armagnac. Machaut's poem is a significant source for Chaucer's Ceyx and Alcyone episode in the *Book of the Duchess*. The text is translated from the *Œuvres*, ed. E Hoepffner, SATF (Paris, 1908–21).

In order to give delight and consolation to myself, and to bind my thoughts to the true love that holds me in those bonds where I shall never tire of being, nor ever say 'alas!', I wish cheerfully to begin something in honour of my lovely lady, which will be gladly received, and delightfully written out of the delightful experience of that true heart which is devoted to her.

Now I beg those who read this to pick out the good from the bad while reading, if there is any good in it. For when a thing is well chosen then people rightly enjoy it more, and ladies and gentlemen who read it must take more pleasure in it and feel among the chosen few. But I don't want to include anything ugly, for when there is rumbling thunder and menacing clouds the weather is dark and gloomy. For this reason I wish to renounce everything base. And I will begin without delay when I have named him for whom I am composing this book, and my own name as well, for there is certainly no reason why that should be left out, as I am constrained to this more than anybody – Fine Loving commands me to do it, and Pleasure wishes that I attend to it, and Pleasure does not desire anything that is trifling. My heart is pledged and my body is a hostage until it is done. Now I will tell you what you should do to discover our names. [*Here in an anagram the author identifies himself and Jean, duc de Berry.*] Now see if I am lying! For truly, if I were lying I should be most perplexed and ashamed.

[55] Now I want to begin on my theme and tell everything that happened, which at first was obscure and frightening to me, but in the end turned out happily for me. Not long ago I was in bed somewhere but not sleeping, like somebody who is asleep yet still awake. I was just dozing on and off, because it was rather difficult for me to get to sleep when melancholy attached itself to my thoughts. But when nature was just about to take its rest in me, I heard somebody lamenting very bitterly, and I could well see that he was not

pretending, because he was complaining and groaning so deeply that I felt a shiver of horror and fear at it. And I heard this two or three times, at which I was very distressed. Then I listened carefully to find out what it could be, for I was not very familiar with that room or place. But as I listened, I imagined in my heart that it was some spirit by which I might be murdered. Then I was extremely frightened and shrank back into my bed – you would have thought I had a fever, for I am more cowardly than a hare, and I trembled and sweated for fear. I lay there in such a bad way, that if anybody had taken my doublet, my belt or my shirt, I would not have stopped him at all! No, indeed, by God! anybody who had taken my body would not have seen me stir. And if anybody says this is cowardice or melancholy I would not care two apples for his opinion, for I have seen braver men than one might ever see or name, whether in this country or overseas, who would not lie in a room on their own for the price of Rheims or Paris. And when they are armed indeed, by God, they fear nothing but dishonour. Because of this I wish to be excused.

Nevertheless I would still like to say – because it has to do with my theme – that if I were armed on the field of battle and saw the enemy advancing to deal his blows, and if I could either leave or stay in the thick of battle, by the faith I owe my creator, I know which I would do! Think of it what you will, but it is not pleasant to be driven out of one's wits, and it is often much better to go after the good things than to die or flee. For I would like to bear witness and say that a cowardly knight, and a clerk who wants to be brave, are not worth a handful of straw in deeds of arms or in battle, for each is acting contrary to what is right. If they do well, it's just luck. And although I am an ignorant, silly, impertinent clerk, I have been, by my two faiths, sometime in such place with the good King of Bohemia (whose soul may God have in His company!) that I was brave in spite of myself, for there was no way I knew how to escape, so I had to be brave. For the country was wild and unknown to me, I didn't know the language, and I was certainly safer if I stayed at his side than far away from him, for I didn't dare go anywhere else in case I was taken for a spy. And if it is thought to be boasting, such praise is very fitting to those brave in arms. When battle plans are made, it is wise to put one's lord in the best and safest place to avoid ill fortune. Whoever keeps close to his lord cannot be dishonoured, and if there are chickens, capons or any other delicacies he has some crumb or part of what is left. For if the lord makes his departure, there is less unworthiness in accompanying one's lord, for to fly can win grace; he makes an honourable pursuit who wins grace through honour, without flattery or deceit, without pillaging and stealing. I speak altogether in general terms without saying anything specific. . . .

[189] But I am putting off too long what I first wanted to talk about, and I now wish to take up my subject again and go on. I listened so long and so hard to this person whom I heard talking in his misery, and I was fortunate in this, for his speech – which I half-heard – gave me very great pleasure. He said in a loud voice, 'Farewell, my lady, I am going away. I am not arranging anything, except that I am leaving you my heart, so that I am going away without a heart. And I do not know where I am going, nor do I have a fixed date to return. I entrust myself to God, to Love and to you, dear lady, whom I love a hundred times more than myself, by my soul. But my lady, before I go far away from you – which saddens me greatly – I shall compose a sad complaint in that severe sorrow which burns my heart, and makes me grow pale and marks my face.

And if God gives me the grace not to make a mistake or do wrong in this complaint, and it is to your liking, I shall be in the seventh heaven, and I shall live so much more happily because of it, for you will know of my feelings.'

Then I immediately felt myself out of my depression, got myself dressed and tidied myself up and lit the candle. But all the time I was listening towards the right of the fireplace, where there was a window through which I could hear his words, for I was near to the window. I took my writing-desk, which is inlaid with ivory, and all my writing implements, in order to write down the complaint which he wished to make. Then he began it very piteously on his part, and for my own part I transcribed it very happily.

The Complaint of the Lover

[235] 'Sweet lady, may it please you to hear my lament, as I go away sighing – sad, sorrowful and overwhelmed with grief – nor can I tell the year or the month of my return. Alas! in this I am losing the gracious company of your sweet eyes, which many times through their sweetness have very sweetly sweetened my sorrow, joyfully turned my tears into joy and given me back my wits and my strength – for of these I was completely deprived when I saw your splendour, which surpasses all others in grace and worth.

'That sweet look was all my comfort: it maintained my spirit within my body, for – if it had not been for that – I would long ago have been dead, because it sustained me against all desolation. Alas, it was the delight of my love, and the true haven of my life and health. It was worth a great deal to me, for when the spirit of refusal came into my lady, this sweet look immediately contradicted it, and sweetly kept me, so that my spirit was reassured and not frightened anymore. Thus my heart always took all its comfort from that sweet look.

'And when I lose the solace and joy of that very sweet look that I used to have, if I lament and sigh and weep I cannot do anything else, for in this world I have a single wish, and I do not wish for anything but that. I was always happy in thinking of that look. Alas! now I do not know if I will ever see the sweet lightnings of her look, through which I was pierced to the heart and set to bearing the sweet enterprise of love, for I must go far away from her. But I will preserve her honour wherever I am.

[283] 'There is something else which is even harder for me, for I am going away, and there is nobody who can mention my sorrow to my pure lady, because nobody knows what I endure. She herself does not know the wound that my heart feels through her sweet face, and that I cannot see, imagine, think, nor conceive how I can have happiness, for I serve and love her without any deceit or baseness. Alas! now I am leaving with very little hope, and perhaps somebody else is begging her for her love who – if she loves him – truly kills my heart.

'And if it should be, my sweet lady, that I am not loved or called lover by you, or if (God preserve me from this) your pure heart is given in love to another, I should be so mortally wounded that sooner or later I should die or go mad because of it. For in that I am borne up by your sweet look – such that I don't care about anything else – and my heart is enamoured by your glance, then if I had a quarter share of your love, as God may keep me, there never was a lover anywhere so highly honoured.

[315] 'And when with a quarter of your love I could be taken out of hell and put into the earthly paradise, if I do not have it I must suffer every pain, for that would be to lose everything in honour and way of life, in heavenly and earthly happiness. For despair, which leads a creature to death in hell eternally, will be within me – be sure of that. But unless you are my sovereign lady, there will be nothing left of me sooner than an empty valley is covered with broom.

'And when my life, my death, and my health lies in you, sweet and lovely lady, if you would deign to be on my side, I am cured. And if it should be that you do not love me at all, or prefer another, or are hostile to my feelings, I am humiliated. It is up to you, and at your pleasure. But when I have been taken prisoner and surrender myself as a captive into your keeping, submissive and true, you ought not to hurt me, I think, when without impropriety I love and esteem you more than Paris ever did the beautiful Helen.

'I do not know how, nor can, nor wish to defend myself, and thus I must wait upon your mercy. Because I do not wish to offend you or Love, I will wait until pity for me gives rise in you to grace and mercy, and until your tender face deigns to turn towards me its sweet look. But I do not know when that will be, which much distresses me, for I am too far away from your pretty body, which will force my true heart to split in two if I do not have mercy – I who have never loved, nor wish to love, nor ever will love another. And, by my faith! I will die, without any mistaking.

[363] 'Alas! wretched me! what is the value of this waiting? And what is it worth that I have put all my hopes in you, when I do not know, my sweet, noble lady, if you recall how desire for your love possesses me? how it burns me, and assails and torments me? how I live in wretched melancholy when it has to be that your beauty, from which all joy springs, and your goodness – which bears up all honour, and which my heart serves, loves, obeys and fears – are absent from me? or when I do not see your noble body, in which there is nothing that is not perfect and which is always pretty and delightful? It is this which puts me and holds me on the path of death.

'This is why I have tasted sadness; this is what slays all my joys; this is what so pierces and kills my heart, and so hurts me that I see nothing that can comfort me. I can think of nothing but of desolation, in which my longing overcomes my hope, and joy does not know the way to my heart, but sadness knows the right way there very well. It is her keep, her principal stronghold, her chief resort: there she lives and reigns as queen and mistress, there she holds my heart in mortal distress, and with great largesse distributes the jewels of death.

'Alas! there is nothing which is not against me, and I see nothing that can make any difference in my situation, so I must suffer my woes in silence. And I am a hostage, and thus can do very little through my honour, for I am young and to be of more worthiness I ought to frequent places where worthiness and valour dwell. Now I am in a cage, which is to say that I am in captivity, where I can perform very few deeds of service, and this will do my name great harm, which I must lament. Thus I am losing my youth, my time, my lady, and my fresh spirits. It would be more honourable for me to be in Carthage or in Cairo.

[411] 'And if I lose your love, my lady – you who control my love and my heart from afar, because you have possession of my life – I certainly believe that this will be because I am worth very little and have won very little honour. But now I cannot seek other labour or other battle, nor can I do anything that is

worthwhile, for I have taken the straw and left behind the grain – that is you, my lady, in whom there is nothing lacking – and thus I fall from high to low. Thus it must be that desire continually assails me, and because of this I say that the hope which love gives me is worth nothing.

'And if I thus have little hope, nobody should be surprised at it, to be sure, for I am poor in honour, worth, and goodness, while you are the flower, the very best of all good qualities – as I know by true experience – root and branch of honour, of prudence and of honesty. If you quickly and rightly refused me, and gave your love to someone better, yet you could still soon set me right through your power, for I am rich in good will, and well furnished with love and loyalty, and desire to do your will only.

'And so I wish to praise and complain on love. I wish to praise love in that without relenting it makes my true heart remain on such a lady in whom all good dwells. But I complain on love because from fearing, serving, loving and desiring unfeignedly I cannot do anything through which I might expect mercy or that she would love me. Alas, unhappy me! this is what constrains my heart, what stains my face and is always changing its colours; this is what is extinguishing both my hope and my strength. For this my heart groans, weeps, and goes on doing so. But my lady cannot hear the complaint of my heart.

[459] 'And even if I am put into confinement, all my hope is not lost, but indeed it is much diminished. Yet Love, from which Hope comes, will soon augment it when she pleases, for all hearts soon change where Love is. And if my lady takes pleasure in my pain, or if – in order to injure me – Standoffish-ness, who hates and despises me, urges her to kill me, or if grace is always forbidden to me in love, which saves many a lover from death, then everything will soon be destroyed, taken, and overcome.

'I have no other hope, and so I sigh and weep, although I well know that love can in a very little time cure a heart which is working towards death. But I have no hope that mercy will come from beyond the sea, or seek to cure me from my woe, nor that love will help me at all from such a great distance, nor that her heart would take my part and be advocate for me, when my heart must always stay in her bonds and never be free of love. Alas! this kills me and makes me say "alas!" This is why I am sorrowful, sad and afflicted.

'Dear gods, how can I last in such a state, how can I endure such evils? Where do these evils come from? They come from beyond the sea and will slay me, for there is nothing on this side of the sea that can cure them, and I have to go there, while my lady would not think of coming there too. It is not fitting. And when she launched the dart of love which wounded me in the heart, to be sure, I believe she did not think to make me fall in love. And thus I believe that my sorrowing heart will never be cured of the wound it has, unless Love sets Pity to work, which has never helped me.

[507] 'Now let us suppose that Love wished to help me, and that Pity wished to soften and change the honest heart of my lady. How can this be? It is not fitting for her to send to me, or show herself friendly towards me, before I humbly beg to have her grace. She loves honour more than a valley full of gold, and well knows how to preserve it everywhere, and she is so wise that she does nothing and will do nothing that harms her honour. And I am far away from her sweet, noble face, and so do not see that Pity will cure me very easily.

'And if I send to my dear lady to say that she has pierced my heart, and that love of her burns it without fire and martyrs it without flame, and that desire more and more enflames it, she will say that I am causing her dishonour, and that I should not tell my pain to man or woman. And if I were to write to her, I do not know if she would read my letter. And from so far away I would not be able to tell her that she is starving me of the very sweet, good things of love, so that I would not know how to pick out the worst of my griefs, for in my predicament I cannot see anything which, by my soul, does not grow worse all the time.

'So I must find some other way, if I wish to know how I can advance this love that I want to keep up, and which quite destroys me. When Fortune caused King Ceyx to perish in the sea, he had to die. But Alcyone, who was his queen, could never enquire enough, or enough consult soothsayers, that she knew the truth of what had happened. And so she had him searched for on the sea; for in truth, she loved him more than anything, with a most pure love. She tore her hair and beat her breast, and because of her love for him she could not sleep.

[555] 'Alcyone's heart was so afflicted by the sorrow she had for her husband, who perished at sea through Fortune, that she said weeping to Juno several times: "I beg you, powerful goddess, hear my sad plea." She offered her many sacrifices and gifts for her beloved, and to know where, and how, and when he died. She was always begging for this very much, so that the goddess Juno had such great pity for her that Alcyone saw Ceyx in her sleep. I will now tell you how it happened: the God of Sleep did it through his command and caused her to fall asleep.

'Juno, who saw and heard Alcyone's prayer, which came from a devoted, humble and true heart, said to her loyal messenger Iris, "Listen to me. I well know that you are prompt and light of foot. Go now to the god who hates noise and light, who loves all manner of sleeping and hates disturbance. Tell him that I send you to him, and tell him of the grief and suffering of Alcyone. Instruct him to show her King Ceyx, and the manner in which he died, and how and why." Iris replied, "I understand you, my lady. I will very gladly take this message, by my faith."

'Iris is immediately ready for her journey: she takes her wings and flies through the air hidden in a cloud. She goes on until she arrives in a large valley surrounded by two great mountains, and with a stream which murmured through the landscape. There was a house there which was marvellously beautiful, and within is the god who sleeps and slumbers so much that there is nothing that can properly wake him. Iris comes into the house, but is greatly amazed that there is neither man or woman awake inside. She herself feels ready for sleep, and is frightened.

[603] 'In the chamber where the God of Sleep is asleep, there is an extremely rich bed. There he lies, lost to the world, in such an attitude that his chin touches his breast. He does not move his mouth, nor a hand or foot. In that place no cock is heard, nor the clucking of hens, nor the barking of dogs. No doctor is needed, nor any special means, in order to sleep well, for there is nobody in that place who coughs or blows his nose. Iris said to him, "Sleeping god of Sleep, I come to you from Juno, goddess of all good." In short, she delivered her message irreproachably well.

'Iris did not wait until it grew light, but came away without leave, for she would not willingly stay there. That place made her weak, sleepy and depressed. She only wanted to get back to the gods, and so she fled away. But the gentle god, who had thousands of his offspring round about him, dreams and fantasies of all sorts, of good and bad, of joys and sorrows, turned in his bed. That noble lord opened one of his eyes just a little and, as best he could, set himself to doing what Iris asked.

'The thousand sons, and the thousand daughters too, who were round about him, transformed themselves at will, for they took on the forms of creatures, so that they showed themselves very diversely in sleep through dreams. By this means people dreamed, and in dreaming saw many things, both sweet and bitter: some are painful, some are hard; one is clear, others are obscure; they know how to speak all languages; they take the shape of water, of fire, of iron, of wood. They have no other occupation, no other concern, and they go everywhere.

[651] 'The God of Sleep calls one of his sons – it is Morpheus – and tells him the news that Iris had brought him from Juno the beautiful: which is that Alcyone's beloved lies dead upon the ocean sand. "Go and show her, so that she sees the death of Ceyx and the loss of his ship." Then Morpheus took the naked shape of Ceyx, much drenched and filled with water, and with matted, dishevelled hair. He comes into the chamber of Alcyone, discoloured, pale, and desolate, and reveals to her everything of the disaster he suffered.

'The God of Sleep through his power caused Alcyone to be sleeping in her bed. Morpheus was before her and said to her, "Dear wife, here is Ceyx, for whom you have so lost all joy and pleasure that nothing pleases you. I have no colour, joy or spirit within me. Look upon me, and remember me. Do not think, fair one, that I am lamenting without cause: see my hair, see my wild beard, see my clothes, which show you a true token of my death." This woman woke up so that she might hold him, but he – who had no power to remain any longer – vanished away.

'In this way, the beautiful Alcyone clearly saw King Ceyx, and knew without doubt the manner of his passing. But she lamented and wept for him so long, with such great, deep sighs, that Juno, because of her complaints, so contrived that their human bodies changed into two birds that fly over the sea night and day. They are called kingfishers; for truly, when sailors are in difficulty at sea and see these birds nearby, they often cause them to have good fortune or storms.

[699] 'Now I must come to my point and say what I want to say: it is certain that in my bed I neither rest nor sleep, and that I have neither happiness nor repose. And this makes me very much afraid, if I may say so, that I shall be called a fool when I am unable to sleep in this way, which makes people amazed, and indeed, amazes me myself. For this reason, I want to beg the God of Sleep that Morpheus so act that in a few words my noble lady beyond compare may know my heart, my sadness, my grief – and that with kindly good will it is kept quite secret.

'If Morpheus transports himself before her five or six times, and pleads with her in my form, which is half-dead, I cannot believe, if he really tells her how much distressed I am, and that I do not take any pleasure in anything, that my lady would be so hard and unbending that Pity will not open the door of her frank heart to Dous Penser – that heart which is empty of all evils, stream and well of all good, the sweet fruit of sense, grace and honour. And Dous Penser is so well instructed, that he will tell her how I am both day and night, and of the mortal anguish that I bear for her.

'In this way, she will be able to know how much I love her, and how her eyes

32

have taken away the spirit from my heart through her look, which is neither haughty nor unworthy. This will be if the God of Sleep wishes it, and Morpheus, who will make her heart completely sure of mine, and will tell her fully how I lament every day for her love, and that I must die for her love – it cannot be otherwise because of the sorrow that possesses me – unless through Pity Love moves her to give help to my worthless heart, which suffers great misfortune and very sorrowful thoughts. Alas, Morpheus! I see how it must be. To you I make my complaint about it.

[747] 'I cannot find nor know any other way, for a messenger, ink and parchment, myself or anybody else, cannot be used. But I imagine that she would see while sleeping that I do not cease to love and serve her with a pure heart, and that in this service I am afflicted and my strength is undermined. If she is hostile, what good will this thing do me? But if she keeps Morpheus's speech secretly in her heart and, in the morning when she wakes, she remembers it and interprets each word for herself, then I believe indeed that my affair will be going well.

'And if Pity wishes to have pity on me, and gracious Love by amorous thoughts reminds her of my sorrowful sorrow, I do not doubt for a moment that she will be more gracious towards me, and more anxious to know how I am getting on. And if all is well, she will be very happy about all this. And if Love, Desire, and Dous Penser unite, and this desire is implanted in the heart, and Morpheus reminds her, she would not be so cruel as not to think of the dream, and the thought would be delightful to her.

'This would be something very advantageous to me, if she thought while in bed and at table, and everywhere that thinking is possible – for indeed, often-thinking should not be something fanciful, but rather it should be something substantial, if there is no changeableness or unreliability. Also, she will see the pains that she causes me if Morpheus justly imitates me; that I love her with a whole, true heart, constant and steady; and that she has pierced me through the heart by the laughing appeal of her sweet eyes – but that bow and arrow are not made of yew or maple!

[795] 'I hope then that the carefree god would not fail me in this moment of need. If he helps me then I shall indeed be in such a state that I shall think quite worthless all that woe of mine that I fear too much, for I shall never have happiness without regaining my lost hope. Nor will I care at all about the onset and assault of desire which pierces and assails me, whether near or distant. And because of that, I promise and give a cap and a soft feather-bed to the god who is so knowing and worthy, in order that he sleeps better.*

'I also wish to pray to the God of Love that he hear my pitiful complaints; and that he so act through his subtle means that Morpheus's speech, when he tells of my tears, my great unhappiness, and my hard sorrows, shall be as clear as day to my beloved rather than a parable; and that he should be pleased to tell my beloved – who is not at all silly or foolish – how she drives me to distraction,

---

*Cf. 'Yif he wol make me slepe a lyte,/ Of down of pure dowves white/ I wil yive hym a fether-bed/ . . . . This shal he have,/ Yf I wiste where were hys cave,/ Yf he kan make me slepe sone,/ As did the goddesse quene Alcione./ And thus this ylke god, Morpheus,/ May wynne of me moo feës thus/ Than ever he wan; and to Juno,/ That ys hys goddesse, I shal soo do,/ I trow that she shal holde hir payd . . .' BD, 249ff.

and that my heart flies to her from beyond the sea to seek for help. Indeed, I cannot go, for I am in prison, where I have enough leisure to put myself to school again, but whatever I see, except what I am speaking of, is hateful to me.

'It is my lady who holds my true heart in her prison – it became hers once despite itself. It is right that it should be obedient, and be so attentive that it will never be ransomed; and that it should die there or have a reward that will cure it, that it will be loved or dead, before it comes out of that prison. Now may it please God that no thought so foolish be in my heart that it thinks any malice or treachery, for it cannot have any better role, and if it serves her loyally and without sin, it will indeed be able to have the gift of her love for service.

'And however much I am troubled and frightened by the amorous wound that she gave me through her gay manner, which desolates me completely, I have no will to retreat, for it seems to me that my hope springs, and my loving heart is not to be despised. This is why. The gods are too clever; my lady has a frank and noble heart; and I love her inordinately. This is a true thing. And though I am now in exile, not everything that lies in danger is utterly dead; and also, I do not know if it is myself that Love is testing.

[859] 'And when my lady has several times seen in her dream the great unhappiness that I have suffered for her, and that there is no pretence in me, nor the pains I have undergone – if her heart is a little moved by that, I do not know how this will be known by me. But now I consider: in Morpheus there is such generosity that he will tell me of her manner and attitude, if she has already been requested in love. For she is so well-bred, she loves honour so much and so hates dishonour, that if she is enkindled with love, this would never be known through her.

'And so I must make my offering to the God of Sleep, and above all worship the God of Love, and humbly give them praise for the good hope that grows in my heart, and beg Morpheus that he set himself to help me, if the God of Sleep commands him. I must also not offend Good Hope and Sweet Thought, because I must be of their company. For truly, whoever fails out with those two, however much he loves, is throwing himself into the mire, and he who upsets or changes them must pay for the damage.

'This is to say, that he must rightly pay for it who does not have Good Hope as his true father, and Sweet Thought too as his dear mother. For whoever makes despair and melancholy his associates, even if he is a king, will live in misery and ensure that he loses honour, generosity and every happiness. But when the lover serves in hope, Sweet Thought makes him attractive and apt, and his love is not reluctant to give him a green hat of happiness. But he who lives in sadness may have his head covered with sad and bitter care.

[907] 'So I wish to forget the evil of madness, for it ill suits me. It goes away on foot, but it comes on horseback, and this saddens me very much, for it has sought me out everywhere and neglected nothing, but has always found my heart loyal, and encouraged by Sweet Thought, and also by courteous Hope. In this way I wish to behave in this trouble, and wisely seek in my heart if I can through Sweet Thought gain joy and delight, and then hold on to them tightly through Hope who secures Sweet Thought in the lover's heart, while waiting for Morpheus who soon comes and goes by night. And if he takes away from me the pain that so torments that it would have destroyed me if it had not been for Sweet Thought and Hope, then I think that no lover ever had such honour

anywhere. For I will have such glory that I would not trade my position for the fine gold crowns of France and of England.

'By God, not all the wealth which abounds in heaven, in earth, and in the deep sea, gems, honours, the future life, all the gold and silver that is mined – all this I do not prize at a stone, compared with the love of the beautiful, blonde-haired lady. Dear lord God, when I think of her beauty I feel in my heart so delightful a wound, that I think she will still be the source of my tears, and Morpheus will say to me as I sleep: "Never regret your sadness, for you have conquered the richest treasure that there is in the world."

[955] 'If this is so, I feel my affair is assured, and truly I assure myself enough about it, for the gods will not be so cruel to me if they remember the pains that I endure for my lady. And they know very well that I love her with a pure heart; and if I say I love her, or swear it, I ought to be believed. Pygmalion made the ivory image, to which he made many imploring petitions and loved without relenting, but he did not have so very noble a victory nor such joy as I shall have if Morpheus makes true that which I think will be true. Because of this, I don't think my unhappiness is worth a rotten pear.

'I wish to be a joyful lover and no longer miserable, and taste the sweet delights that Hope and Sweet Thought give me, which make me happy, for I always have these two as companions. And it often happens when I am alone that somebody speaks to me, but I am so preoccupied that I do not utter a word, for I am thinking too intently of that fair good creature who is the sum of all good qualities – and this makes me embarrassed. But my heart is so fixed in thinking of her that it sees no other lady that is of any value to me, however beautiful, or even if a queen. . . .

[1003] 'My sweet lady! – whose picture I carry impressed in my heart, painted there by pure love with the brush of memory and surrounded by loyalty, so that nobody else will be painted there because of her beauty – through memory, I quickly answer the call of my earthly god. Without ever changing, I shall die here, for her eyes which are neither proud nor wicked have given me so many joys – I often utter and often repeat this complaint.

'Do not be offended, lady, if I do not rhyme any further, for any spring could be exhausted. I have put one hundred rhymes into this complaint, whoever cares to count them. I was inspired to them by your beauty, which keeps me awake from the evening through to early the next day. But in a thousand years I will not tell the tenth part of your beauty. It surpasses everything. Everybody says so: duke, king and count. Now may it please God that I never so shame myself in service as to have an unworthy thought, for this quite wears away, stains and overcomes beauty. Nothing is to be compared, for through her all ills are overcome.'

[1035] He stayed there for a very long time without saying anything, and I really listened in case he wanted to say any more, but there was nothing further, so I left off writing. Then I half-opened a window to see what hour it could be, but it was almost day-break. I did not delay very long, but dressed and got myself ready. I fastened my cloak at my neck, and put my hat upon my head. Then I read all the way through the complaint that I had written, to see if he had repeated any rhymes, but I did not find one, and I very thoroughly examined it, and marvelled that there were one hundred different rhymes. This done, I got up from there, blessed myself, washed my hands, and then I went out without waiting to ask and learn who he was that I had heard. I went straight towards the chamber where he lay, and I well remember that there was a young lord awakened by a bird. And as it was truly day by now he saluted me first in French and not in Latin, and I responded politely that God give him good fortune, and that he had had great trouble to stay awake all night in this way. But he said to me, 'Nothing troubles me, but on the contrary it is a joy and a pleasure to me, and also in true trust my lord has commanded me to do it.' And he named him by his right name.

[1075] I asked him where he lay and he told me, 'Here truly is the chamber where he lies, so privately that of all his household he only has one knight there whom he very much trusts. You will very soon see him come, if you would like to stay beside me and if it will not trouble you, because I am certain that he is getting up.' And I said I would wait. I looked through the place, which was very splendid and spotless, to where there was a great company of knights and retinue in groups, all waiting to go and divert themselves. But I did not wait very long, for on several sides I heard both great and small saying: 'Here is my lord!'

[1097] Then I turned a little and set my eyes and my wits to examining his manner, his body, his state and expression. But never in any day of my life did I see a more handsome manner in man or woman, and physically he was perfect, for he was tall and straight, well-built in every way, noble, handsome, young and graceful. I well believe that his heart was pierced and wounded by the arrows of love, and that he knew all the necessary points of the life of a lover. He had a very gracious, pleasant, cheerful, simple and gentle face, but it was a little pale because he had stayed awake and suffered all night long. And normally he had a good colour, if he was not weary from staying up. On his head he had a chaplet, and on his finger a ring which he looked at anxiously. But the chaplet truly suited him very well – I don't know where it came from. And indeed, I thought when I had considered his face, his body and his manner, that he bore himself nobly and that he prized honour and good renown more than mere material gain. For suddenly he made this gesture, which certainly did not displease me:

One of his neighbours sent him a very fine horse, a good mount and finely saddled; also a very fine sparrow-hawk, well-trained for hunting; and also a little dog – I never saw such a good one. He prized the gift very highly and received it politely, saying, 'Here is a splendid gift: it is indeed worthy of a reward.' And to the servant who brought it he gave fifteen of his florins. But the present did not stay very long in his place, for very soon the dog, the bird and the horse were all sent and presented by a servant to a lady whose honour and spirit God preserve, for I hear her very well spoken of, and everybody also said, 'My lord, you could not make better use of them, or send them to a better mistress.' And also, briefly, he was so splendidly attired that he seemed to be a king's son, or born the sovereign lord of all the land.

[1161] But such a person may be rich in beauty and poor in loyalty, and such a person is strong like Renard, who is recreant and cowardly; and such a person is rich who is poor in the goods of this worldly life; and such a person often thinks himself wise and has no better knowledge than a page. I am saying all this for great men: they cannot govern well if they are not true and valiant men, brave, and also generous like Alexander in distributing their great wealth, and wise too in seeing and foreseeing their great affairs, without any games of dice or drinking. They should take up arms gladly because it is their true calling, for the prince who arms himself will win valour for himself. They should uphold justice and guard the church, orphans and widows. Alas! it is nowadays a great reproach to them that justice is uncertain and in flight, and the church is quite destroyed. Widows and orphans do not have their property, their houses and mills – alas! for they have lost everything. If He who is prince and lord of kings, of kingdoms and empires, did not in His great compassion remember such people, I think they would fare very badly. But He is always merciful and compassionate to both body and soul. Now I wish to leave this subject and return to my original theme, for sometimes one makes things worse to talk of good and truth.

[1205] With the other people I followed him; but truly, I did not know anybody there, and I would gladly have spoken to him a little longer by ourselves. Yet I thought I would go on, and so went forward, and did not go too far from him, but knelt down a little way away. And when he saw me like this, in his goodness he did not hesitate at all, but left his company, quickly came towards me, took me by the right hand and reproved me because I was kneeling. I said that I ought to do this. Then he drew me to his side away from the others after he had raised me up from my knees. So he led me along while talking for a long time, and as we went along he asked me where I came from, and wanted to know everything about how and why I had come to his house. And when I had heard his speech, without pretending to be clever, I replied to him in this way:

'My lord, as God give me joy, I wished to see you more than any lord in this world, because of the good that abounds in you. I heard tell of it so much every day, that reason drew my will to love and obey you and gladly see you. But the guest who brings nothing with him and knocks at the door acts madly or presumptuously if he is not well known there. My lord, I have acted in this way and you will correct my mistake, for I have come without being asked, in order to commend myself to you. But I have been told that you love me and often call me, and it is this which moved me to come when I knew of it. And certainly, I should never have dared to come like this if it did not please you. But I love you a great deal, such as a poor man can love, even if the love of a poor man is worth little or nothing. But whether or not it is worth little, I wholly deliver up to you my heart and body to your bidding. Now give your commands boldly, for if I prized any gift most dearly I would most willingly give it to you.'

[1271] He replied very sweetly, 'Sweet friend, by my troth, you are very welcome. You have held yourself back for a long time from visiting and seeing me. But since you are in my power – by the faith I owe to Saint Mary – you will not escape me before you tell me your news, for I well believe and think that it will be courteous and delightful, fine, gentle and honourable. But I thank you five hundred times when you wish to love me so, that you give yourself wholly and abandon yourself freely to me in this way. And by my faith! if I can, I will very willingly deserve it, for I value this gift more highly than two thousand silver marks.' And so we went hand in hand until we found ourselves at the entrance of a very lovely park. A knight brought him a very beautiful bow, but he did not wish to draw it and said, 'Go in joy, for this place delights me very much.' He led me by the hand across lush grass to a very beautiful fountain which fell, sweet, clear and pure, into a bowl of dark marble. But no sheep, dog, deer, or other animal drank at all at this fountain because the story of Narcissus was set up there on a pillar of ivory, and so subtly inlaid and enamelled that, by my faith, I thought when I saw it that he was alive.

[1313] On the marble of the fountain were carved Venus, Paris and Helen, and all aspects of their affair, and how she was abducted and taken off to Troy by ship. Paris made his suit to her; Venus was the bawd, and so kindled Lady Helen with the brand that burns without smoke that she did not know what to do to defend herself. Helen's weeping was so well depicted that it seemed very lifelike. The battle was also included, how Achilles fought against Hector in the combat, but could not win at all nor withstand his mortal blows; and the marvellous archer killed so many people that it was a marvel. Troilus, too, was depicted, suffering greatly for his Briseyda, the daughter of Calchas of Troy. What should I tell you? I never in any day of my life saw so accomplished a piece of work. In the middle was set a golden serpent with twelve heads, through which by means of machinery and conduits the fountain spouted ceaselessly day and night. There were beautiful meadows very well set out all around the marble fountain, and the trees were planted with such masterly skill that the sun had no dominion there and everything was instead beautifully shaded and green. But I never heard such singing, nor such great melody, as from the birds that were there, for they so strove to sing that the whole place, the woods and meadows, echoed with their songs. Every fruit, every flower, every plant that one could name, whether from this country or from overseas, was there in great abundance. I do not know who planted them. For this reason I firmly believe and declare, that in the whole world there is no place, no earthly paradise, that could be more beautiful or more noble.

[1371] The lord sat down and made me sit, to see and listen to the fountain, which was the very antithesis of everything rude and base, and also the surrounding area, which was properly set out. And then he started to ask me if there was anything that could be bettered. I said, 'By my soul, nothing at all, my lord.' And then he told me that this was formerly the haunt of Cupid, the god of love, and that Jupiter and Venus came there many times to take pleasure, to embrace and kiss, to have that pleasure that nature took most pains over, and to have more than enough joy and solace, for sometimes one is plagued, as with rain after fine weather. Jupiter set up the garden and contributed the golden serpent, and truly, Venus had the marble and ivory carved by Pygmalion, who works with great skill and accomplished all this work. Cupid made the rest, which is beautiful and pleasant, and the nymphs and fairies held their assemblies there, and still often came there to hold their gatherings, their games, festivities, and dances, and also their schools of love. It is also ordained that if any mortal creature drinks of this fountain he must become inclined to love. 'Its fame is current in many places, and for this reason it is everywhere called the Amorous Fountain, which has made many a lady joyful and caused many lovers to complain and weep, when for all their service and adoration they cannot win mercy. And it makes them love so much that some have died a pitiful death without any help. Now I have told you the whole truth about the delightful fountain, and I beg you, my friend, to get up and drink of it.'

[1425] I replied that I would not, and that I was already so much inclined to love that the fountain and its power could not put more love in my heart than was there, and that Venus knew this very well, who is lady, queen, and mistress of lovers, and their goddess. But I told him that, if he pleased, he should rise and drink from it. He replied that he would not, and that he would never drink of it, for he had drunk so much of it that he thought himself deceived.

And then he said to me, 'Sweet friend, since chance has brought us together it is fitting that whoever has something worthy to say should say it. I will tell you of the sickness that pierces my heart and soul: I love a lady so marvellously good and beautiful that she has no equal in the world. But I cannot speak to her, and I have to go far away from her and have no set time to return. Because of this, I do not know what is going to happen, for she does not know the suffering that martyrs and slays me for her. And truly, it is not fitting that there should be any approach made or message sent to her. For by my soul! I would not dare, nor reveal this love to anybody, for it would displease her, I suppose. For this reason, I have lost hope, and live in such great misery that nothing in the world can comfort me. For this reason I do not expect to live much longer, and I have been in this state for a long time. And I have to go away into captivity and leave my true inheritance. In captivity? – rather, into exile, which completely desolates me. That beautiful creature will soon have forgotten me, who will never forget her. Forgotten me! Lord! will she remember that I love her more than a hundred thousand others? I believe yes; but indeed, no. I know and see that she does not remember me at all, and I must die for her. And so I have no comfort. For truly, if she was aware of it she would have some compassion. Was there ever any fate so sorrowful and cruel? And I cannot go back, for I cannot do it. It could not happen, it is just impossible. For I will love her always with my whole heart, and afterwards, when I am dead, I believe that my spirit will not die with my body, but rather will pray for my lady when my body is in its grave, that God preserve her and her honour, and always have her in His protection.

[1501] 'For this reason, my friend, I want to beg you to be so kind as to set yourself to making for me a lay or complaint about my love and my sorrow. For I know very well that you know all the theory and practice of true love in all its aspects, and its fierce assaults and onsets have given you many pangs sharper than the skin of a hedgehog.'

I was very happy indeed when I heard him speak in this way, for I knew very well that he was the self-same man with the very subtle intelligence, whom I had heard making complaint in his bed, and sorrowing and lamenting. I put my hand into my wallet, took out his whole complaint and said, 'Receive, my lord, your request: here it is, all ready.' He took it and read it all through. He never stopped or hesitated over what was written, word for word as he had composed it for me. And when he had finished reading it, he began to laugh very graciously, blessed himself with amazement, and said, 'My heart is greatly amazed and troubled by this thing, for I kept it so secret that I cannot think or understand how any man alive can know of it. Tell me, friend, how you came across this, for I truly need to know it.' I briefly related to him the truth of the matter: how I heard him from my bed; the fear I had of it in my bed where I lay. I did not conceal the truth of what I have recited above, and he was greatly amazed at it. He rested his head and arms on me, and very gently went directly to sleep in my lap. I looked all round, but there was nobody about. And so I started to think of my lady, and as I was in this sweet and joyful thought, I bent my head. And because I had not slept enough, and because there were only the two of us there, I also went to sleep. But first I covered him with my cloak, because of the breeze which was blowing, for the morning was very dewy, and the stream from the fountain, full of joy and sadness, made the air and the

39

green grass more dewy and fresh. And when I had completely fallen asleep and left my thoughts, I dreamed a dream while sleeping, that I do not think at all false. Rather I consider it truthful and good [1568].

[The poet now has a lengthy dream. Two beautiful ladies appear, one with a golden crown and carrying a golden apple with the inscription: 'To be given to the most beautiful.' She reproves the knight sleeping in the poet's lap – she will ordain that he will have his wish. Then she undertakes to explain the golden apple to the poet. She now tells the story of Peleus's wedding to Thetis, attended by all the gods, including Pallas, Juno, and herself – she identifies herself as Venus. Discord – offended at not being invited – comes and throws down before the three goddesses the golden apple with its inscription. The three goddesses each lay claim to the apple. Jupiter will not risk displeasing any of them by giving judgement, and allots that task to Paris, the Shepherd of Troy.

Mercury conducts the three goddesses to where Paris is all alone as a shepherd. Mercury tells him he is not really a shepherd, but the son of Priam and Hecuba. When pregnant with Paris, Hecuba dreamed that the child would be the undoing of Troy, and Priam ordered that the child be killed at birth, but Hecuba, when she saw the beauty of the baby, arranged for it to be brought up secretly. Paris then determines the judgement and awards the apple to Venus.

Venus now complains that the sleeping duke has no trust in her, nor does he make any sacrifice to her of bull or heifer. She brings his lady to him to comfort him, who takes him by the hand and calls him her lover.

Now follows *Le Comfort de l'Amant et de la Dame* (2207–2494): the lady comforts the lord with declarations of love. He will take her image with him in his heart into exile. Hope will keep her well. By thought she will be near to him. She reproaches depression and self-pity. Venus's help should be relied on: she helped in the love of Danaë and Jupiter. He should trust Venus rather than Fortune. He should not worry about being unable to do knightly deeds, for she would rather have him in good health. He should think of his return, love firmly, take heart and comfort, and he will soon be in the haven of peace and joy. He should not think her coming to him improper, for Venus caused her to come to him.

His lady kisses him more than a hundred times and exchanges her ruby ring for his diamond one. Then Venus and the lady depart. The two men awake, to find to their amazement that they have had the same dream, and to find the ruby ring on the lord's finger.

They rise and wash in a stream from the fountain. The lord praises and thanks Venus, and says he will sacrifice to her in a temple that he will build to her, together with a temple to the god of sleep. The lord recalls his lady. The poet recalls the 'Istoire des Romains', where one hundred senators have the same dream. The lord is comforted by his dream.

One of the lord's knights approaches and reminds him that his meal is getting spoiled, for they have been there half a day. They go to the duke's castle and dine. After dinner the duke asks the poet to accompany him as far as the coast. When the duke boards his ship he sings a rondel, and afterwards gives the poet a gift of jewels, which the poet declares were more than was really proper for him. The duke sails away over the sea, not forgetting his ruby ring, and armed against desire, sighs and tears. 'Thus he departed. I took my leave. Now tell me, was this well dreamed?' (2848)].

Le Paradys d'Amours

Jean Froissart

Le Paradys – probably one of the earliest of Froissart's poems – is a major source for the dream framework of the *Book of the Duchess*. The opening section closely parallels the opening of *BD*, while the balade at the climax of Froissart's dream ('Sus toutes flours j'aime la margherite') is part of the tradition of Marguerite poetry that lies behind Chaucer's own reverence for the daisy in the Prologue to the *Legend of Good Women*.

Jean Froissart was probably born in 1337 in Hainault, and at the age of twenty-four went to England, where he was appointed secretary to his compatriot, Queen Philippa of Hainault, wife of Edward III. Froissart remained attached to the English court with few interruptions until Queen Philippa's death in 1369, and so during this period both Froissart and Chaucer – near contemporaries in age – were in attendance at the court. Froissart did not visit England again until 1395, and died sometime after 1404. While his *Chronicles* have assured Froissart's fame, his poetry shows the influence of Machaut, and *Le Paradys d'Amours* recalls Machaut's *Remede de Fortune*.

The poem is translated from the *Œuvres*, ed. A. Scheler (Brussels, 1870–72), where the figure of Plaisance is explained as 'la personnification de la première sensation de bien-être, qu'éprouve un coeur frappé par les charmes d'une femme', and the figure of Jalousie is explained as 'irritation, mécontentement, désenchantement; c'est la contraire de plaisance, satisfaction intérieure' (Vol. I, pp. 364–5).

I can only be amazed that I am still alive, when I am lying awake so much. And one cannot find a sleepless person more tormented than myself, for as you well know, whilst I am lying awake sad thoughts and melancholy often come to torment me. They bind my heart tightly, and I cannot loosen them, for I do not want to forget the fair one, for love of whom I entered into this torment and suffer such sleeplessness.*

*Cf. *Book of the Duchess*: *I have gret wonder, be this lyght,/ How that I lyve, for day ne nyght/ I may nat slepe wel nygh noght;/ I have so many an ydel thoght,/ Purely for defaute of slep,/ That, by my trouthe, I take no kep/ Of nothing, how hyt cometh or gooth,/ Ne me nys nothyng leef nor looth./ Al is ylyche good to me – / Joye or sorowe, wherso hyt be – / For I have felynge in nothyng,/ But, as yt were, a mased thyng,/ Alway in poynt to falle a-doun;/ For sorwful ymagynacioun/ Ys alway hooly in my mynde. . . . 1–15.*

And yet not long ago I did want to sleep and prayed so much to Morpheus, to Juno, and to Oleus, that they should send me sleep. I did a wise thing, for if I had not asked them and made sacrifice to Juno of a golden ring, I think I would still be lying awake without sleep.* But the dear and noble goddess sent her messenger Iris for me to the noble God of Sleep, and that sweet god did her command, for he sent through the air one of his sons, Enclimpostair.† As soon as he entered my bedroom – and how he came in I do not know – I fell asleep and had such reflections as will be related to you.

Whoever wishes to assay the experience of gentle love must not lose heart, for there are many consolations in it. I never wish to renounce it as long as my soul is in my body. In my sleep it seemed that I was in a beautiful wood where there was an abundance of lovely plants, with flowers and fruit-bearing trees. There was a great sound of bird-song for the birds were singing without ceasing, as they do on a beautiful early summer's day in the month of May. I, who was in love indeed, took great delight in the birds, and so wandered about up and down until I came upon a stream, around which there were many bushes and shrubs. It was a very pretty spot: columbines, roses, and lilies all grew round about there, and nightingales were singing their hearts out with one accord, so that even if someone had never felt inclined to love before he would have to begin. In order to hear the birds better, I sat down beneath some hawthorn boughs all covered in blossom. Love, who by his dominion controlled my heart and my body, then made me think a lot about my life and my youth, my joys and miseries, and made me feel the pains of all my loves. I well remember, alas! what pain I then felt: I nearly despaired in my hopes. Nevertheless, I complained very much upon Love, and in my complaint I said:

'Love, I have done you homage for the most beautiful, the most wise, the best at heart, as it seems to me, that ever lived in my age. And you took my heart as a token and urged me in such words as these:

"I retain you as my servant henceforward. Serve loyally, and I tell you that you will have mercy, although I don't know when."

'Alas! what a payment I have received! I have served for a very long time and obeyed your command in everything without success. I don't know what to take comfort in, for my sweet radiant lady does not wish to listen to my prayer, and when I want to make known to her the great grief I have to endure, without saying a word, she is so very cool and reserved with me, and gives me such hard looks that I can tell from her manner that she would much rather have me on my bier than look at me any more. I do not know what I should request when you wish to go back on your earlier promise to me.

[107] 'If you had said to me then when I gave you heart and body utterly without holding anything back, "You will never have any solace from your lady", it would have been different. But when I sorrow over the great hopes of joy which you held out to me at that time and of which I have had none, then I sigh for them and well know that you will kill me by such trials. When I am

---

*Cf. 'I wolde yive thilke Morpheus,/ Or hys goddesse, dame Juno,/ Or som wight elles, I ne roghte who,/ To make me slepe and have som reste, – / I wil yive hym the alderbeste/ Yifte that ever he abod hys lyve. . .' 242–7.
†Cf. There these goddes lay and slepe,/ Morpheus and Eclympasteyr,/ That was the god of slepes heyr,/ That slep and dide noon other werk . . . 166–9.

42

dead, what will you have gained? You will have killed one of your servants who has served you in everything, loyally and with all my strength.

'Alas, and with this my struggles are soon ended! I do not know who to complain upon except you, and I shall consider you a traitor. I will never, for an hour or a day, do you honour, but will do all in my power to upset and dishonour you. I have the heart and the will for it, for I cannot see that I could receive anything other than sadness through you. From my long service, evening and morning, my heart is overcome, pale and gloomy, and the thing which cures my sorrow is tears.

'Remember then, I beg you, that when I first saw you and submitted to your service, you told me that I should always have with me Hope and Memory and also Sweet Thought; and I seemed to see them here. I do not know where each of them has fled, but I am poorly served by all three, and I fare the worse for this, I tell you. Ah, Plaisance, you made me do all this and told me that I would have success in winning grace. Now I am sure that you have betrayed me.

[155] 'I certainly have reason to complain: I believe that never did lover have greater reason, for I cannot see other lovers having the least of my torment. Love makes me grow pale and change colour, and extinguishes all joy in me. I used to spend my youthful hours in delight. Alas! now Love constrains me otherwise, when she whom I love ardently, utterly, with my whole heart, does not wish to change or cease her hardheartedness towards me.

'It seems to me that I must rid myself of my sorrow and make a poor will and testament of my health, when I cannot win mercy from the delightful gracious one, who by her very sweet face has wounded my heart. Hey-ho! would that she were pleased by my prayer and gave some pleasing gift in reward for my hard times, for I have suffered pain and hardship both winter and summer, and must a heart that suffers such affliction keep silence?

'Oh, Plaisance, I suffer a great deal of sorrow because of you, for through your fair welcome I have received a pain great enough to kill me. In an evil hour I ventured out to where my eyes and heart were condemned by your pride to suffer so much. Why did you make me offer and give myself unreservedly to this lady who makes me languish? I used to honour you, praise and cherish you, but now I curse you vehemently. Death, come and take me soon!'

[203] With that I finished my complaint. And what I did then, I know very well. I stayed there like that with head bowed low for some time, for my grief and misfortune overwhelmed me. The birds who were brightly singing did not cheer me at all, and nor would all the birds from here to Alsace have done, as I very well know. And this is only as it should be, for at the moment when the true lover is conscious of all that he has suffered his heart is so utterly prey to all sorrow that his tears are all the less. I have had so much to reflect upon that I know this very well.

And so in such a state as I then was, I thus tormented myself like a desperate man, at my wits' end and at the end of my strength. I was not aware of anything that could comfort me, but then I heard the bushes rustling a great deal nearby me, and I felt a little afraid, for I feared that people were about and that I should be discovered. So I then concealed myself in the bushes and peeped out a little to find out what it could be. But very soon there came up to me on my right two of the most refined and courtly ladies, with complexions finer than were ever painted in a picture, and I do believe that both God and Nature took a very special interest in their creation. They were most regally attired, and I would never come to the end of describing to you their great beauty and their apparel.

They advanced upon me briskly, and one of them said, 'I've found him! – the false wretch, the lost soul, the transgressor! Over here, my friend, at him! at him! He has certainly deserved to be beaten, for he has come here to delight in the private arbour that our lord has laboured in planting with his own hands, and then he spoke more evilly of him than anybody ever did.'

[256] When I heard them say such things I was quite terrified. I would gladly have fled away if I could, but – in a few words – I couldn't do so in any way at all. I thought that by gentle manners and entreaties and references to love, I would appease the two ladies, and I would beg them for mercy. Then I threw myself on my knees and said, 'Ah, ladies, I implore you for mercy if I have given offence, when you found me here all alone in order to divert myself, to find some comfort and to reproach my love for the pains that I have had. I see you so very well provided with understanding, with magnificent apparel and with noble bearing, that you will receive kindly my entreaties and will tell me, if you please, what sort of a man your lord is, and whether he is the son of a duke or a king, for you certainly reveal by your clothes that you belong to a great lord. There can only be sweetness in you, my dear ladies, to be sure. Please be so gracious as to receive my prayers.'

Then the one said this to her companion, 'I advise that we should be merciful to him. For in truth, we are not born nor established in this world, except to grant mercy to the supplicant who acknowledges his transgression and begs for mercy. Pity is fostered within us, and our lord wishes it so. Let us show care for this man, for he asks us so sweetly that his prayer wins our hearts, and we ought to have compassion on him.' The other lady said, 'If you wish to do your duty in comforting him, I am glad to agree, yet he has today grossly slandered me, falsely accused me and raged at me.'

[301] When I heard them speak thus, I greatly rejoiced. With these words, one of them came forward, raised me by the right hand, and said to me as she raised me up, 'Fair friend, come forward now. My companion here is graciously pleased that we should have compassion upon you. However, you have transgressed very gravely against our lord, and also against me, if one interprets the drift of your speech.'

'Alas, my lady,' I said, 'by my faith, I was just speaking very carelessly – it would be a great kindness if you would take it as that. And I should be very glad if I could know truly the name of your lord and also your own name. Since he has his dwelling in such a beautiful garden as is enclosed here roundabout, he is a very great lord and much to be honoured and respected. And you too, my dear lady, I do not recognise you. No, indeed, by my soul, I don't know if I ever saw you.'

And the lady spoke then and said, 'My friend, according to your speech, which isn't anything other than straight to the point, you know our lord well. You say that he has bound you in his chains and that you did him homage, and also that I made you do it. You have certainly given a good account of the matter today from beginning to end. But you have fallen into a mistaken opinion, which will do you no good. And it is for this that I laid hands on you. Truly, you did him homage irrevocably in your heart, for I was there at that moment – in proof of which I tell you that I was wearing clothes like those I still wear. I opened the door for you by which you entered into the place. Now you are talking about me in such a way that whoever believed you would never wish to love. In this you will never be believed. Friend, my name is Plaisance, and my companion here is named Esperance. And indeed she is my cousin german, and I tell you that it was she who led me straight here. She pitied you. And our lord, whom you know so little, is the god of love and the king of honour, of grace and of largesse.'

[358] 'My lady,' I said, 'now I am overjoyed since you are named Plaisance: your renown is spread abroad everywhere and that of your cousin just as much, too. Through you are found many gracious means to the God of Love, your dear master. For without you no heart can be happy and joyous in thought nor given to feelings of love.'

'This is true,' replied Plaisance, 'but you have today defamed our role too much.'

'My lady, in what way, why, and how did I do this? You will have to remind me.'

'I'll gladly tell you. You have railed against your lord. And have you no memory at all of the day you did him homage? You know that when you became his man I was standing at his left, and he took you by the right hand and said to you:

"Friend, step forward. I retain you for my servant: serve truly and you will have mercy always."

'Now what did this speech mean? I will interpret it to you without getting annoyed. It is the will of my lord that the lover should be very loyal, patient, obedient, and very properly acquiescent in all that Love sends him, nor must he take any other way than that which Love sends him. And if he grows too intoxicated with burning desire and becomes bewildered in his emotions, then he may see that the grace of compassion may come slowly. This is something, I warrant you, which throws the lover into jealous irritableness, and from this both night and day he is full of cares and burns within and tortures himself, for Jealousy now rules him. I am no longer his companion for he is now removed from my company: I am no longer to accompany him. I want to make it clear to you that a lover can err in very little. His heart, his thought, his eye must all be obedient, completely compliant and patient; he must be ready to accept whatever his lady likes, to be sure, whether she is hardhearted or haughty. It just is not right that a lady should grant her grace at the very first assault. Love will not have it so, but introduces a certain order into these things, and often causes the lover to be tested. And if the lover is found to be true and loyal and really steady, then Love makes him his own true officer, and puts him in possession of all that he rules and, if the lover can wait patiently and advisedly, Love has him take in an hour greater delights, I assure you, than he dared to imagine, to wish or to suppose. But as soon as a lover wavers and looks discontented because he is having to wait, as it seems to him, much too long, then very great distress builds up in his heart, just such as you have shown today. Then it never occurs to lovers to remember how much I have laboured to give them happiness and joy. Really, my friend, it delights me when I see a true lover who wishes to obey the commandment of my rightful lord and master, Love, whom I serve, love and adore, and who endows me with the powers that I have, for without him I cannot live.'

[445] 'My lady,' I said, 'you are very wise, and when you encountered me I considered myself happy. My lady, I have a heart disposed to love, and I well know that it was through your powerful influence that I first came, like a vassal,

45

to knowledge of it. I know that it was through you that I was dazzled and enkindled by the spark of my lady, who is so lovely that her equal cannot be seen. But I marvel over one thing in how I came to enter on these paths of love, and I would very gladly hear more about your powers and your ways, and what the God of Love has been able to teach you, to make use of and to spread solace in love.'

Plaisance replied without delay, 'I shall willingly tell you. Love has settled upon me the power, as my inherited right, that at the time whenever anybody approaches him to do homage and express his obligation, then I am the spokesman and mediator for everybody, and I advise the God of Love and say to him, "Lord, it would be a good thing to accept this offer." I also possess another power that I rather boast about – indeed, I almost have it in my coat of arms! When God and Nature have created people in this world and given them life and soul – be they man or woman – and they come to the proper age to do homage to my lord, then I endow them with proper bearing and with restraint.

[480] 'Now tell me, is this not an order of things which is reasonable and as it should be? For I fashion bodies so very capable, so graceful and so pretty, that it seems to each lover that he will not find the equal of his love. Through their eyes and ears I cause that beauty of which I am the minister to make its impression, and then Cupid takes his bow and with his arrows he wounds with love the gentle hearts with which he is concerned. He sends the arrow through the eye into the heart, just as Achilles in former times was enamoured of the beautiful Polyxena simply by seeing her, as was also Neptune, the God of the Sea, for the young girl Leucothea. And Leander, too, was so utterly taken with the lovely Hero whom he so adored, that through his love he drowned in the sea. If I wanted to bother, I could name to you a thousand such lovers, in whom I have been the principal agent at the moment when they fell in love. And as soon as lovers see each other it is fitting that their hearts be impressed and pierced with sweet looks. And then I so suffuse their being that there is no part of their flesh and blood down to the tiniest vein which is without sensation of me. The more they know me, the better they are pleased with the lifestyle which grows in them through me, and also through my master, and so it is said: "There never was – do not imagine it – an ugly lover or an ugly lady." Since I wish to dwell with them they cannot prevent me from bringing them to mercy.

'And my lord – thanks be for it – loves me above all his servants, and has told me that I serve him well everywhere and in every respect. The gentle god has also said to me that he could do nothing without me. He so prizes my noble conduct and that influence he has instilled in me, that he does not wish that this authority should be moved from me. For he is so knowledgeable that he realizes very well that things would not go so well, and he would never receive the homage of lovers, if it were not by means of me. I am the true mediator between all lovers and also all ladies, whether married or maidens. I am so clear-sighted that I can tell in a moment if they want me to stay among them, and when they have received me they address my lord, and make their laments and complaints to my master, who is so full of love, of feeling and nobility, that he recompenses them for their great sufferings when they serve him loyally. He does not do otherwise, and he pays no attention to flatterers. He knows the sort of people he will reward: those who are obedient to his order, who have put at his service their heart, body and soul, and everything they· have, without hesitation or deception or wrongdoing. Now believe me, my dear friend, if you

46

have not given over your whole heart to serving truly your rightful lord, then you should do so, for you cannot have any greater lord than he. He does not want your possessions, but he desires to have your heart for his own.'

[562] 'My lady,' I said, 'by St Maxien, I could not put my heart and body to better use than to put them entirely at his mercy. Would you care to advise him that he should give me some relief? For I endure great suffering, and I think you know this very well by the signs you have observed. You ought to know, my lady, that she whom I love more than my own soul does not wish to show mercy to me: I have nothing from her but refusal. I am quite distracted with this, and I believe that if you do not exert yourself on my behalf, and if some comfort does not come my way, then I do not know what will become of me. However, I now certainly recognize your power and goodness, for truly, through the sweetly perfect, pink-and-white face and graceful features of my lady I was in a moment so captivated that my heart still remains completely enthralled.

'It was the flashes of lightning from her eyes which did this to me, and the effect of her looks never leaves me for a moment. Then I flew without delay to my sovereign, the God of Love, and said to him: "Ah, dear Lord, I love a flower lovelier than any other flower, but I do not know if it is madness, for I never told her of my love." The God of Love then told me that I should immediately do him homage. I did so in the sight of his whole company of barons, and I then considered myself very happy; but since then, as a sorrowful man, I wonder if I have annoyed him. He has not advanced me at all, but has abandoned me to this suffering without letting me see if his grace is imminent. If I could talk to him about this, I would very gladly point out to him the peril into which he has put me who am his humble servant and lover.'

[609] Then Plaisance replied to me, 'Fair friend, through your ignorance you could well lose your whole cause. Why do you not know how to set yourself to be steady and constant and not so very changeable?' Then Plaisance turned graciously and said, 'My friend, Esperance, I beg you: there has been too long a delay. Do talk to this man. He takes far too little account of the great good that Love has done him. He would prefer that as soon as he thinks to have a thing he should have it. But I tell him truly that if he does not believe our advice, I consider all his labours to be in vain.' I listened intently to this speech.

Then Hope spoke, and said to me at first as follows, 'My friend, I pity you very much for I see you in great distress, and as I ever loved or helped to comfort any man, I wish to cheer and encourage you. You know – or ought to know, for there is much intelligence in you – that when one has undertaken something and has not learned how it is going to end, whether for good or for ill, then one must bear it wisely without grieving oneself in an evil mood. So calm and temper your heart, then. Do you think I hold a man wise who loves *par amours* and who frets about it all the time? Certainly not. On the contrary, I consider his behaviour extremely foolish and silly. For, you know, the life of loving, which is so delightful and beautiful, needs to be very finely carried on, and if it is in any way mismanaged then all one's time is wasted. I tell you this truly, and I will prove it through your own example. Jealousy is a very remarkable thing, and a dangerous force which can confound the heart: one should fear it as one fears a tempest. Although some who are fluent in speaking of love would like to dispute the matter, there will never be a real lover who is not a little jealous at heart, for Jealousy is well known for this. But God

47

preserve you from its fire, which is neither pleasant nor good. A spark from that fire would make you a little more thoughtful, solicitous and attentive in pursuing your affairs of the heart, but if you are given over too much to that fire you will be doing something stupid, I can tell you. I think that since the day that you did homage to Love you have tasted some of Jealousy's drink. Now tell me if I have spoken truly, for I would certainly like to know, and after a false confession false absolution is given.'

'My lady,' I said, 'by St Francis, you have so comforted me that I can tell you nothing about it, for so great is my sickness that I would not be able to say anything, nor would I tell the truth because I was in such pain.'

And Esperance who strove to comfort me in every way said, 'I will be your advocate, be it to Love or to your lady. But if Jealousy wounds your heart – as I very much believe that your heart is bound in jealous bonds – then whatever I advise you, I shall be wasting my words. For a jealous man has so sensitive a heart that he wishes to listen to nothing except to his melancholy; and indeed, through such folly you have today made complaints and laments. You are a young man all full of cruelties, I tell you truly, who should not have anything but pleasure and joy, for every amorous disposition wishes for nothing that hurts him.'

[710] 'My lady,' I said, 'by your nobility, put me back on the right path, and just as if it were written down on parchment I will stay with you always, and my love-affairs will go the better for it. In this you will be doing a very courteous thing, for truly I am at once seized and struck by jealousy: I got too far involved with it. Your consolation is very necessary to me.'

And she replied, 'By all means. Don't trouble yourself over anything that may happen, but remember me every day. Whether you are on foot or on horseback, whether you are traversing mountain or valley or water, and you fall into any kind of danger, whether you hunger or thirst, life will always go better with hoping, and it will never be that you are not in happiness, whether in youth or old age. There is nothing that hurts me, nor those who put their trust in me: all fortune they defy. Only think how strong I am: in one hand alone I carry more than forty ships. You will be fortunate, if you want to love and believe in me: good medicine must be drunk to restore one's health. Those who have trusted in me and been of my company have reached their goal. But you must wait through days and hours before the reward comes. Remember my teaching: when ardent desire assails you, and jealousy would confound you with its boldness, then say in this way: "Oh, kind mother Hope, comfort me in this necessity." Then shall I come with clenched fist to your aid, and I shall slay your foes, nor shall one of them be spared. With me I shall bring Atemprance, Avis, Manière and Cognissance, Franchise and Debonnaireté, Sens, Pité and Humilité who will all bear my banner. Friend, a woman esteems good sense and moderation in the heart of man. That man is held a fool, and called so by everybody, when his lady sees him lacking in good sense. What has a sensible woman to do with a foolish man who reveals his affair and lets it be known here and there? An honourable lady never loved a foolish man with a big opinion of himself, and if she does love him she gives it up (and I think it very sensible of her), when she understand the nature of the man, which is neither good nor gracious, but far too dangerous, and something for which she could be blamed. A lady loves a discreet man who wisely knows how to behave tactfully and how to foster their love affair in sweetness and courtesy without a trace of jealousy.

And since you wish to have the benefits of love, remember, my friend, my teaching, and never go pestering too much with your attentions a lady who has a worthy and spirited heart. For if you wear her out too much with your courtship, and begin to flounder in such excesses, you will miss your time, and rightly so.

[787] 'I am Hope, the courteous one, who is easy and light to carry and who fits into a very small space. Yet, by God, it is said that my power is such that it is worth the gold of five hundred cities, for I am needful to all people; and whoever makes use of me will never be discouraged by anything that happens to him. Now listen, for you can find good counsel here. If you believe me, you are cured; if you fail in this you are lost.'

'Indeed,' said I, 'my dear lady, I so much esteem you and your expression, and your sensible teaching – in which your great good sense instructs me – that I shall always fare the better for it. But tell me where is the place, the beautiful residence, where the god and king of love is staying? If it is so, that mortals can approach that place, I beg you to lead me there, and I shall be very fortunate, for I should very gladly see him and show him my state.'

'Friend,' Hope said to me, 'Plaisance looks after everything, for she is lady and gardener of the place, and I believe that if she heard you utter your prayer she would let you go in. For you wish for nothing there but flowers – roses or lilies or violets. These are not very dear things, and she will not refuse your prayers.'

Then I bowed towards Plaisance and said, 'Lady, may it please your worthiness to grant that I may have the delight of seeing this garden in your company.' She replied, 'Sweet friend, I grant it to you gladly.'

[832] Then, very happily, I was taken by those two young ladies who are so blooming and lovely; and then we set off on the way. By my faith, it is true that one sees in a man who is accompanied by ladies who have names such as this Plaisance and Hope, that he has in him everything that is necessary for joy and consolation. And as we were going along, I was asked by those sweet ladies, and begged from their lovely mouths, that I would recite a rondel, and nor would I have refused for anything at that moment. Then we sang it, all three of us, as I record it for you here:

'Since Plaisance agrees – and Hope as well – to take me away from care, it is right that I recite it, since Plaisance agrees.
For my heart is full of happiness. It fills me with delight
to live in this way, since Plaisance agrees.'

As soon as I had recited it to them, Plaisance said, 'By the Body of God, that pleases me very much in every way; now let us all three sing it again.' Then we sang loud and clear, like the ladies of Vauscler, once, twice, three times. The hour of terce had already passed, and by then I had no sadness in my heart. We came across a hunting-station, where a very gracious lady was holding two very beautiful hunting dogs. As we passed, Plaisance called to her and said, '*Doulc Penser*, is my lord where I left him yesterday?'

'Not at all, my lady, by St Richier, you will find him further on at the fountain of Narcissus.'

Then we set off again on our way, and Plaisance once more invited me to perform a *rondelet* again. 'My lady,' I said, 'it must be done, since you wish it; it is right. I will do it first, then all three of us, if you like.' As Plaisance urged me, so I made a pretty *rondelet*. For the love of her, you shall hear it:

'One must suffer in silence, and accept everything willingly that Love ordains, in truth; and if one feels grief or hate, one must suffer in silence. For Love can bring about every comforting thing through his great power; because of this I say with a good will: one must suffer in silence.'

When I had finished, Plaisance said, 'To me this *rondelet* is just right, and I prize it very differently from the one before.' The three of us sang it there in unison without any wrong notes. And all the while we were going through the forest, sometimes through the shade for an hour and then through the open meadows, until we came across a spinney where we found a companion holding three hunting dogs on a leash. I said to Plaisance, 'I would gladly know his name.' And Plaisance replied to me, 'He is called *Beau Semblant*, and his brother *Bien Besongnans* is near here, for I see him, and I hear one of my own brothers blowing the horn – I recognize him very well by his note – it is *Douls Regars*. At this season Love follows the hunt. I do not know what he is hunting after at the moment, but he scarcely rests or stops for an hour in the day. Further off I see *Franc Voloir* who is waiting for him with three hunting dogs, and at that other hunting-station I can see *Desir* and *Oïr*, by my faith, and *Souvenir* a little further away.'

[926] 'My lady, as Jesus help me,' I said, 'there is great delight here! Very gladly do I hear all the noise and the barking of the dogs. But tell me – because I know nothing about it – are all these huntsmen the men of our lord, the God of Love?'

'Yes,' answered Plaisance, 'he has more than thirty times more at his disposal. There are counts, dukes and kings, knights, and from all peoples, and with their number his company is fine and gracious, for whoever is not of very gentle condition cannot be one of my lord's men, nor be entered in his register. And all those that I am bringing to your notice are good huntsmen all the time, and they sing all day without ceasing. The hunt of love pleases them so much that each one seeks after his delight where he thinks to have it, and each one of them so strives in his duty to pursue what he has undertaken that it seems that everybody burns with effort, with difficulty, with concern. I also help them where necessary, for otherwise – although I tell you myself – their lives would be too hard for them, and they would not be able to support the pains they have to suffer.'

[957] Then I looked into a clearing and I saw a great company of ladies and young maidens, radiant and beautiful, and also a great number of young men, handsome and inclined to love, who were all stopped there and very richly attired. All were dressed in green, without any exception. The ladies had very rich embroideries, all in intricate patterns and thickly sewn with pearls, while the men had ivory hunting horns, all edged with fine gold.

'My lady,' I said, 'may I know who are all these people that I can see there?'

'Yes,' said my priceless lady, 'Troilus is there, and Paris, who were sons to King Priam, and he who you see laughing is quite certainly Lancelot. And because I love you so much I will tell you the names of the others and will not lie about them. There are Tristan and Yseut, Drumas and Perceval the brave, Guirons, and Lot and Galahad, Mordres, Melyadus, Erbaus, and he with that beautiful golden sun is called Melyador. Tangis and Camels de Camois are there further within the wood, Agravain and Bruns and Yvain, and the good knight Gawain. And among the ladies there is Helen, and the Châtelaine of Vergi, Guinevere, Yseut, and lovely Hero, Polyxena and Lady Echo; and Medea, the lover of Jason, you will see there in this copse. All of them are joyful in these places where the gentle God of Love is lord and master. His kingdom and his empire extends everywhere in this region. Very near here is the entrance to the paradise of my lord, where he has his sure place of repose.'

[1005] And thus in conversation between ourselves and taking in the scenes of delightful joy that there were within the wood, the three of us came, as it seems to me, into a clearing. Then I asked Plaisance what the place was called, and she drew me to one side and said, 'Friend, step forward: do you see these trees here in front of us? There is the pavilion of my lord towards whom we are journeying, and within is the lord who will be the doctor to cure you. Now give some thought to what you will say, and how you will speak to him.'

'My lady,' I said, 'in truth, I do not know. Give me your advice, for I have need of it.'

Plaisance replied, 'Gladly. You are well enough practised in composing a lay, I think. Now set to work with all your diligence, and make your need known to him through a lay, for it is very necessary for you. He will receive it very favourably and will seat you on a step at his feet – you will not be anywhere else whilst you recite your lay – and then he will give you his answer according to the counsel and appeals of those people who will be around him.'

'My lady,' I said, 'I would need a long day to compose a lay, and yet I have already for my own pleasure composed one about my situation. Since by chance I have this one by me, I think it best if I recite it.' Plaisance said, 'I agree.'

We came quite quickly to where the God of Love himself was within his beautiful tent. Plaisance, who very much wished that I should receive consolation, said to me, 'Listen, fair friend: you see the God of Love, our master? draw a little towards the left and I will introduce you to him and to those at his table.' I then did as she commanded, and Plaisance very softly set herself on her knees in front of the gentle god, and then said to him, 'My lord, here is your son, who says that he lives in great peril since the hour that you wounded him with an arrow, and since you have wounded him and you know all this very well, please listen to his prayer.'

[1064] The God of Love was kindly disposed to answer and said, 'Willingly.' Then I approached and straightaway I started to recite my lay. At the beginning, indeed, he made me sit at his feet. I could not see, but Plaisance told me later that she had seen him many nights and many days in his joyful diversions, but she did not see him move his eyes or lips in the slightest, so very agreeable was the matter to him. Now I begin my lay in this way in the form that I made it:

'When I first saw my very sweet, dear lady, her great beauty so rushed to wound me that, unless Pity concern herself – who must be the confidant and messenger of my ills – then I have suffered too hard a beginning. Now I beg her humbly that she look with joyful countenance on my lady and urge her that I may have some relief. About our meeting I shall be very discreet, nobody will know of it but she.'

'For her sweet looks have wounded me and pierced my heart, and I am in a distress too great to be able to return to health. They have shown me a fair regard without wishing to, for they have diminished such that I cannot in truth give any good or true reports. Alas, that Loyalty and Pity do not speak to my lady and say to her, "You have with too great injustice slain your servant, who has always so much loved, served, obeyed and feared you, and been faithful to you. And now your eyes which are his comfort show him cruelty. In our view Love will not thank you for it."

'There is no season which does not impose some sacrifice, nor is there a beggar who is not put to some test. It is right that I have great pain for – in a true figure – I am like Pygmalion who loved the statue. Although the foolish man cries and weeps, and tells the statue his sorrows, and dresses it in gold and in silk, there is nothing that he gets out of it except in imagination. In this way, Plaisance wounds me: she has given me a wound in the heart which troubles me too much. I do not know where to take myself to be cured of it, except to my cause in love – at once so bitter-sweet – which immediately cheers me up again. I am enclosed in the thicket where Melampus barked for his master Actaeon.

[1139] 'I am not Orpheus, who by his songs and his sweet melodious playing put the gods to sleep down below, but I am the wretched Tantalus, whose chin touches the water and who can see the water but cannot be quenched. And thus was I wounded by sight of her fair hair, her delicate and slender fingers, her perfect eyes. Achilles nor Narcissus, nor Eucalious, Tristan, Paris, Lot, nor Jason had anything greater than I.

'This sickness which is growing in me and binds me with melancholy will not be cured or arrested, I see, for any day of my life, if Pity does not implore and undertake it, for joyful Plaisance and beautiful Beauty have fostered it within me. And for this I weep and cry, "Ah! Love, help! out of your courtesy, for Jealousy which is attacking me cannot for a moment even claim lordship over me, for his company gives rise, whatever is said, to madness and weariness."

'Now it is clear a man must consider how to do away with this evil by governing himself wisely, by loving well yet by concealing and moderating it, by having a pure heart and keeping himself from evil-doing. There is nothing else to be done in the lover's condition, a state so beautiful, perfect, and furnished with every good thing beyond price. Ah, gracious Pity, cast your gaze upon me.

'I must keep quiet about what I am, but I declare that there is nothing in me but sorrow, pain, and torment. Now it is most necessary for me – to restore my spirit – that it please you to approach her who wounded me through the heart by her sweet look, and wisely make her realize my sorrow and affliction. And in order to make everything well, I beg you to talk to her in this way:

' "He is so utterly given up to your love that night and day he sees your lovely face, and calls your worthiness and sweetness a paradise filled with honour and delights, so much so that every day, my lady, he lies weeping in bed in such sorrow and such passion that things go badly with him. Neither Achilles nor Paris had a greater passion, they who in former times were completely taken through such a struggle and such a means.

[1263] ' "Now consider the substance and great power of Love and how, at your instance, there remains here somebody who has suffered a great deal for many a day. Now be gentle with him, and give him some relief out of courtliness, so that his tears and laments may turn into joy, and the hope he has had does not turn into despair, for fear holds him back and disconcerts him. If obedience did not keep him in company with fair perseverance, he would have been severely assailed by so many ills.

' "For it often happens that when you are present, and Plaisance presents him, your excellent manner and gay mood are a form of bond – just as Hippomenes felt for Atalanta, if the truth be told. So much does he love and fear you – and with a love that is always increasing – that he becomes so frightened that he lacks strength, will, or wit to say anything, but is silent and absents himself from you, and laments distractedly all alone by himself. And thus he is kept by ardent desire which tries him, and he goes through this agony repeatedly. I know very well that, however much Plaisance torments him, he speaks about it to nobody, and for this reason – in order that he should be happy and not repent of his love – it is necessary that your own gracious spirit should have some knowledge of his situation by such a means as I am, my noble lady, for he is spending too sad a life."

'If Pity, who very well looks after all those for whom she cares, wishes to deliver me from the burning which, to my way of thinking, comes to me from the piercing wound of love, then she would accomplish a splendid cure, for I lie in a dark prison at the point of defeat. And may there be a change in the nature of Refusal and Standoffishness, for through these two I endure so much pain and hard anguish that there is nobody who would not swear that they wish to drive me to death; I am in such great misfortune! Now quickly! Pity and Justice, speed to my lady, and tell her of this wrong without delay.

'And say to her how these two, who are harder than stone, have at their command in order to encourage their followers, more than a hundred envious folk, who are positioned about thickly on all sides and are so posted all along the way that one does not meet anybody else. They contrive so many impediments for me that my happy time is put back, for their malicious tongues go more busily than windmills. They often anger me, and I do not know how to overcome them whether by gift or by entreaty or by being joyful.'

[1355] When I had recited the lay, the God of Love said immediately, 'I can certainly tell by your words, friend, that you have given yourself up entirely to serve both myself and your lady. And, by the faith that I owe to my own soul, you shall have for it such a reward as a true lover ought to receive, for never has a heart served me that I have not rewarded, and you may well trust me in this if you will. And you will find by experience that my words are true, if you are not undone by your own negligence, or by foolish impetuosity. If there is any subtlety in you, you can certainly believe this will increase: I will say no more about that. Your lady is in my protection, as well as you, and if Desire burns you and enflames your heart I cannot guard you from death, except that I so much wish and so arrange that Hope gives you comfort and is with you every day in that pain that Desire gives you. If you trust in Hope you are safe: you will never be overcome by any fortune that assails you. Now tell me, is this enough for you?'

'Yes, my lord,' I replied, 'I thank you, and tell you that always, whatever happens, I will not fail to remember you and your nobility, which have brought me every happiness.'

Then the God of Love called the two ladies that were there, Plaisance, and Hope as well, and said to them, 'My daughters, here is my servant, and I consider him to be such in word and deed and bearing. Bear him company graciously, I charge and beg you.' And then each replied to him, 'Dear lord, we will do so wholeheartedly, in mind and body, since you wish it.'

[1402] The God of Love said, 'Now go and divert yourself in this garden. I give you leave to do so.' Then the two ladies took me – may God preserve them, body and soul! – and they said to me, 'Let us leave here, since it is our lord's wish. We will take you to find joy elsewhere.' I did not wish to argue with their speech. 'My ladies,' I said, 'I wish to do what you please.' Then we left that place and set off on our way amid the green and shady wood. Plaisance laughingly begged me, 'Friend, at my request you must recite a virelay.' 'My lady,' I said, 'I anticipated this. It is right that I should compose it and sing it when I have seen my lord face to face, the God of Love and the true king, who has brought me understanding and assurance.

'Love, I thank you with a humble will when you have placed all my care in your power. For I would never have had any alleviation of my pain, if you had not remembered me; and when, through your power, you have worked for me in this way, I know in truth that you wish to receive me as your friend. Love, I thank you . . . *etc.*

'In my need you have helped me – as I very well realize – and richly provided for me with consolation and with hope; and thus furnished with hope I now say, and will say, that I may very well have joy through you. Love, I thank you . . . *etc.*'

[1445] And when I had recited this virelay Plaisance said, 'By God's Body, it is very well written. Now let us sing it, in the name of peace.' Then we sang it with one voice, very clearly, between the three of us, and all the time we went on through the wood, gathering flowers. We went through the wood at our own pleasure, until we came to a meadow where it was beautifully green and pleasant, all set about with red roses, columbines and lily plants, and there the nightingale was singing delightfully. It gave me tremendous joy to hear its song. Then Plaisance said in a low voice, 'Let us all go in there, the three of us.' I then did her bidding, so as to have more delight. I did not think to find anybody there except the little birds, and Plaisance, and her good friend Hope, but happily I found there *Bel Acueil*, who was making a chaplet of flowers, with two young girls who were helping by gathering the flowers. Then I went without delay to kneel in front of my lady and greeted her. She returned my greeting and I listened to her very lovingly and very humbly. 'Lady,' I said, 'Love commands me to ask for your grace, for I have languished for a long time without receiving grace or mercy, joy, hope or comfort. Dear lady, it is too hard for me to live very long unless Plaisance deliver me, for I feel that to have only tribulation where all consolation ought to be is too cruel a destiny for me. If it pleased you to soften my pain through your great courtesy – for you are in a very good position to give me grace and comfort – then I would have come to land in a fair haven.'

[1501] Then my lady began to laugh and very sweetly said, 'Friend, what do you want? It is sensible to present your request well, so now make your petition in the courteous way. In order to give you some relief I should like to use all possible mildness, but make sure you do not go beyond what is proper, for otherwise you would make a very grave mistake and never obtain grace, whether for love or pity – I tell you that truly.'

Now I tell you, by the faith I owe my own soul, that my lady's answer struck me as ambiguous, but I had never transgressed her command. 'My lady,' I said, 'I see well enough that you will go on keeping me in fear and subjection, and you can well see with what love I love you and have done always, with little consolation relative to my deservingness. Now may it please you, my sweet lady, just this once, to speak one word unequivocally, and I shall be very greatly comforted by this.'

'What word, friend,' she said immediately, 'do you wish me to say? It seems to me that I act courteously when I look and behave pleasantly towards you.'

'That is true, my dear lady, but – in order to give me more encouragement – may it please you that from henceforward you consider me your faithful servant, and that through what you say I can assure myself of this favour?'

Then my lady said easily, 'Do you wish that this be so?' 'Yes, my lady.' 'And I wish it, too.' Then her gentle eyes very sweetly put me at my ease. It is just that I should be pleased with such an answer, for I never had anything greater, and she then set me on the way to win my rich reward. The heart which has long been raised on hardships and pains must greatly rejoice when it is made happy with so very much. I very gladly heard these words of my lady's, and so did Plaisance, who had been guiding me with her advice. Then that lovely, good, wise lady – who is accustomed to do all that is good – when she saw me so happy, so overjoyed, so eager to engage in all delights, she said to me (and it was very good advice), 'Friend, my friend, keep your joy within proper bounds – do not be over-hasty. Any favour, great or small, can be lost through presumptuousness. He who does not carry on completely with his love-service, or does not perform it well, gains nothing. You should know that I am not so silly, so rash or unwise that – although I have willingly spoken affectionately to you – if you do not do your duty I should soon take everything back. I want you to be happy, and more joyful and comforted than you were before, but you should have true obedience and loyal perseverance, without asking for anything, whether in public or in private, that could cause me harm or displeasure.'

[1583] 'My lady,' I said, 'as God preserve me, I will never have any other care than to serve you loyally, in order to deserve the pleasure that you have granted me here. You will find me loyal and discreet, obedient and humble, and very bashful in all that I ask. If I do well, you will reward me; if I do badly, you will punish me.'

My gracious lady declared herself extremely content with this speech. Then she took me by the hand, and we began to stroll on the fresh, new grass. My heart began to brighten because of the pleasure it felt and in seeing my lady in joy, in sport and in amusement.

'Haven't you composed anything new?' she said very sweetly. 'Yes, my lady, out of my own feelings and with a heart happy and in love I have composed a balade.' She said, 'I would like to hear it and – in order to give you greater pleasure – whilst you recite it seated beside me, I will make you a chaplet of sweet and pretty flowers such as this season provides.'

[1614] Then we were both seated, and Plaisance and Beauty-without-Envy,

55

Franchise, Honour and Gaie Vie, Manière, Sens and Attemprance, Cremeur, Avis and Pourveance, are all seated with us. With her sweet and delicate fingers alone, and without any other instrument, my lady made the chaplet from the little flowers that we call daisies, which were growing in the meadow. And whilst I attended to her doing this, I recited this balade to her:

'Above all other flowers the rose is held to be loveliest, and after that, I believe, the violet; the lily is beautiful and so is the cornflower; the gladiolus is delightful and beautifully formed, and many people are very fond of the columbine, the peony, the lily of the valley, and the marigold. To each person each flower has its special quality, but as for me, I must tell you that above all other flowers I love the daisy.

'For in all weathers, rain, hail or frost, whether the season be fresh, or gloomy, or bright, this flower is graceful and ever new, sweet, pleasant, white and red; it is always open and blooming or closed up just at the right moment; you will never find it dead and colourless; all goodness is inscribed in it; and thus when I reflect on it, above all other flowers I love the daisy.

'And the sweet season is just now burgeoning once more and brightens this gentle little flower; and I see seated beneath this horse-tail-bush two hearts wounded by a delightful arrow, and may the God of Love come to their aid! With them are Plaisance and Courtesy and *Douls Regars* who is very busy between them. And so it is right that, at the making of the chaplet, I should say that above all other flowers I love the daisy.'

[1654] Laughingly, Plaisance made an arrangement for this balade, at which my lady began to smile. And Plaisance said to her, 'What are you laughing at, my good and lovely lady? This balade is quite new, for I have never heard it.' And my lady, who was just as much pleased that Plaisance was speaking, as for the song that had been performed there, replied gracefully and with the heart of somebody in love, and said, 'The balade is very good, and it is right that I give the chaplet to him who composed it.'

Then my lady very deftly unfolded with her beautiful fingers the chaplet all entwined with that flower I so delight in, and which I have named to you as the daisy. The chaplet was exceedingly pretty. Then my lady with great joy made me kiss the chaplet, then she kissed it and put it upon my head, and then said, 'Let us go, let us go to enjoy ourselves somewhere else.'

Whether it was by a movement or a look of that lovely, gentle lady, it seemed to me that Plaisance touched me, and for that reason I trembled, and with that my dream left me. And when I had thoroughly woken up, I was greatly amazed at what had happened to me. I groped about quickly in my bed to discover where I could have fallen asleep, and found that I had lain down on my own bed in order to rest. And I began to think over what could have caused me to have this dream.

[1696] I though about it so much that I remembered that I had been accustomed on going to bed to pray to Morpheus, the delightful and true god of sleep and dreams, that for love and pity, and out of his kindly graciousness, he should cause me – who was at that time not sleeping at all – to fall into that sleep that is slept by those who are tormented and discouraged in love. And now he had done what I asked him, thereby much softening my pains, for he caused me to fall asleep into such a dream where there was nothing that was not true. I thanked him for it, and also Orpheus, who showed me both the art and the practice of singing the balade and rondel, the virelay originally composed there, and the very fitting lay. I also thanked Iris, messenger of the sleepy god Morpheus, through whom all true lovers, as is right, are comforted in dreams and visions. Thus was I once ravished into the Paradise of Love.

Remede de Fortune
Guillaume de Machaut

The *Remede de Fortune* is the source for Chaucer's material and his diction in a large number of lines in the *Book of the Duchess*, and Chaucer's borrowings are indicated below by being cited near to their source lines in footnotes. This extract from the opening of the *Remede* is translated from the *Œuvres*, ed. E. Hoepffner, SATF (Paris, 1908–21).

[1]. He who wishes to learn any art must attend to twelve things. The first is that he should choose something to which his heart is most drawn, or to which his nature inclines, for nothing will turn out well that one tries to do against the grain of one's heart and contrary to nature. He should love his teacher and his calling above all, and he must honour, obey, and serve, without thought of serving himself; for if he loves them they will love him, and if he hates them, they will hate him. He cannot get on otherwise. He should receive instruction humbly, but should take good care that he keeps at it, for knowledge half-heartedly grasped is easily forgotten. He should have care, thought, and desire to know, and he will be able to possess knowledge. And he should undertake it at a young age, before his heart turns to wickedness through too much experience.* For the true state of innocence exactly resembles the white, polished table, which is able to receive without any interference whatever one wishes to paint or portray on it; and it is also like wax, which can be written upon, and which retains the shape or impression just as it has been imprinted upon it.†

Thus it is indeed with true human understanding, which is capable of receiving everything one wants, and can conceive of everything that one wants to put to it, whether of arms, or of love, or other art or letter.‡ For nothing can be so strong that it cannot master it if it wishes, as long as it is prepared to work as I have said above.

---

*Cf. '*For-why I tok hyt of so yong age/ That malyce hadde my corage/ Nat that tyme turned to nothyng/ Thorgh to mochel knowlechyng,*' BD, 793–6.

†Cf. '*Paraunter I was therto most able,/ As a whit wal or a table,/ For hit ys redy to cacche and take/ Al that men wil theryn make,/ Whethir so men wil portreye or peynte,*' 779–83.

‡Cf. '*And thilke tyme I ferde ryght so,/ I was able to have lerned tho,/ And to have kend as wel or better,/ Paraunter, other art or letre;/ But for love cam first in my thoght,/ Therfore I forgat hyt noght,*' 785–90.

[45] Because of this I have said that when I was still at the innocent stage, when youth governed me and idleness kept me, then all my behaviour was unstable.* My heart was changeable. I cared very little about anything, except that my heart and all my thoughts were always inclined towards my lady, who is universally considered beautiful and good above all others. Everybody by right gives her this name.† She is so well endowed with all the goods that Nature can grant to any creature that she is the sovereign flower above every human creature.

For that reason my heart was inclined towards her, and I think Nature taught it this, for certainly, to my youthful understanding, I saw her very gladly.‡ For all my ways and paths, my play, my thought, and my recourse, were always round about her, and without seeing her I could not have complete happiness.

And when Love saw that I was in this state, she did not wait before intervening in such a way that, above all that God has made, I love her and shall always love her in heart and in deed, obey, serve, and honour her, and at all times and all hours am utterly hers.§ For she was my first love, and she will be the last. For this, I shall finish my days in serving her, and I will never love another. Now God grant that her love be mine, for in this world I would not wish for anything else.

[87] Thus, by its art, Love – which gently burns many noble hearts – caused that when I first saw my lady her great beauty ravished my heart. And when I was kindled by love of her, I was young and untaught, and had a great need to learn when I would undertake such an affair.** What am I saying? Thus I took it on. I took no counsel and asked no leave, except from my heart and from her eyes, that have in many places laughingly begged that I should love her, so tenderly that I dared not, nor could not, refuse their wish.†† My heart wished that I were all hers, and I also wished it, and this was the counsel I took. In this way, as God preserve me, I was taken by her sweet laugh and sweet look. And indeed, if I were as wise as Solomon, and the whole world were given to me, and I were as valiant as Alexander or Hector (who was scarcely less than him in valour), and if I had the honour of Godfrey of Bouillon, and the beauty of Absolom, and the great patience of Job, the firmness and constancy of Judith and of Socrates, which was always unchanging (for he did not change either for

---

*Cf. 'For that tyme Yowthe, my maistresse,/ Governed me in ydelnesse;/ For hyt was in my firste youthe,/ And thoo ful lytel good y couthe,/ For al my werkes were flyttynge/ That tyme, and al my thoght varyinge./ Al were to me ylyche good/ That I knew thoo,' 797–804.

†Cf. 'That was my lady name ryght./ She was bothe fair and bryght;/ She hadde not hir name wrong,' 949–51.

‡Cf. 'I trowe hit cam me kyndely,' 778; 'For wonder feyn I wolde hir se,' 1101.

§Cf. 'And Love, that had wel herd my boone/ Had espyed me thus soone,'835–6.

**Cf. 'But wherfore that I telle thee/ Whan I first my lady say?/ I was ryght yong, soth to say,/ And ful gret nede I hadde to lerne;/ Whan my herte wolde yerne/ To love, hyt was a gret empryse . . .' 1088–93.

††Cf. '. . . she ful sone, in my thoght,/ As helpe me God, so was ykaught/ So sodenly, that I ne tok/ No maner counseyl but at hir lok/ And at myn herte. . . ' 837–41.

59

gain or for loss), and if together with this I had the humility of Esther and the faithfulness of Abraham, in truth, I would still fall short in the love of such a lady.* But Love made me do it and gave me freely, when I first saw her, so that I am hers unreservedly, whatever becomes of me, and will be for as long as I love, and will never love any other.†

[135] And when Love so worked that I was taken, and was a true lover, she clearly recognized my youth, my innocence and my simplicity. And because I was a child, she took me under her governance.‡ She showed me the right way, how I should love my lady, serve, obey, honour, humbly believe and adore her, and fear her above everything else as my love and my earthly god. I should always be concerned to work for her advantage and according to her will, protecting her honour and her peace. And if, in the activity of loving, I experienced pain, sorrow, melancholy or sadness, I should accept everything humbly and take no account of my misfortunes. And I should also take good care that this love should continue, and that always, both far and near, I should have desire, thought and concern for her love, and seek her grace, without desiring or seeking after any other, and that I should be loyal and discreet. These are the points and steps that Love taught me when she took me under her governance, and I have learned them so well that I have not erred in a single one.

Also, my very sweet lady – whom, by my soul, I desire and love with all my heart, without any unworthy thought, more than Paris did Helen – was to me a mirror and example of how to desire and do all good things.§ And for the good that I saw in her I strove to do well, and did all I could to keep myself from making any mistake for which I could be reproached, for her goodness gave me the heart and the will.

[179] And her perfect humility was to me a shield, defence and guard, so that pride (which raises up and engenders many evils) could not take me by surprise, and that I behaved myself very gently and humbly towards everybody. And truly, I can certainly say that she is fountain and well of humility. No dove, no lamb, no young maiden, could be purer of pride than her, or more full of humility accompanied with pity, in every way and every place. This is true and very right, for it descends to her in a direct line without any falling away from the ancient stock.

I learned from her easy manner (praised by everybody), her fine bearing, her noble behaviour** – which have no equal, in my opinion – just as the child is

*Cf. '. . . I wolde thoo/ Have loved best my lady free,/ Thogh I had had al the beaute/ That ever had Alcipyades,/ And al the strengthe of Ercules,/ And therto had the worthynesse/ Of Alysaunder . . ./ And therto also hardy be/ As was Ector, so have I joye,/ That Achilles slough at Troye. . . .' 1054ff.
†Cf. 'And yet she syt so in myn herte,/ That, by my trouthe, y nolde noght,/ For al thys world, out of my thoght/ Leve my lady,' 1108–11.
‡Cf. 'After my yonge childly wyt,/ Withoute drede, I besette hyt/ To love hir in my beste wyse,' 1095–7.
§Cf. 'For every wight of hir manere/ Myght cacche ynogh, yif that he wolde,/ Yif he had eyen hir to beholde./ For I dar swere wel, yif that she/ Had among ten thousand be,/ She wolde have be, at the leste,/ A chef myrour of al the feste,' 968–74.
**Cf. 'She had so stedfast countenaunce,/ So noble port and meyntenaunce,' 833–4.

taught by its teacher. For in brief, when I was far from her, bearing, manner and expression often came better to me when I remembered her. And when I saw her face to face, and saw again her bearing, her conduct, her manner – which are more sound and accomplished than any other I ever saw – it was certainly right that I should retain from them some important instruction, when by the memory alone my manner was many times improved through Sweet Thought.

[217] And her gracious way of speaking, which was not strange or silly or shapeless, which was lofty, yet finely controlled, perfectly collected for every occasion, based on absolute truth, and so sweet and agreeable to hear that it made everybody happy – this way of speaking of hers put a rein on my own mouth, and made me refrain from saying anything which could be considered wrong. For nobody should say anything about others that he would not wish to hear about himself. She forbade me to talk too much, and commanded me always to speak with propriety, without presumption, and without boasting, without lying and without flattering. For it is a very honourable thing to be truthful in what one says, for truth seeks only what is open and has no time for gossip.*

Her honour and her great courtesy forbade me from doing anything base, and desired that I should honour everybody and esteem myself very little. For he who acts with honour has the honour of it, and not he to whom the honour is done. And if the Gospel is not wrong, he who exalts himself is humbled, and he who humbles himself is exalted. For this reason, the name of my lady is exalted throughout the whole world, as she who abounds in humility, in honour and in courtesy more than any lady alive. And although everybody gives her the prize and crown of honour, she has so much honour that she thinks herself to be the least among the others. She knew nothing of rash, spendthrift extravagance, nor of stinginess, nor of the misery of avarice, which is a great vice in the human heart. But always, when she gave, she arranged her gifts wisely, and certainly knew what, when, how, to whom and why she gave. She did it promptly and gladly, and in this her gifts were more complete, for whoever gives promptly gives twice. In all this, she was a good teacher to me, who taught me very effectively that I should not rashly give largesse (but not have avarice or stinginess, which without pity hates generosity), and above all, that there should not be in me either the iron head nor the wooden shaft of the dart of avarice, which causes all other good to perish everywhere that it can strike. For no man is so honoured and respected that he would not lose all good because of this, although he has esteem, sense, honour, spirit, praise and reputation.

[281] And her great sweetness in no way left my heart, for its being there made it both night and day for me. And just as the sweet salve treats and softens

*Cf. 'And which a goodly, softe speche/ Had that swete, my lyves leche!/ So frendly, and so wel ygrounded,/ Up al resoun so wel yfounded,/ And so tretable to alle goode/ That I dar swere wel by the roode,/ Of eloquence was never founde/ So swete a sownynge facounde,/ Ne trewer tonged, ne skorned lasse,/ . . . ther was never yet throgh hir tonge/ Man ne woman gretly harmed;/ As for her ther was al harm hyd –/ Ne lasse flaterynge in hir word,/ That purely hir symple record/ Was founde as trewe as any bond . . .' 919ff.

the pain of a wound, so her great sweetness softened the pain that Love and Desire caused me, who attacked me very severely, at which I neither complain nor grieve, for I have no pain or sorrow in it, but rather I accept them humbly, gladly and happily.

[295] And her very sweet, pleasant look drew my heart too, by its gentle allure, just as the magnet attracts the iron. And this kept my heart in joy, for when I saw that sweet look nothing could find room in my heart which was contrary to happiness.* And her all-surpassing beauty bound my heart and binds it more and more, day by day, to her service and her love, and teaches me through its power to be acquainted with Sweet Hope, and to desire the mercy of Love, for which I am very grateful. For indeed, I did not know Hope or Desire, when her beauty set me on the way to know them, to augment my love and my joy, so that Love encourages Desire and Hope brings joy.

And her noble and beautiful array which is, as everybody says, simple, elegant, graceful and lovely, taught me and still teaches me how I should conduct myself elegantly, properly and handsomely, neither too much so nor too little – for indeed, there is nothing good in making a pretence, but he who can hit on a mean is most certain to keep to it.

[327] In the same way, her excellent goodness, and her perfect humility, her manner – which is not changeable – her noble bearing, her wise conduct, her beautiful speech, her lofty honour, her faultless courtesy, her generosity, her sweet friendliness, her gentle look, her pure beauty and her beautifully instructed way of behaving – all these things were a great education to me, if I can retain them. And although I saw all good things in her and retained very little of them, I must be the better for it, or indeed I should have done very badly. And if I had acquired any of these good qualities in myself through example, I would not willingly tell of it, because praise grows dim in the mouth of he who says it of himself. And nonetheless, I very much want to say – without boasting or speaking ill, and to her praise alone – that if there is anything worthwhile in my life it will come precisely from her, to whom I surrender heart, body, and soul.

[353] And thus I am taught by the very noble instruction, so very precious and pure, of my beautiful lady who possesses instruction in all that is good. And I served her for a long time with such a loving heart that I paid no attention except to the love of her that filled me. But she knew nothing of all this, nor of how she had captured me. For I would not for anything make known to her the love of my heart, nor ought I to have done, nor could I have made myself known, and if I had wished to I would not have known how.† Thus I bore this love in secret, without making any complaint or cry about it, so very much enflamed with love I was. Nonetheless, when I felt the very sweet gaze of her look I lost all strength through its power and influence, and it made me change colour and grow pale, shake, tremble, and start. Then one could well perceive

---

*Cf. 'So mochel hyt amended me/ That, whan I saugh hir first a-morwe,/ I was warished of al my sorwe/ Of al day after, til hyt were eve;/ Me thoghte nothyng myghte me greve,/ Were my sorwes never so smerte,' 1102–7.

†Cf. 'On hir was al my love leyd;/ And yet she nyste hyt never a del/ Noght longe tyme, leve hyt wel!/ For be ryght siker, I durste noght,/ For al this world, telle hir my thoght,/ Ne I wolde have wraththed hir, trewely,' 1146–51.

that I truly loved her more than five hundred thousand times more than myself, without any pretence and with a lover's heart. And thus I spent my youth for my very gentle, gracious lady, in sweet thought, in memory, in hope of attaining to her grace, which I desire so much that I have no other desire.

[387] In this way I felt many pricking wounds, one hour sweet, another sharp, sometimes pleasant, sometimes painful, sometimes sad, another time happy. For a heart that feels the wound of Love is not always in the same state, not secure in joy or in pain, but rather it must live according to the fortune of Love. But with my head bowed like a bear I received her sweet will, be it of joy or sorrow, in humble fashion like a perfect lover, amorous in word and deed. And because I was by no means always in the same state, I betook myself to making songs and lays, balades, rondeaux, and virelais, in accordance with my feelings, amorous and not otherwise.* For he who does not compose from out of his feelings counterfeits his work and his song. I also could not show the woes of love that I felt to my lady, who in singing seemed to me so enchantingly lovely. And all the songs I composed, I made in praise of her, thinking that if it so happened that my song came to her ear, she would be able to know how much I love her and am at her command. And my heart took great delight when my lady led me out of love for her to sing to her praise and honour. For singing is born of happiness of heart, and tears come from sadness. And because Sweet Thought is enclosed in my heart – together with Memory and Good Hope, and Loyalty, where I have my trust so entirely that I have it nowhere else – I composed this poem that is called a lay [430].

[In his lay the poet asks Amour that his lady may know how much he loves her. It happens that his lady sees this lay and asks him who wrote it. All abashed, he says nothing and goes away to the beautiful Parc de Hesdin, where he sits in a garden beside a fountain and makes a complaint upon Amour and Fortune. This lengthy complaint has some lines in common with *BD*: The poet-lover complains on Fortune's wheel (918): 'Le sormonté au bas retourne' [cf. *'That ys broght up, she set al doun,'* 635], and later (1052–4) he complains that Fortune 'dazzles and blinds the eyes of many people to whom she makes large promises' [cf. *'The trayteresse fals and ful of gyle,/ That al behoteth, and nothyng halt,'* 620–1]. He declares (1113–4) that 'Fortune has more than a thousand contrivances with which to pain and deceive her people' [cf. *'For Fortune kan so many a wyle,/ Ther be but fewe kan hir begile,'* 673–4], and he compiles a list of her antithetical attributes, saying (1138) of Fortune: 'C'est l'envieuse charité' [cf. *'She ys th'envyouse charite,'* 642]. He touches on the iconography of Fortune – that (1162) 'with one eye she laughs and with the other she weeps' [cf. *'She ys fals; and ever laughynge/ With oon eye, and that other wepynge,'* 633–4], and also (1167) that 'she has one sound and one lame foot' [cf. *'She goth upryght, and yet she halt,'* 622]. Again, 'she so delights in her sport that when she is winning she says "Check and Mate!" in a proud voice' 1190–2), [cf. *'Therwith Fortune seyde "Chek her!"/ And "Mat" in myd poynt of the chekker,'* 659–60], and thus the poet's own joy has all disappeared and (1198)

*Cf. *'But, for to kepe me fro ydelnesse,/ Trewly I dide my besynesse/ To make songes, as I best koude,'* 1155–7.

63

'my laughing is changed into heavy tears' [cf. *And al my laughtre to wepynge*, 600]. Much later (1467–9) he complains that Desire so enflames his heart 'that there is no man or woman in the world who knows the cure, unless it is my lady' [cf. *For there is phisicien but oon/ That may me hele*, 39–40].

[*After his complaint the poet is visited by Esperance who educates and corrects his attitudes at length, and he is eventually rewarded*].

Le Dit dou Lyon

Guillaume de Machaut

Machaut's *Dit dou Lyon* – perhaps the original of the now-lost 'book of the Leoun' that Chaucer mentions among his works in the 'Retractions' at the end of the *Canterbury Tales* – offers several analogues to the *Book of the Duchess*, most especially in the parallels between the behaviour of the 'whelp' in Chaucer's poem and that of the amiable lion in Machaut's work. The following extract is translated from the *Œuvres*, ed. E. Hoepffner, SATF (Paris, 1908–21).

It was the season when winter is losing its hold, since by rights in winter nothing is naturally inclined to be happy and joyful. For many people, including myself, love spring very much more than winter. Even the animals, and the creeping things that come forth out of the earth to meet the spring, rejoice at its coming. The birds are also filled with joy at the arrival of spring and constantly, evening and morning, they prettily pay it its rightful due in their language: each one sings or descants and celebrates spring's coming, because up until then they have been in winter's prison. Nature commands them all to give themselves over to singing, so that throughout meadows and river-banks, open country and woods and thickets of elder-trees, throughout mountains and valleys, they all sang with open mouths, pouring out many sounds. For all of them threw themselves into their singing when they saw the wood covered with blossom and fresh green leaves, and the hawthorn that does not scratch their little throats with thorns when they eat the seed.

In this sweet season that I am describing to you, on the second day of April, 1342, I was tremendously sleepy, and I was tucked up in bed because I needed to be. But I didn't stay there very long, because a long way before daybreak I was woken up by the sweet nightingale which is so pretty, together with the goldfinch, the linnet, the parrot, and the sweet song of the calendar lark, which is of such a noble nature that, when anybody lies ill and the lark is brought in, it can be told immediately from the lark whether the sick person will recover or die. For if the lark looks at him it is certain that there is nothing to fear, and if it turns its head away it is clear that death is near.

[57] As God preserve me, it is like this with my lady and her look, for I am safe from all ills when she looks at me, and I have no fear of death. And alas! I have no hope of cure and am in fear of my life when her look signifies my death – that is when she turns her gaze elsewhere, which gives me great pain. However, I want to drop this subject and come back to my first theme, and

from now on I shan't rhyme about it any more, because I have other things to put in rhyme.*

As I say, then, the fresh songs of all the birds could be heard there, for each in his own way rendered praise and service to spring. I listened to their singing for a long time, with such pleasure that I could not sleep and forgot my rest. The place where I was lying was far from people and roads, set by a clear, pure, gentle river, which ran by a garden so beautiful it surpassed all wishing, for it contained an abundance of all sorts of fruits, trees, plants, flowers, seeds, and herbs, springs, all species of animals from big to small, and every good thing from here or overseas. There was never any rain or wind, but a continuous spring, nor did the sun at all lessen with its heat the colour of the grass, always green beneath the shade of the trees.

[107] And I, who had come there because I had heard tell of the garden and its uniquely marvellous property – for it is so strange a place that no false person goes there who does not change – without more delay I rose, washed my hands and went towards the garden, which was surrounded on all sides by the river – it needed no other fortification.

When I came to the bank I saw no bridge, plank, or way over by which I could cross, and I began to think hard how I could reach the garden, for the water was deep and broad, and I could find no boat there, which greatly annoyed me, because the garden attracted me so much that I never desired anything so much as to be there, and I sighed a great deal. I quite wore myself out, for I went up and down, and I had no horse. But in the end, I came across a beautiful spot, and indeed, on that third day of April I saw in the shadow of a tree a boat so beautiful and rich that it was fine enough for the Duke of Austria, or the Pope, or the King of France, and it was splendidly adorned, and covered with a canopy of green silk, so that I thought – as God help me – a better could not be wished for.

[151] I was very happy when I saw it, and do you know what I did? I ran towards it, for I never thought I would be on the other side of the river, and got in very cheerfully. But I didn't find anyone there but myself. Then I untied the boat, looked all round, and found an oar to propel it. But indeed, I didn't know anything about how to do it, and wasn't very good at it. Nonetheless, I managed to reach the far bank, and if I had had the whole Empire I would not have been happier when I saw I was safely over to see the strange things contained in that garden.

Then I jumped out of that graceful boat and tied it up fast to a willow. I thought I would be able to find it when I needed it for the return. And when I had secured it, I went through the garden without company and light at heart, taking a little-trodden path full of lush thick grass all dewy, for it was a beautiful morning.† I walked along for a while, noticing how well the garden was laid out: there were many trees but all equal in height, and many birds in them. As I listened to the delight of the birds, Love, who taught me to do his

*Cf. *Book of the Duchess: For there is phisicien but oon/ That may me hele; but that is don./ Passe we over untill eft;/ That wil not be mot nede be left;/ Our first mater is good to kepe. . . .* 39–43.

†Cf. . . . *And I hym folwed, and hyt forth wente/ Doun by a floury grene wente/ Ful thikke of gras, ful softe and swete/ . . . And litel used, hyt semed thus . . .* 397ff.

sweet pleasure with pure heart and true desire, caused me to think of my lady, without any unworthy thought, for her very sweet image is so strongly imprinted in my heart that it will always be there and never leave.* I am completely hers, who is my heart, my belief, my desire, my hope, my health, my joy, my comfort, my worth, my sorrow, my pain, all my happiness, my peace, my sustenance, my resort, my trust, my death, my sickness, my hold on life, all that I love and desire. At her will she can make and unmake me and with a single look restore me. All I have comes from her: always I remember her, see her, adore her, serve her, honour her. Nothing stops me thinking of her, seeing her, and feeling her great sweetness within my heart. In short, she makes me laugh and cry and be happy as she pleases, and I only want to do her will: she can make me live or die. This is all, for I am entirely hers.

[249] And should God give me the name of lover of the lady I love much more than myself, I should ask for no other reward for my humble devotion than that my service should please her, and she should know I am hers, and love her, without any unworthy thought, more than Paris did Helen. I am unworthy of my wish and have not served enough to deserve it, for if I served her a hundred thousand years I would not deserve a hundredth part, yet my heart indeed strives night and day to the end that she should truly know that, as long as I live, I shall faithfully be hers with a true will. My greatest fear is that my life will not be long enough to serve her, for I have irrevocably committed my energy, my heart, and all I can do to serve her, and I should serve her all my days.

Thus I went over and over in my thoughts how I would serve my lady. I thought about this so deeply – without paying attention to anything else – that I lost my path in the garden, and stumbled into a place full of brambles and thorn bushes. In the middle was a very thick bush, and I shuddered terribly, for a lion with a great mane sprang from out of it. This hurled me from my reverie, for I thought he must be going to kill me. I didn't know what I should do, for I had no knife, sword, axe, or any weapon to defend myself. And the lion without more delay came bounding towards me. But yet, however much I feared him and would have preferred him to be elsewhere, I was not so utterly out of my wits that I did not have the memory – which Love caused to come to me – of my very sweet, dear lady, whom I love with heart, body and soul. When he came near me, he tossed his head very fiercely, and when I saw this I cried out, 'Dear lady, I commend myself to you!' I don't know why or how, and whether it was through the power of my lady, for certainly, as soon as I had said this he had no will to harm me but stopped in front of me and looked at me. I devoutly thanked both my lady and Love, for I would have come to my end if I had not remembered them.

[352] Then the lion came towards me very nicely, and as meekly as if he were a little puppy, and when I saw this I said, 'Good boy,' and put my hand on his head. But he let me do this more sweetly than any other animal and joined his ears together. It absolutely amazed me that so fierce a beast behaved so gently. I watched what would happen and what the lion would do, for he frisked amiably round me for a long while, which pleased me very much. He looked

---

*Cf. 'And yet she syt so in myn herte,/ That, by my trouthe, y nolde noght,/ For al thys world, out of my thoght/ Leve my lady; noo, trewely!' 1108–11.

67

around me and took the edge of my coat in his teeth, as wisely as if he had understanding – then he went on in front and I followed behind. But he held me so tightly that he seemed to want to say to me, 'Come with confidence, fair sir! for you are in my safekeeping.' I was delighted, for I was quite sure that this was some good fortune, and I followed him very willingly.*

But he led me for a long way through a pathless region, among brambles and nettles and thorns sharper than needles, which pricked me in several places so that they made the blood flow. I would never have thought there was such a spot in the garden, but it was for the wild animals that did not like the good places. This did not prevent me going along with the lion, for I was engrossed to know what he would do. But as we came out of that place where there were so many brambles, thorns, and nettles, I certainly had need of my lady, for by my soul, if I hadn't said as I had said before 'Dear lady, I commend myself to you!' I am certain I would have been dead and could not have escaped. For I saw there many kinds of cruel and savage beasts, dragons, serpents, scorpions, of all types, wild bulls, camels, tigers, panthers, elephants, leopards, bears, lynxes, foxes and vixens, beavers, various mastiffs and hunting dogs, as well as asps and unicorns. And there was another beast there with two horns, very strange, dangerous, and venomous, for I feared it more than the others and I still fear it very much. I don't know its name. I think it comes from overseas, and I wish it would return and be drowned in the process and all the others too, and then I would have a less anxious life!

[407] It seemed to me all these beasts were assembled to harm the lion, each in its own way, for they all cried and yelped after him in their babble, and I was sure they would strangle him if they could or dared. The noble lion would very well be able to take his revenge if he deigned to, but I could see from his expression that he wanted no revenge. They made such a storm it made my head ache and displeased the lion, for he glowered so, that if he were wounded in a hundred places he would not be so disturbed. For two or three times I saw he was so strongly attacked he nearly died. But this did not stop him from continuing to go on his way with his head bowed towards the earth.

Thus I was led for a long time by the lion, who put himself to great trouble to arrive where he wanted to be. He found a path to the right, and entered on a small path by a little stream which came down from a spring. The lion lapped and drank deeply here, and I too, who was very tired, felt the need to drink some of it. Then we went on our way, and eventually went so far along the stream that we found a fine and beautiful fountain, and beside it there was a rich and beautiful pavilion very well pitched and surrounded by lush grass, in a meadow so beautiful that I never saw a lovelier.

[453] Between the tent and the spring, to which I had come with great difficulty, in great fear and danger with the noble lion, there was a carpet of exotic workmanship made in the Carthaginian manner, and some cushions of fine, rich silk and gold. There sat the finest and gayest lady that man or woman

---

*Cf. *And as I wente, ther cam by mee/ A whelp, that fauned me as I stood,/ That hadde yfolowed, and koude no good./ Hyt com and crepte to me as lowe/ Ryght as hyt hadde me yknowe,/ Helde doun hys hed and joyned hys eres,/ And leyde al smothe doun hys heres./ I wolde have kaught hyt, and anoon/ Hyt fledde, and was fro me goon;/ And I hym folwed, and hyt forth wente. . . . 388–97.*

ever saw, I think, in body, manner and face, in sweet look and simple expression, in bearing and wise comportment, in nobly laughing and playing and every other disport that a good lady should know. And because I don't have the knowledge to be able to tell properly of her excellences, or describe the beauties in her sweet face, I shall keep quiet. There isn't anybody, nor ever was or will be, however much he studied, who would know how to do it, and for that reason I am silent and will stay so. But yet I will say that I know God gave her everything needful for a good and beautiful woman.

She was much surrounded by knights and squires, ladies and maidens, young, noble, gay and lovely, and she was as beautifully dressed as if she were a king's daughter. I certainly believe she was a queen, for she had on her head a crown of pure gold with the finest stones I ever saw in my life, but the priceless golden crown seemed better and more beautiful because of her beauty.

[499] And when the lion saw her he never had such great happiness. He now raised his head and began to celebrate. He had his ears up very straight, and wagged his tail amazingly. He was very eager to run, and made such great bounds that I was amazed. I certainly saw he was very happy. With his claws he was scratching the earth. He cared very little for the attack by the animals who wished to harm and destroy him. Thus the lion was full of joy, and I was very happy too, when I could see face to face the lady I described to you. For she was a hundred times more beautiful and well-taught than I can say. But the lion bounded away again and left me, and without delay, softly, meekly and courteously, he drew towards the lady he much feared and obeyed, and knelt before her. I could certainly see that he cared for her a great deal, and he had his tail between his legs. But he took no notice of all the other ladies, and handsomely, with trembling heart, approached the lady so that her robe was touching him, and laid his head upon it. And the lady, whom God honour! smoothed with her white hand the fur of his head [538].

[When the lady's attention is diverted to the two-horned beast the lion becomes quite dejected and even contemplates suicide. The poet asks the lady to explain to him the joy and torment of the lion and the strange beasts, and she calls on a wise old knight to explain the garden to him. In his ensuing discourse (853–1800) the knight reveals that no one false in love can enter that garden, for the lion prevents them. An ancestor of the lady had the boat and river constructed for this end. Previously, many people had flocked to the garden, both true and false lovers, and he lists and describes many types of false and insincere lovers – but among the true lovers are those who fight abroad for their lady's honour (1368ff.) from Cyprus to Alexandria . . . to the Dry Tree . . . to Prussia . . . to Tartary, among very many other places.* Because so many unfaithful lovers and betrayers of love came there the defences were created, and the old king who had them made named the place 'L'Esprueve de fines amours' (1778). He concludes by saying that as a faithful lover the poet will be able to come and go. When he finishes the lion comes up to the lady who strokes

---

*Cf. 'Ne sende men into Walakye,/ To Pruyse, and into Tartarye,/ To Alysaundre, ne into Turkye,/ And byd hym faste anoon that he/ Goo hoodles to the Drye Se/ And come hom by the Carrenar,/ And seye "Sir, be now ryght war/ That I may of yow here seyn/ Worshyp, or that ye come ageyn!"/ She ne used no suche knakkes smale. . . .' 1024–33.

him, but the two-horned beast appears. The poet asks the lady to explain. She recalls to him that Envy cannot perish, and its evil effects are everywhere. She brought up the lion from young, and still feeds him and prevents him from revenging himself. The poet feels the lion's position is too difficult, but the lady replies that he will conquer everything through suffering. The poet humbly thanks her for her answer and takes his leave. The lion accompanies him back to the boat, and as the poet gets in the lion bows to him. The poet returns to his company – he has been away a day and a half. He tells them his adventure, at which they are amazed, and determine to go there themselves. The poet is unsure if they will succeed. He gives his name in an anagram and prays to Amour (2204)].

II

Sources and Analogues of 'The Parliament of Fowls'

The Dream of Scipio
Cicero

Cicero's Dream of Scipio was originally part of his *De re publica*, Bk VI, and although the whole work was not known in the Middle Ages, the *Somnium Scipionis* itself was preserved in the Commentary on it by Macrobius (*c.* 400 A.D.), and exerted a very great influence. For the text and a full account, cf. *Macrobius; Commentary on the Dream of Scipio*, transl. W. H. Stahl (New York, 1952), and also *Cicero; De re publica*, ed. C. W. Keyes (Loeb Classical Library, 1928).

[1] When I arrived in Africa under the consul Manius Manilius – as military tribune in the Fourth Legion, as you know – my greatest desire was to meet King Masinissa, who for excellent reasons was a great friend of my family. When I came to him the old man embraced me and wept profusely, and after a short while, looking up to heaven, he said, 'I give you thanks, oh highest Sun, and you other heavenly beings, that before I quit this life I see within my realm and under this roof, Publius Cornelius Scipio, by the mere sound of whose name I am refreshed, for the memory of that excellent and invincible man has never faded from my mind.'

Then I enquired of him about his kingdom, and he asked me about our commonwealth, and the whole day was spent with much to say on each side. Later, when I had been entertained with royal splendour, we prolonged our conversation far into the night, the old man talking of nothing but Africanus and remembering not only all his deeds but also his words. When we parted to go to bed sleep took a stronger hold of me than usual, as a result both of the journey and of staying up so late. Then (I think because we had talked of him – for it often occurs that our thoughts and conversation give rise to something in our sleep, such as Ennius writes about in connection with Homer, of whom he would often think and talk while awake) Africanus appeared to me in the form more familiar to me from his portrait than from himself. Upon recognizing him I shuddered, but he said, 'Take heart, Scipio, have no fear, and commit to memory what I am going to say.

[2] 'Do you see that city which, compelled by me to be obedient to the Roman people, is renewing its previous hostility and is unable to stay at peace?' – and from a place on high, splendid and bright and studded with stars, he pointed out Carthage – 'that city against which you come to fight, with a rank little higher than that of a private soldier? In two years' time you yourself, as

consul, shall overthrow it, and will win for yourself that surname which hitherto you have had as an inheritance from me. After you have destroyed Carthage and celebrated your triumph, you will be censor, and you will go as legate to Egypt, Syria, Asia, and Greece; you will be chosen consul a second time in your absence, will bring a great war to a close and destroy Numantia. But when you come in state to the Capitol in your chariot, you will find the commonwealth disturbed because of my grandson's policies. Then, Africanus, you will need to demonstrate to your country the brightness of your character, talents, and judgement. But at the time I see your way forward uncertain between two destinies, as it were. When your age has fulfilled seven times eight recurring circuits of the sun, and these two numbers have made up their destined sum in your life in Nature's circuit, then the whole state will turn to you alone and to your name. To you the senate, all good men, the allies, the Latins, will look; on you alone will the safety of the state depend, and, in brief, as dictator you will need to set the commonwealth in order, if you escape the wicked hands of your relatives.' – At this Laelius cried aloud, and the rest groaned deeply, but with a gentle smile Scipio said, 'I beg you not to rouse me from sleep, and listen for a little while to what followed.'

[3] 'But be sure of this, Africanus, so that you may be the more zealous in protecting the commonwealth: for all those who have preserved, assisted, or enlarged their fatherland there is a special place set aside in heaven where the blessed enjoy themselves for ever. Nothing that occurs on earth is more pleasing to that supreme God who rules the whole universe, than assemblies and associations of men bound by the rule of law, which are called commonwealths: their rulers and protectors derive from this place and return there.'

Although I was then terrified, not so much by fear of death as by fear of treachery among my kinsmen, nevertheless I asked him whether he and my father Paulus and others whom we think of as dead were still alive. 'Indeed yes,' he said; 'those are alive who have burst forth from the chains of their bodies as if from a prison – indeed, what is called your life is death. Do you not see your father Paulus coming to you?'

When I saw him I burst into a flood of tears, but he embraced and kissed me, and forbade me to weep. As soon as I could stop weeping and start to speak I said, 'I entreat you, most excellent and most revered of fathers, since this is life, as I hear Africanus say, why do I remain on earth? Why do I not hasten to you here?'

'Not so,' he said. 'Unless that God whose temple is all that you see has freed you from the prison of the body, the route here does not lie open to you. For men are created under this law: that they should tend this globe called Earth which you see in the middle of this temple; they have been given souls from those perpetual fires which you call stars and planets, which globes and spheres, animated by divine intelligences, complete their circuits and orbits with marvellous speed. Wherefore, Publius, you and all pious men must maintain the soul in the custody of the body and must not abandon human life except at the command of him by whom it was given you, lest you should seem to have shirked the duty assigned to man by God. But Scipio, cherish justice and duty as your grandfather here and I who begot you did: justice and duty are owing to parents and kin, but most of all to your country. Such a life is the road into heaven and to the fellowship of those who have already lived and, released

74

from the body, dwell in that place which you see (it was a circle of brilliant splendour shining out among the stars) which you, taking the term from the Greeks, call the Milky Way.'

When I looked out from this point, everything appeared to me surpassingly brilliant and marvellous. There were stars which we never see from earth, and of greater magnitude than we ever imagined. Of these the smallest [i.e. the Moon] was furthest from heaven and nearest the earth, and shone with a borrowed light. The starry globes easily surpassed the magnitude of the earth. Then the earth itself seemed so small to me that I was ashamed of our Empire, which only covers a single point, as it were, on its surface.

[4] As I gazed more intently, Africanus said, 'I pray you, how long will your thoughts be fixed upon the ground? Surely you see what regions you have entered? In nine circles, or rather spheres, all things are connected. The outermost sphere, which contains all the rest, is the celestial, and is itself the supreme God, enclosing and holding together all the other spheres in itself. In it are fixed and revolve the eternal courses of the stars; beneath it are the seven other spheres, which revolve in an opposite direction to that of the celestial sphere. That planet which on earth is called Saturn possesses one of these spheres; next comes that shining light, benevolent and beneficial to mankind which is called Jupiter; next the red one, terrible to the earth, which is called Mars; then below that the Sun holds almost the middle region, lord and chief and ruler of the other lights, the mind and guiding principle of the universe, of such magnitude that he reveals and fills all things with his light. The Sun is, as it were, accompanied by his companions, the spheres of Venus and Mercury, and in the lowest sphere revolves the Moon, kindled by the rays of the Sun. But below the Moon there is nothing but what is mortal and subject to decay, save for the souls given to the human race by the goodness of the gods, while above the Moon all things are eternal. The ninth and central sphere is the earth, which does not move and is the lowest of all, and towards it all bodies are drawn downwards by their natural inclination.'

[5] I gazed in astonishment and when I recollected myself I said, 'What is this great sound which so fills my ears and is so sweet?'

'That,' he replied, 'is produced by the onward rush and motion of the spheres themselves: their being separated into unequal but properly proportioned intervals, blending high notes with low, gives rise to various harmonies; for such mighty motions cannot be so swiftly carried on in silence; and Nature has so arranged that at one extreme the spheres give out a low note and at the other a high. Therefore, that highest sphere of heaven, which bears the stars, as it revolves faster, is moved with a high, loud note, while the lowest revolving sphere, that of the Moon, gives out the deepest note; for the ninth sphere, the earth, remains fixed motionless at the centre of the universe. But the other eight spheres, two of which [Mercury and Venus] move at the same speed, produce seven distinct notes – a number which is the key to almost everything. Learned men, by imitating these harmonies on stringed instruments and in songs have opened up for themselves a way back to this place, as have others who during their earthly lives have pursued divine studies with outstanding ability. Ever filled with this sound, the ears of men have grown deaf to it, for there is no duller sense in you than hearing, just as at that place called Catadupa where the Nile rushes down from highest mountains, the people who live near that place have lost their sense of hearing on account of the greatness of the noise. But indeed, so great is the sound of the whole universe, revolving at the highest speed, that human ears cannot catch it, just as you cannot look directly at the Sun, for your sense of sight is overpowered by its beams.'

While marvelling at these wonders, I nonetheless kept turning my eyes back to the earth.

[6] Then Africanus went on, 'I see that you are still gazing at the region and home of men. If it seems small to you – as it is – then always keep your gaze fixed upon these heavenly things and contemn those that are human. For what fame can you win from the speech of men, or what glory that is worth the seeking? You see that the earth is only inhabited in a few, very small places, while between these inhabited "spots", as we may call them, lie vast deserts; and those who inhabit the earth are not only so widely scattered that there can be no communication between them, but some of them dwell in parts of the earth that are oblique, transverse, or even directly opposite to your own, and from such, indeed, you can expect no glory.

'In addition, you will notice that the earth is girdled and surrounded by certain belts, of which you see that the two that are most widely separated and lie under the opposite poles of heaven are overwhelmed with frost and snow, while the middle, and broadest, belt is scorched by the heat of the sun. Two are inhabitable; of these the southern – the footsteps of its inhabitants are opposite to your own on their side of the earth – has no connection with your people. Of this northern region which you inhabit, notice how small a portion belongs to you Romans. For the whole land which is inhabited by you, narrower at the ends and broader at the sides, is really only a small island surrounded by that sea which on earth is called the Atlantic, the Great Sea, or the Ocean – and now you see how small it is despite its grand name. From these known and settled lands has your name or the name of any of us been able to cross the Caucasus, which you see there, or swim across the Ganges? Who in those other lands of the rising or the setting sun, or the extreme North or South, will ever hear your name? With all these left out of account, you surely see into what narrow confines your glory is eager to spread itself? And how long will even those who do talk of us now continue to do so?

[7] 'But even if future generations should desire to hand on to their successors the praises of every one of us that they have received from their fathers, nevertheless, because of the floods and conflagrations which necessarily happen on earth at certain times, we cannot achieve even a long-enduring glory, let alone eternal. But what difference does it make that you should be spoken of by those who are born after you, when you were never mentioned by those who lived before, who were no less in number and were certainly better men? – especially as not one of those who may hear our names can retain any recollection for a single year. For men usually measure a year solely by the return of the sun, i.e. by a single star. But when all the stars return to the same place from which they started off and have restored over long intervals the original configurations of the heavens, then indeed can the returning cycle be called a year. I scarcely dare say how many generations of men are contained within such a year. For as once the sun appeared to men to be eclipsed and extinguished when the soul of Romulus entered those regions, so when the sun shall again be eclipsed in the same quarter and in the same season, and all the constellations and stars have returned to their original positions, you may

believe that a year has elapsed. But you should understand that not a twentieth part of such a year has yet passed.

'Consequently, if you despair of returning to this place, in which all things are given to great and outstanding men, of how little value is that glory among men which can scarcely endure for a small part of a single year? Therefore, if you will look on high and contemplate this place of rest and eternal home, you will no longer attend to the chatter of the common herd, nor put your hope in human rewards for your exploits. Virtue herself, by her own charms, should lead you on to true glory. What others say of you is their own business – they will say it anyway. But all their talk is limited to those narrow regions which you see, nor will any man's fame long endure, for men's words are buried with them and extinguished in the oblivion of posterity.'

[8] When he had spoken in this way, I said, 'If indeed, Africanus, a path to heaven, as it were, is open to those who have served their country well, I shall strive much more keenly with the prospect of such a great reward, even though from my boyhood I have walked in your footsteps and those of my father and have not failed to emulate your glory.'

He replied, 'Indeed, you must go on striving, and believe that it is not you that is mortal, but only this body. For it is not really you that is declared by your outward form, but the mind of man is his true self, and not that physical figure which can be pointed to by a finger. Know, then, that you are a god, if a god is that which quickens, feels, remembers and foresees, and which rules, and restrains and moves the body over which it is set, just as the supreme God does this universe. And just as the eternal God moves the universe, which is in part mortal, so an immortal soul moves your frail body.

'For what is always in motion is eternal, but that which communicates motion to something else, but is itself moved by another force, necessarily ceases to live when this motion comes to an end. That alone, therefore, which moves itself never ceases to be moved, because it is never deserted by itself – indeed, it is the source and first cause of motion in all other things that are moved. This first cause itself has no origin, for all things originate from the first cause, but that first cause itself cannot be born from something else, for that would not be a first cause which originated from something else. And since it never had a beginning, then indeed it will never have an end. For if a first cause were destroyed, it could not be reborn from anything else, nor could it create anything else from itself, if indeed it is necessary for everything to originate from a first cause. Thus it happens that the beginning of movement begins with that which is self-moved, and this can neither be born nor die, or else the whole heaven must fall and Nature come to a stop, meeting no force to impel them to motion again.

[9] 'Therefore, since it is clear that what is self-moved is eternal, who is there who will deny this to be the nature of souls? For everything which is moved by an external impulse is inanimate, but whatever possesses a soul is moved by its own inner impulse, for this is the peculiar nature and property of souls. And as a soul is unique in moving itself, it certainly has not been born, and is eternal. Use it, therefore, for the best things. And the best tasks are those that serve the welfare of your fatherland; a soul busy and trained in such concerns will fly the more swiftly to this its resting place and home. And this flight will be still more swift if the soul, while still confined within the body, will rise above it and, by contemplating what lies outside itself, detach itself as much as possible from

the body. For the souls of those who have given themselves up to the pleasures of the body and have as it were become their slaves, and who at the instigation of desires subservient to pleasure have violated the laws of gods and men – their souls, after leaving their bodies, fly around the earth itself, and do not return to this place except after many ages of torture.'

He departed, and I awoke from sleep.

De Planctu Naturae
Alanus de Insulis

For the text of Alanus' description of Nature, cf. J. P. Migne (ed.), *Patrologia Latina*, Vol. 210, cols. 439–40, or Thomas Wright (ed.), *The Anglo-Latin Satirical Poets and Epigrammatists of the Twelfth Century*, Rolls Series, 2 vols. (London, 1872).

[*The description of Nature . . .*]. Now the virgin, as was said before, came forth from the realms of the celestial region, and was carried in her bright chariot towards the humble abode of the suffering world, and drawn by Juno's own birds, which were not controlled by any yoke except their own willingness. A certain man, tall enough to tower over the virgin and her coach, and whose countenance expressed not the common quality of earth but the mystery of godhead, assisted the weakness of her feminine sex and guided the regular approach of the chariot. When, to behold this beauty, I had assembled the rays of my eyesight, those soldiers of my eyes, they – not daring to venture before such majesty and overcome by the impact of such splendour – fled with fear into the tents of my eyelids. At the coming of this virgin you would have thought that all the elements were holding a festival, as though they were renewing their nature. As if to light the virgin's path with his candles, the firmament ordered his stars to shine more brightly than usual, and daylight marvelled at their boldness when they insolently appeared in his presence. Phoebus as well, assuming a gladder countenance than usual, poured out the treasures of his light to greet her. To his sister – from whom he had taken away the adornment of his shining – he gave back the apparel of delight, bidding her to meet the approaching queen. The air put aside the weeping clouds, and with clear face smiled at her approach; previously buffeted by the north wind's anger, it now relaxed in the embrace of Favonius. By natural inspiration the birds delighted to sport with their wings, and gave sign to the virgin of their deference. Juno, who had shortly before scorned Jupiter's advances, was now so overcome with joy that with many darting looks she drew her husband on to the pleasures of love. The sea – previously chafed with storms – made a festival of the maiden's coming, and promised perpetual calm; for Aeolus, in order that his winds and storms should make no turbulence in the virgin's presence, bound them in their cells. Fish came close to the surface, as far as their limited sensual nature allowed, and showed their delight at their lady's coming; and Thetis, at sport with Nereus, thought then she would conceive another Achilles. And maidens whose beauty not only stole away a man's reason, but

79

also made the heavenly beings forget their divine nature, came forth from places where streams rose, bringing tributes of gifts of aromatic nectar to the arriving queen. Indeed, the earth, which was previously stripped of her adornment by the robbery of winter, gained from generous spring a dress of bright flowers, so as not to appear unfittingly in her old clothes before the virgin.

Teseida, Bk VII, 50–66

Giovanni Boccaccio

The *Teseida* extract is translated from the edition by A. Limentani in *Tutte le Opere di Giovanni Boccaccio*, ed. V. Branca, Vol. II (Milan, 1964). Chaucer follows the Italian closely, and the line numbers in brackets which follow after the translation of each Italian stanza refer to relevant lines in the *Parliament of Fowls*. A few variant readings are given from the corrupt Italian text cited by Skeat (*Works*, I, 68–73) which seem to preserve readings closer to those Chaucer may have encountered in his own text of *Teseida*.

[50] Just as the prayer of Arcita had sought out Mars, so that of Palemone went to merciful Venus on Mount Cithaeron, where the temple of Venus stands in a somewhat shady place among very tall pines; and as she [the prayer] drew near, Desire (*Vaghezza*) was the first she saw in that high place.

[51] As she went along with her, she saw that the place was mild and delightful in every way, in the form of a leafy and beautiful garden, full of the greenest plants, fresh grass, and every newly-opened flower; and she saw clear springs [*var.* living and clear springs] rise there, and amongst the other plants with which the place abounded it seemed to her that there was more myrtle than anything else. (183–9)

[52] There she heard almost every kind of bird singing sweetly among the branches, upon which she also saw them happily making their nests. Then, among the fresh grasses, she saw rabbits going quickly here and there, and timid young red-deer, and roe-deer, and many other kinds of little animals [*var.* dearest little animals]. (190–6)

[53] Likewise, she seemed to hear there every instrument and delightful song. And passing along with not too slow a step, somewhat bemused in herself and gazing about intently at the lofty place and its beautiful adornments, saw that almost every corner of it was full of spirits flying hither and thither to their places. While she was looking at these, (197–8)

[54] among the bushes, beside a spring, she saw Cupid making arrows, having placed his bow at his feet. His daughter Sensual Pleasure (*Volutà*) was tempering some selected arrows in the water. Seated by them was Ease (*Ozio*) whom, together with Memory (*Memoria*), she saw tip the arrows with the steel that she [*Volutà*] had first tempered. (211–16)

[55] Then passing by she saw Grace (*Leggiadria*) with Elegance (*Adornezza*) and Friendliness (*Affabilitate*), and Courtesy (*Cortesia*) who was completely at a loss; and she saw the Arts which have power to force others to commit folly, in

their appearance much disfigured from the likeness or image of ourselves; and Vain Delight (*Van Diletto*) she saw standing alone with Nobility (*Gentilezza*). (218–24)

[56] Then near her she saw Beauty (*Bellezza*) pass by, without any adornment, looking at herself, and she saw Attractiveness (*Piacevolezza*) going along with her, each of them praising the other. Then she saw Youth (*Giovanezza*) standing by them, living and adorned, and making merry; and on the other side she saw mad Foolhardiness (*folle Ardire*) with Flattery (*Lusinghe*) and Procurement (*Ruffiania*) walking together. (225–9)

[57] In the middle of the place she saw a temple on high columns of copper, and she saw dancing around it finely dressed youths and ladies beautiful in themselves, with their hair and their clothes flowing free, barefoot, and spending the day in that alone. Then over the temple she saw many sparrows fluttering about and doves cooing [*var.* and doves sit and coo]. (230–8)

[58] And close by the entrance of the temple she saw my lady Peace (*Pace*) sitting quietly, and lightly holding in her hand a curtain in front of the door; near her, very wretched in appearance, Patience (*Pazienza*) sat discreetly, with a pale face; and on all sides she saw about her Promises and Artfulnesses (*Promesse e Arte*). (239–45)

[59] Then when she had gone into the temple she heard a tumult of sighs which whirled about all fiery with hot Desires: this lit up all the altars with new flames born of Torments (*Martiri*), each one of which dripped with tears caused by a cruel and wicked woman that she saw there, called Jealousy (*Gelosia*). (246–52)

[60] And she saw Priapus occupying the highest place there, dressed just as he was when anybody who wished could see him, that night when by its braying the laziest of animals awoke Vesta, to care for whom he was not a little inclined and towards whom, in that fashion, he was going; and likewise, throughout the temple she saw garlands of many different flowers. (253–9)

[61] There she saw many bows of the followers of Diana hung up and broken, amongst which was that of Callisto, who was made into the northern Bear; and the apples of proud Atalanta were there, who was supreme in running, and also the arms of that other haughty woman, who gave birth to the fair Parthenopaeus, grandson to the Calydonian King Oenus. (281–7)

[62] She saw stories depicted there all about, among which – of the finest workmanship – she clearly saw all the acts of the wife of Ninus [Semiramis]; and she saw at the foot of the mulberry tree Pyramus and Thisbe, and the mulberries already stained; and along with these she saw great Hercules in the lap of Iole, and sad and pitiful Byblis going to entreat Caunus. (288–9)

[63] But as she did not see Venus, it was told her – nor did she know by whom – 'In the most secret part of the temple she takes her delight: if you want her, enter quietly through that door.' So without more delay, she humbly approached the door to enter into her, and perform the mission entrusted to her. (260–1)

[64] But when she first came there she found Wealth (*Richezza*) guarding the door, who seemed to her very much to be respected; and when she was allowed by her to enter the place seemed dark to her at her first steps, but when she had stayed there a while a little light appeared to her, and she saw her [Venus] lying nude on a great bed which was very beautiful to see. (261–6)

[65] She had golden hair, fastened around her head without any tress; her

face was such that the most highly praised have no beauty by comparison; the arms and bosom, and firm, high breasts, like raised apples, were all to be seen, and the other part was covered by a garment so fine that scarcely nothing was concealed. (267–73)

[66] The place was fragrant with a thousand perfumes; on one side of her sat Bacchus, on the other, Ceres, with her well-savouring foods; and she herself [Venus] held Lasciviousness [*Lascivia*] by the hand, and in the other hand the apple that she, preferred above her sisters, won in the Valley of Ida. And having seen all this she made her prayer, which was granted without denial. (274–6)

Visions and Questions of Love

Li Fablel dou Dieu d'Amors (mid thirteenth century) represents the earliest surviving 'love-vision', and is related to the poems that present a *débat* on the merits as lovers of knights or clerks. Perhaps the earliest of these poems is the Latin *Altercatio Phyllidis et Florae*, which gives rise to the thirteenth century French poem *Florence et Blancheflor* or *Le Jugement d'Amours* (together with the fragmentary and closely similar *Hueline et Aiglantine*, not translated here), and also to the Anglo-Norman poems *Blancheflour et Florence* and *Melior et Ydoine.– Li Fablel dou Dieu d'Amors* is plagiarized in another French poem, the *De Venus La Deesse d'Amor* [ed. W. Foerster (Bonn, 1880)].

In the *Altercatio* Phyllis and Flora go to a meadow one fine spring morning. They sit by a stream in the shade of a pine tree, and talk of their loves. Phyllis praises the knightly life; Flora praises the life of 'clerks'. Phyllis disparages clerks' easy life; Flora contrasts the knights' hard and poor life. Phyllis praises the valorous knight riding to battle; Flora is unimpressed. They agree to appeal to Cupid. Their journey and arrival at the court of the God of Love is lengthily described. They present their case to the God, who decides in favour of the clerk.

The *Florence et Blancheflor* reproduces the plot of the *Altercatio* (which is therefore not translated here) until the ladies arrive at the palace of the God of Love, where a parliament of birds is called who debate the issue. The Anglo-Norman *Blancheflour et Florence* and *Melior et Ydoine* also contain an assembly of birds and trial by combat.

The following four poems are translated from *Les Débats du Clerc et du Chevalier*, ed. Ch. Oulmont (Paris, 1911). Cf. also the edition of the *Fablel* by I. C. Lecompte, *MP*, 8 (1910–11), 63–86.

Li Fablel dou Dieu d'Amors

Whoever wishes to Love, according to my understanding, should take much care when he begins that he knows what he is doing, and that nothing is mixed up in the affair which could be criticized. Now listen, noble knights, barons, ladies and young girls, and hear what I have to say. I am going to tell you my dream, and I don't know whether it is true or not.

One morning I was lying in my bed – I was thinking of love and had no other pleasure – when I fell asleep a little with my thoughts. I dreamed a dream which delighted my heart.

I got up one morning in May to the sweet song of the birds, the nightingale, the thrush, and the jay, and when I had risen I went into a meadow. I will tell you what the meadow was like: the grass was thick beneath the dew, and there was every plant and flower you could ask for. There ran a stream from paradise through the meadow, which was so clear and beautiful that there is no man so old in any city or castle who, if he bathed in it, would not be made young. Nor is there any lady so loose and faithless that, if she were to taste a little of it, would not be a virgin before she left the meadow. The gravel was all of precious stones of many different types – I do not know which to say are dearest.

I went through the meadow with delight beside the river, all along a bank. I looked up towards the gleaming sun, and saw a garden to which I hurried straightaway. The garden was arranged to have all the trees we hold dearest, pines, laurels, cypresses, and olive-trees. There are flowers and leaves always on the branches, and the rose-bushes are heavily laden with roses. They will never be disturbed by winter, and do not fear February anymore than May. A moat enclosed the whole garden about, the water being channelled there by artful contrivance, and the bottom was paved with marble. The wall was of carved porphyry and ivory. There was no sand or chalk, but everything of strongly-linked gold. In front of the gate the drawbridge was drawn up, all worked of pure gold, and the columns, which will last forever, were all of dark marble. If any person of low birth came there and wished to enter despite his degree, when he came to the bridge the drawbridge was drawn up and the gate shut. They did not wish that any *vilain* should enter there, and as soon as he went away the gate was opened and the bridge lowered. And if a courtly person wished to go inside into this garden to give delight to his body, he would find the gate open for him to enter, and there would be no trouble about raising the bridge.

[69] This garden is forbidden to those of low birth, for it is the garden of the King of Love, and each year, either two or three times, he dispenses justice and adapts his laws. I entered inside without any opposition. There were innumerable birds there, and each was singing of love according to his own sense of it. I entered within, without anybody gainsaying me, when I heard the song of the

85

birds, and had no care for any other song or poem in that place. There is no man under heaven, however base he might be, who would not be forced to love if he heard them sing. I sat down there to take my pleasure beneath an inestimable tree. This tree is of such a nature that three times in the year it flowers, spreads and dies. It cures the man that honours it of all ills except death, against which there is no security.

When I was seated in the garden beneath the tree, and listened to the cries of the birds, my heart was so filled with joy that it seemed to me I was in paradise. The nightingale was crying in his language: 'Fortunate is the man who receives encouragement from his beloved: in this he is like the ship which with a good wind sails exactly where it wishes.' Then, singing in his own language, he called all the birds of his own type, and they all came there promptly. When all were assembled before him, he said, 'My lords, it seems to me that love is deteriorating, and is not what it should be.' The sparrow-hawk spoke first, 'My lord, it is those unworthy, low-born people who abuse love; if they were courtly people they wouldn't do so. Sir nightingale, it would be right and proper if low-born people had no concern with love, for if they do love, to some extent it is just by chance. Nobody should become involved with love, except clerks who well know how to talk, to dally and to sport with their loves, and knights who go to joust for them.'

[117] 'Sir hawk,' then said the thrush, 'What you say doesn't seem true to me – that nobody will have delight in love unless he is a clerk or knight.' 'This,' said the jay, 'can very well be true – that if a man loves, and is well loved in return, he is worthy and wise like a learned clerk and a knight armed with love.' The nightingale listened to the barons' argument and raised his voice and spoke. All were silent: 'My lords, he who will love well will speak ill of nobody, but will be worthy, wise and courteous. If he strives in love, there is no man on earth who will not become gentle and courteous. For this reason I beg you to leave this dispute, for great evil can come of a small thing. I say to you all, great and small, return home and take your pleasure with your loves, for I think it is past midday.' With this word they all left. Each bird went to his pleasure, and I remained all alone without delight, beneath that tree where there were both leaves and fruit. I committed to memory what the birds had said whilst I slept. After I dreamed this, I dreamed another dream. Give me a drink, and I will tell it to you.

[149] I was sitting all alone beneath that tree – he who sits alone laments to himself very willingly. I was watching the whole garden, and I saw coming along a path a noble young lady. She was far away and I did not recognize her, but when she came close I knew that it was my darling. 'Ah, God!' I said, 'by St Mary, do I not see here my death and my life?' She was dressed in ermine-fur with a tunic over the top, and on her finger she had a ring of pure gold. When she recognized me she bowed her head. At this I was very happy, and not at all slow, but jumped to my feet: 'My sweet love, welcome!' She said, 'Greetings to you, sir!' I embraced her in my arms becomingly, as she did me. I drew her towards me and kissed her gently, more than a hundred times, I think. She spoke as an honourable young lady, 'Sir, there is no man, woman, or creature here: I beg you, by the glorious, heavenly God, do not do anything that could do me harm.' 'I will not, my sweet, fair love. But tell me now, how you have come here unaccompanied?' 'How I came here? . . . You wish me to tell you?' 'Tell me.' 'I came here by wishing. It is a marvellous thing, but it is certainly

true. . . . You are not angry?' 'No, indeed, you have done very well.' 'All the time I am longing for your love, and am afflicted with my thoughts and desires. Your love has driven me to death, and I do not know how I shall find peace. I am doing a very foolish thing in telling you my thoughts, yet I should do so, to you whom I have as my lover. And if I can follow what I am thinking I shall never have any other husband than you.' Then the fair one finished her complaint.

'Fair lady,' I said, 'I am held fast by your love. He who is ill can do nothing but complain, and by this means it is known indeed that he is not making a pretence. I complain to you, fair lady, of my sorrow. It makes me unwell, and my colour has changed. I think of you night and day, and this often causes me great joy and great sadness. And I am sorrowful and full of great violence when I think of you and I cannot see you; and when I can embrace and feel you, I am then indeed joyful.'

[201] When I had described my feelings to her, I saw a great flying dragon coming raging through the garden, four-footed like a wild beast. It came rushing, seized my darling from my side, and ravished her away. 'My sweet lover,' she cried out in a loud voice, 'help me, save me from death!' When I heard her begging for help and I could not aid her – for I was on foot and the dragon was flying – I was desolate. 'Ah, dragon,' I said, 'ferocious creature! why are you carrying away something I hold so dear?' I grew as rigid as a stone with grief and rage, and became greener than an ivy leaf. I could say no more, and for sorrow I fell into a faint, awakening after a long time, pale and tormented. 'Oh, earth,' I said, 'open up and swallow me! Alas, wretched me, I have no sword here to finish my life. All my blood should be shed, for this blow should have finished my love. Ah! God of Love! he is a fool who serves you. If I do not have back my life again, because I deserve it, I shall consider you a wretch forever!'

This speech was not ignored by the God of Love, whom I have served so much, for I soon saw him come on a well-harnessed horse. His horse was all covered in many different coloured flowers, and his mantle was woven up out of thread of love and the green days of May. The trimming was all made of the new time, and the collar from the high song of a bird; the tassels were made of embracing, and the clasp and buckle were made of two kisses. 'My friend,' he said, 'the God of Love comes to your aid! Tell me what is the matter? What do you lack? And why are you making such a great lament in this wood? Such sorrow as you are making will do you no good.' 'I have told you why I have such sorrow, but you, who have so many flowers, tell me what man are you?' 'I am the God of Love, and come to help your lady. It is already late. Are you worried? She will come to no harm. You will come with me through this valley – jump up behind me on my horse – through flowery fields to my main castle.'

[253] When I heard his words, I jumped up behind him, and with him I came through fields of blossom and dismounted at the stairs before the door, as did the God of Love saying, 'Friend, here is my court, my hall and my house! You will go in to rest, and I will go into the garden. If I do not rescue your lady, it is wrong. She will be rescued, for I am mighty and strong. I must not stay, for day is fading.' 'My lord, start on your way.' He strikes the horse with spurs of pure gold, and I stayed behind and looked at the palace before entering. I do not think there was, or ever will be, another like it, and if you will be quiet for me for a little while, I shall tell you how it was built.

First, I want to tell you how the entrance was devised, of the moat that surrounded it, and the wall with which it was enclosed. The bridge was made all of refrains, and all the planks of poems and songs. The pillars were of the sounds of the harp, and all the flooring was of sweet Breton lays. The moat was of complaining sighs, and there was a spring of running water of tears, wept by lovers when they remembered tender kissing. Never think that the door was made of wood: it was made of the sorrows and woes and torments suffered by lovers. And the great door, and the bar, and the lock, were of prayer and sweet asking, through which all love may be won. He who does not do this cannot love without strife. A bird was the porter of this gate, which was born without father or mother, and when it is old goes into a fire by which it renews itself and reappears. It is called the phoenix, as the text says. And this bird, as porter, signifies love in good faith, which tells its feelings to nobody but keeps its own counsel and acts rightly.

[305] I came to the door and wished to go inside. It was closed. I knocked for it to be opened, but it remained shut. Not wishing to be long, I moved the ring, which was made of thought. When the porter heard the ring, he knew very well that it was a summons. He came to the door and said welcomingly, 'Friend, do you wish to enter this castle?' 'I wish to enter if you commend it.' 'I certainly do, if you can guess what it can be that was born without a mother. If you can say this, I know that you are in love.' 'I do not ask to enter if I am failing in anything. If I do not speak, you will say that I am worthless. You are making a riddle about yourself. I know you, for you are called Phoenix. You have no father and mother, but I will not make a long discourse about your birth. Open the door, and seek no other pretext.' 'Truly, I shall seek none,' he said. 'You have said what I asked you. You are a wise man, and henceforth I will serve you. Please enter and see the palace.'

He opened the door, and I went into a palace made with great wit – if I had the intelligence of all people I could not tell how noble it seemed. But I want to give you my impressions of how it was built and furnished. All the twelve months were there – January, February, March, April, May and the others – for they were the pillars on which the palace was set, and bore it up by their strength. On the right side were the summer months adorned with flowers. Whoever saw them, if he had not already loved, would not fail to love now. On the left dwelled the months of winter, cold and gloomy, that would chill anything however hot. The twelve months were the pillars of this palace, the paved floors were of sweet loving and the benches of service. The roof was constructed of humility and sweet reason, with a covering of stolen love. I could not tell you what it was made of. What I am saying may seem incredible, yet it is perfectly possible that I saw it in my dream. I came into the hall where there was great delight. There I found a very noble company of youths, each with his love, and all playing chess and tables with each other. Whoever beat his partner had no other reward or money, except that he took a kiss. When I came in and was received, I was much loved and cherished by everybody, and all greeted and said welcome to me. For love of me they left off playing and came to disport themselves with me. We sat down by the nearest pillar to amuse ourselves. I told them all about my journey, how I lost my love through the dragon, and the help that the God of Love gave me, to whom great joy belonged. They replied, 'Never fear: you will get her back. Do not be sad. You should sing to us: it is our time, and you owe us this payment.' 'Lords,' I said, 'this is a fine payment. I shall sing but am not much in the mood – I am rather sad about my love.'

[389] All the barons said, 'He has spoken well!' Ladies and maidens and the whole house were hushed to hear my song: 'In the month of May, when the rose is in bloom, the birds sing. The time is sweet and calm. There is no youth that has so good a life if he has a loyal love! I say this for myself. I love a maiden, and indeed I never saw a fairer. I cannot forget her, and thus it is always new to me and seizes my heart beneath the breast. And indeed, for her sweetness I shall love her above everything always. Now I beg the fair creature, by her consent, that she will show some concern for me, for she is a little hard towards me, and this is very wrong. The refrain that I have made will go and tell my lady without flattery that I am her prisoner and do not know if she will love me.'

[413] With this my song was finished, and much praised by all. There was nobody there, however much he loved in secret, whose thoughts were not made to change by it. When I had recited this, I wished to leave that place. A maiden took me by the right hand: 'Sir,' she said, 'come to see us!' and we went into a room on the left. This room was that of the God of Love: there was his bed and his place of resort. There I saw two quivers, hung with flowers, and above hung the bow of love. In one of the quivers there were arrows with leaden heads – he who is wounded by them will never have love in this mortal world. In the other quiver were arrows tipped with pure gold, and these cause an inclination to love. When the God of Love goes to divert himself he wounds with these arrows whom he chooses – nobody can argue against his arrows: the one causes hate and the other causes love.

We came out of the chamber hand in hand, and calmly out of the hall. There we found, not far away at all, a grassy and extensive meadow. In the middle was a beautiful tree, and many kinds of birds were singing there. At the foot of the tree there was the tomb of a noble youth. There were birds round about, and for the soul of the lord who lay there they sang of true love. When they were hungry each would kiss a flower, and then they would have no hunger or thirst for that day. 'Gentle lady,' I said, 'now tell me who was this young lord buried here and when did he live?' 'Sir,' she said, 'he was my beloved. He was a noble man and son of the king. He loved me for my beauty, as I believe.' 'How did he die?' 'He was killed for me.' 'For you? . . . How? . . . who did this, and why?'

[457] While weeping she told me simply about her lover, whom she loved sincerely. 'Sir,' she said, 'I loved him truly. My family often said to me: "Foolish girl! Leave this love. He will not take you as wife. He came into this country to bear arms and will leave when he pleases." I loved him more, the more I was blamed for it. He sent to me secretly, that if I went with him to his country he would make me a crowned queen. I said to him: "Sir, for love of you I will do it. Let us go on the first of May." And this long wait was tedious to us. "Let us go in the morning!" he said. In the morning I went off with him into the country, and we had no concern for anybody. Passing through a meadow in a valley, we encountered a proud vassal. "Friend," he said, "give me that horse. You cannot take that maiden through here without harm. You must leave her and the horse, and unless you defend yourself at arms, I shall sever your head with my sword." "Sir," said my lover, "you may threaten too much. It is unworthy in a man to make such great threats. I shall not go out of my way for you. He who flees finds somebody to pursue him." Then he drew his sword, and put up his strong shield.

'When I saw the battle beginning for me, I armed my beloved with a single kiss, then I went to sit in the shade of a laurel tree, and let my horse wander at will. I prayed very sweetly to the God of Love, "Lord, by your commandment, if I ever did anything that pleased you, now keep my lover from pain." With this they began striking each other and hit each other with lances. They jumped up again like strong men but both were wounded. They began to strike with swords of steel, and shed some armour in order to fight. Neither could gain advantage over the other – and both died. When I saw my beloved lying on the sand, wounded and dead in such a way, more than a hundred times I kissed his face and chin. "Ah! my joy and my delight. By what folly, sweet love, are you dead? If I kill myself for you, this is wrong!" More than a hundred times I fainted over his body.

[513] 'After a long while, when I revived from my faint, I saw a noble lord approaching: the God of Love at the head of his company came riding across the sand. The God spoke first, "Fair one, if your lover has died through his boldness, you will have a hundred more among my company." "Lord," I said, "I will never have a lover, but please have these two bodies carried from here." "Very willingly, and you mount your horse, and come with me into the field of flowers." With this, I mounted, and the knights took the two bodies, and we came to stay in the flowery field. That night we watched over the bodies, and in the morning had them very richly buried, with reading and singing. There lies my one good, and here the other that I love so little. And the birds always pray in their way that God will have mercy by His most holy will. And now I have told you, sweet friend, by my faith, how he died, who did it, and why. Now let us go and enjoy ourselves in that hall where there is great happiness. I shall not have such joy there for I am sorrowful for my love.'

[541] When the young lady had told me all this, we proceeded hand in hand through the meadow. We came to the hall, but before we went in I looked across the garden, and saw a noble lord approaching, the God of Love. In front of him on his horse he was holding my love, who was unharmed. I was overjoyed when I saw their approach, for I could not think of living without her. I ran towards her, and she got down. 'My lord,' I said, 'I owe you great thanks when you have saved my love from death, and given me back my joy.' 'Friend,' he said, 'I would have been very wrong if I had not helped you, when you believe in me. You have served me and done my commands from before you were seven.' 'I certainly should, for you are mighty and I would not be unfaithful in serving you.'

When he had put down my love from his horse, I felt that I was cured from death, and never before in my life was I as happy as I was then. Because of the great happiness I had, I roused from sleep, and so I woke up when I had slept for some time. I was very sad that the dream lied to me.

Here ends a dream of the God of Love.

Li Fablel is followed closely in the *De Venus La Deesse d'Amor* (which is narrated in the third person) until the assembly of birds, when the Amant frightens away the nightingale with his own long complaint. After he has lamented, Venus approaches on a mule accompanied by three maidens 'and three thousand birds were assembled there, who all beheld the lover who was so afflicted' (st. 121), and all the birds join in begging the Goddess to help this 'true lover in great distress' (126). Venus asks the lover if he wishes to be free of love, but he passes her test by declaring that he does not. He describes his lady at length, and Venus agrees that there must be pity in such a creature. She tells Amant that he is like the gerfalcon that scorns five hundred other birds except the one he desires. Venus agrees to put the lover's case at the court of the God of Love. They set off, and the palace is now described. As before in the *Fablel*, the maiden now shows Amant the tomb of her beloved. But in addition he also witnesses the embalming and funeral of another loyal lover. After Amant's petition to the God, the nightingale draws up a charter ordering the lady to love Amant on pain of the God's displeasure. And after a restless night of anticipation Amant finds his lady compliant to the God's commands. [*De Venus* also takes over some lines from a didactic poem *Dou Vrai Chiment d'Amours*, ed. A. Långfors, *Romania*, 45 (1918–9), 205–19].

Florence et Blancheflor

Of courtesy and valour he has more than enough in his heart, who is going to present this tale that you will hear me relate here. The prologue prohibits whoever hears it from telling it to cowards. To unworthy people and to boasters one should not speak of love, but rather to clerks or to knights, who will gladly hear of it, or to a sweet young girl, for she has something to do with it.

[15] One morning in the month of May, two maidens went into a garden to amuse themselves. They were both proud at heart, beautiful, and of the same rank. They were dressed in two cloaks made on an isle by two fairies, not worked in wool and without any unworthy workmanship. The fabric was woven up out of sword-lilies, with thread of May-roses, and the borders were of love. The fastenings are very well-fashioned out of two kisses, and the tassels are very rich, and fastened with bird-song. Through the garden on the side of a slope they went along enjoying themselves. In a valley they found a stream that ran gently through the meadow, and there they looked at their faces, which often changed colour because of love. Then they sat down beneath the olive-tree which was planted beside the gravel. One of them spoke first, like a wise and worthy person, and said,

'What a good life the lover would have who kept his beloved secretly all alone without the company of other people. If they both really loved each other they would not seek for anybody else, and would be able to do what they wished.' The other replied, 'What you say is true; would that it pleased God the king that both our lovers were here! We would not be able to forbid them to kiss and embrace, but we would not allow them any sport that tends to baseness, for we must take good care that nobody can joke at our expense. When the tree has its leaves, it is loved and held dear, and when the foliage has fallen the tree has lost its beauty. And it is just so with the young girl who leaves her chastity behind: however highly born she may be, she will sink into great contempt.' The other replied, 'What you say is true: I love honour better than great possessions.'

[69] They spoke a great deal, both of wisdom and of folly, and of everything that pleased them. If the one had been sister to the other, they would not have been better matched in company and in counsel, but before the hour of prime had been rung, they fell out very violently. For little enough reason, they took leave of their senses.

One of them was called Blancheflor, who had not been in love before, and the other was called Florence, who began the argument that day. Very gently, and out of love, she asked Blancheflor, 'Now tell me, my noble young girl, you who are so pleasant and beautiful, to whom have you given your pure heart, faithful and good? You ought not to conceal from me the man you must love.'

It was not surprising that she then turned both pale and red. Yet she replied courteously about the fine, handsome lover she had – in answering she did not cease to be courteous. She said calmly to the other young woman, 'I will tell you to whom it is that I have given the flower of my heart and my love. I have given the gift of my love to a courteous clerk, handsome and good. He is very good-looking, but his goodness is worth a great deal more than his good looks. I should never be able to tell you everything of his goodness and courtesy.'

The other replied, 'I am amazed that you have taken such a course. I mourn very much for your courtesy when you are the lover of a clerk. While your lover is at church he will turn over the pages of the psalter, and he will not be doing anything else than this for you. Whereas I have a fine and noble lover: when he goes to the tournament and beats another knight he presents me with the horse. Knights are of very great worth – above all people they possess worthiness, renown and lordship. You poor thing, why are you being so silly as to love this clerk, this puny wretch, this foolish, tonsured creature, all shaved on top?'

[126] Blancheflor answered her angrily, 'It is base and unworthy of you to criticize my lover, but you are much more foolish than myself in loving the knight – and I will tell you why. Knights are very cowardly people. I shall prove it clearly before all the people in the world, that clerks should have lovers more than anybody else, for they know more about courtesy than other people, and what knights know is worth nothing compared with a clerk who takes delight in love.'

Florence, extremely annoyed that Blancheflor contradicted her, said, 'By my head, there is nothing else for it: I invite you to come in fifteen days time to the court of the God of Love – there we shall go to seek judgement.'

The other replied graciously. No more words were said, and they left the garden. Each went to her own home, and the day came that they had said. There was no argument that they should go to seek judgement. Then they rose swiftly and attired themselves sumptuously in rich and beautiful clothes such that the like were never seen. They had robes of fine roses, girdles of violets, and mantles of yellow flowers trimmed with two kisses of love, head-dresses of fleurs-de-lis, and chaplets of lily-of-the-valley and of wild rose. When they were thus adorned they mounted on two palfreys, which were whiter than snow, with very rich harnesses – the bridles put on the horses were all of solid gold. The different parts of the harnesses are also of such workmanship. And there were bells of gold and silver which by enchantment were always ringing a new sound of love. God never created such birdsong at dawn which compared with the sound of these bells. There is no man so ill that, if he heard this melody, he would not be immediately healed. The saddles are not of wood, but of ivory worked with gold, and chequered with love.

[195] When they had ridden until past noon, they saw the tower and palace not made of stone, where the God of Love holds court. It was covered with white flowers, with roses intermingled, the laths of beautiful workmanship with nails made of gilly-flowers trimmed with cinnamon. The rafters are of sycamore and the walls round about are made up of the darts of love. You should certainly know that no base or unworthy person can pass the postern-gate if he does not bear the seal of love.

The maidens arrived there and dismounted beneath the hall, under a pine in a meadow. Down from the pine tree came two birds, who approached the maidens and led them up into the palace to where the God of Love was, lying in a beautiful bed made of fresh flowers. When he saw the maidens approach, he rose swiftly from the bed and received them very courteously. He took them

93

both by the hand and seated them beside him, and then asked them, 'What necessity has brought you from so far?' Blancheflor – who was well-educated, and enflamed with love of the clerk – said to him, 'Sir, I shall tell you. One May day we went into a garden and both talked of our loves, so that it happened that I said, as I thought, that clerks know more about courtesy and are more deserving of love than any knight or other person. This lady would not agree to this, differed violently, and said that compared with knights clerks knew nothing of pleasure and delight. And thus we come to seek judgement in this.'

[246] The king replied to them briefly, 'I shall assemble all my barons, and we shall tell you the truth of the matter.' The king assembled his court and related the dispute to them, and then said to them, 'Do not hide your view: which is the better lover, a clerk or a knight?'

The sparrow-hawk spoke first, 'Sire,' he said, 'I will tell you the truth, for I know it well – I know all the laws of love. I say that knights are more courteous than clerks.' The nightingale replied, 'You are lying about that, sir hawk. A knight will never know as much about delight and courtesy as the clerk who has a lover.' The falcon rose to his feet, 'By my head,' he said, 'you are lying, sir nightingale. It cannot be that any clerk, priest, or anybody else, should know as much as a knight. I openly assert, before counts and kings, that knights are more courteous than clerks or other people.' 'You are lying all too clearly, sir falcon,' said the lark. 'I say, in the hearing of all these barons, that love would be better given to a clerk than to a knight or duke or king.' 'You are lying, by my faith, lady lark,' replied the jay, 'for above all people knights are worthy and brave.' The goldfinch jumped forward, 'Sir jay,' he said, 'you are lying about this, and you are crazy, wicked, cruel and presumptuous, to lie in the hearing of us all here. Everybody in the world knows that knights know nothing of delight or of nobility unless they have learned from a clerk.' 'By my head,' said the oriole, 'you lie, sir goldfinch. Whatever comes to pass, it will never happen that a clerk will excel a knight in pleasure and in courtesy. A clerk ought not to have a lover, instead he ought to have a great psalter where he can read and chant psalms. The clerk should pray for souls, and the knight should have ladies and maidens at his will. For knights know all the power of pleasure more than other people.' 'You are lying all too clearly, sir oriole,' said the thrush. 'Accursed be the body and face of whoever taught you to judge. It can never be that knights should know anything compared with clerks about courtesy or good. Clerks are courteous, worthy, and generous. One clerk is worth a boatload of knights, I can tell you.' The starling got up, 'Sir thrush, you are wrong about this,' he said. 'Knights are highly trained, wise and courteous, worthy and brave. Clerks know nothing worth knowing about delight compared with a knight.'

[324] Thus throughout the hall all debated the issue. Then the nightingale arose. 'My lords,' he said, 'listen to this. Love has made me counsellor and judge in the royal court. I will tell you what I think. I say there is no man in the world that compares with a clerk in solace and delight. Nature gives them and teaches them all good and all courtesy. Knights cannot compete with clerks in love, and I tell you truthfully that love would go downhill if it were not kept up by clerks. I declare this before you all, and if anybody wants to gainsay me, I will prove it in battle and fight for it, body against body.'

The parrot rose quickly, 'Listen, my lords,' he said, 'I say that the nightingale is lying. I present myself for battle, and I will pay with death or with honour.' He gave his gage, and the king took it, and the nightingale jumped forward and delivered his glove to the king to confirm the battle, and the king had them armed without further delay. Their hauberks are of hollyhocks, and their helmets of primroses, their doublets are of glass. The neck-guards on their helmets were studded with gilly-flowers, and their swords were made from juniper-flowers and from roses. When they were completely armed, the king allotted them a hall, all painted with flowers, where they were to do battle. When the knights were on the field of battle, they were equal in fierceness, and had proud hearts. The nightingale spoke first, 'Sir parrot, I defy you, and tell you most certainly that I shall give you a mortal blow if you do not defend yourself well.'

[382] Then he drew his sword, rushed at him impetuously, and gave him such a blow on the helmet that the parrot was stunned, yet he returned such a blow to the nightingale's head that the helmet was damaged, and I can tell you he would have died if love had not sustained him. But the nightingale struck the parrot in great rage, and pressed on until he had knocked him to the ground by force. The parrot did his utmost beneath him, but cannot help himself and sees he must concede defeat when he cannot fight anymore. 'Sir,' he said, 'take my sword. You have won the battle. I acknowledge and give my word that clerks are worthy and courteous, and all good abounds in them, more than in anybody else in the world.' Then the king made them get up. Florence was to be seen crying, tearing her hair and beating her breast. 'God,' she cried, 'Death! Death!' Then she fainted three times and the fourth time she died. All the birds assembled there and buried her most delightfully. They put her into a rich tomb beautifully painted with flowers, and placed a stone above inscribed with these two lines: 'Here lies Florence,/ Who was the knight's love.'

Here ends the judgement of love.

Blancheflour et Florence

Here begins the tale of Blancheflour and of Florence.

The other day, happy in my love, I went to enjoy myself into a meadow where there was a very sweet fragrance, and very fine fresh flowers of all sorts of aromatic species. There is no illness, quartan fever or palsey, that worsens in a man's heart, that would not be diminished by a drop of the dew that is found on the grass there. I went into a garden full of love and joy, as has already been related to you. There were citoles and vielles, sweetly accompanied by wind instruments which help to make love new.

There were all sorts of musical instruments there: tabors, trumpets, flutes, gitterns, and rotes were played delightfully; rebecs, horns, psalteries, harps and drums accompanied sweet motets and dances; timpani, organs, bag-pipes, flageolets and cymbals sounded notes of great sweetness. Saracen horns and high trumpets and other sweet-sounding instruments were being played in unison.

There was a murmuring fountain feeding four streams that flowed over bright gleaming gravel. You could find abundance of amber, carbuncle, and chalcedony, onyx, ruby and sardonyx; and beryl, garnet and crystal, pearl and coral, potent emerald, amethyst, and sapphire all lay there in the gravel. There were jasper and diamond, that could heal from pain, and you could find topaz, chrysolite and toadstone, with all their qualities.

[52] I saw many trees there, among them: berberis, thorn, cedar, aloes, and olive and rose, maple, plane, oaks and poplars, sycamore, hawthorn, hazel, medlar, and peach-tree, cherry-tree, pine, yew, ivy, nut and pear trees, cypress, osiers, and many others, including holly, elder, chestnut, laurel and plum-trees, which I found grouped around a fountain set about with ash, holly and fig trees.

I heard the sweet music of birds singing in these trees, and among the birds were goldfinches, buntings, sparrows, nightingales, blackbirds, shearwaters, plovers and pheasants, larks, wrens, orioles, starlings, woodcocks, eagles, thrushes, partridges, wild geese, egrets, herons, merlins, falcons, sparrow-hawks, tercels, cranes, doves, pelicans, wag-tails and quails, lap-wings, corncrakes, jays, bitterns, parrots, all of whom night and day were sounding new notes of great sweetness.

[93] And it was the season of May when plants give out sweet scents and are very fresh and green. Beside a fountain I noticed two young ladies who were refreshing themselves and lamenting their loves. They both seemed of high rank; they were daughters of the prince or the king, as appeared by their bearing and their handsome faces. The names of the two sisters were Florence and Blancheflour, and they were of a tender age. Blancheflour said she wished

she had her lover in her arms, within the leaves of the wood, to embrace and kiss and perform the sports of love. 'And what would I leave him for? There is no sword so brightly shining, nor no potion in all London, that I desire so much.'

'But let us be discreet,' Florence said pleasantly, 'so that there is no gossip about our talking of love, because there will always be people who gossip about this. For when the linden tree has its leaves and the beautiful wood is everywhere covered with flowers, then to be there is delightful. But when the branches are bare, and the leaves are withered that used to be lush and dense, then the path is tedious. And it is so with a young girl: however noble and beautiful she may be, and of honourable parentage, if she once should go astray, that which was previously so much desired will be hateful to all.'

Blancheflour agreed with this and said it was very true, for the most wise clerk said that it was better to possess little in honour than have a great house and live in shame. Then Florence asked her, 'Who is it that possesses your heart? Who is he and of what family, to whom you have given yourself utterly, all in all, at his will? For you are of such high worth that he is a lucky man that can embrace you at his will.'

[148] At this Blancheflour grew pale, then became green, then reddened and her colour changed very often. For this is a way that women have, that they often change colour when they hear their lover mentioned. For when a woman loves completely and somebody speaks of her lover, then she has to show her feelings. And Blancheflour sighs at this, and draws breath before she can express her thoughts to her sister. 'I love one man with all my heart, and am given wholly to him. He is a lord of great goodness. All my wit and being, all my love, I have given utterly to him. He is a clerk of great learning, and I should always do his will.'

Then Florence said, 'It seems to me that you have set your heart too low, as a woman who has shamed herself in loving such a silly good-for-nothing, without marriage, and in dishonour. You have misplaced your affections very badly. May Jesus curse the mistress who taught you to love a clerk with a whole heart. For when the clerk goes to church he sits in his surplice and thinks of churchy stuff. And with his hands which are so blackened and dirty he handles the graduals and tropers, and brays to God. All his honour comes from this, and he eats and drinks like a pig – so much for his life! But I have a most worthy lover: he is a knight of great honour to whom I am drawn. He is my lord and my lover, of very sweet looks and well-nurtured. I am utterly his. When he hears tell of a tournament, he heads there immediately, like somebody who is of great initiative. When he encounters a knight he soon does battle with him, and soon unhorses him completely. Then he brings me the horse. I should certainly love such a man with all my heart who is of such nobility. Then the reward is declared to be given to my lover, completely and without any pretence. If you did as I wished you would quickly change your present way of thinking, which is foolish and tainted. For clerks are rarely of good birth like other people and are marked out as recreants.'

[211] And Blancheflour grew angry, and said she thought what Florence had said was stupid, because she said she had given herself heart and body to a knight, in sickness and in health. 'For when he comes back from a tournament, well beaten-up and in weak state, all bloody, his legs and his arms wounded and weakened, and all his body injured, if you wish to soothe his pain you must

97

prepare warm muck in which your lover may be plastered. Meanwhile, I shall embrace my love and have my wish of the longed-for joys, whilst your beaten and disfigured knight lies buried in the dunghill. And for that reason I would not give a shelled egg for all their pride.'

Florence replied to this, 'You should know for sure that what you have learned from your lover, through art or divinity, will not help you at all. But now let a date be set eight days from now. We will appear before the God of Love, and from him we will discover which love is more appropriate.' Then Blancheflour agreed, and the two of them went away to a room weeping a great deal.

[247] When the time was come, they clothed themselves very richly as I remember, for they had surcoats of samite, and saddles and riding habits, and I could not describe all the gold and precious stones with which their clothes were variously worked. They had splendid crowns of diverse gleaming stones set in pure gold, so that there is no night so dark, as would not seem clear day, such great light did the gems give out. The horses that they rode upon resembled each other in their coats and their form. Then, when they were on horseback and had the reins in their hands, all who saw the maidens marvelled at their beauty. They rode directly, as if they had very often ridden by this route.

Both beheld, at the hour of prime, a fine and noble castle, secure and handsome. The walls which surrounded it seemed like ruby, battlemented with pure lilies, roofed with fleur-de-lis and draped with love. They were not afraid of arriving at a bad moment, for whoever may approach the castle will find such joy there, where the gate will never be shut. But you can be sure of one thing, that any person of unworthy birth will be intercepted at the gate, for nobody passes through the gate unless Love commands it.

When the maidens arrived there, they dismounted before the door and then entered the castle. Two knights met them and greeted them courteously, and led them into a chamber where the lord God of Love always remained both night and day. There was much singing and joy, and pure, spicy flowers. The God was lying on his bed, which was ornamented with flowers of such beautiful and varied colours that it seemed more like paradise than any earthly thing. The chamber was walled with beauty more than can be described. When the God saw the young ladies, he jumped to his feet and took them in his arms. He made them sit down on a seat, and then he began to ask them what had brought them.

[313] And Blancheflour, who was the elder, replied first, 'On a Monday, in the month of May, by a fountain in a garden, as the sun was rising in the early morning, I was amusing myself with my sister. She asked me: "Which love is more fitting and which lover more true – clerk or knight – where both are prudent and accomplished?" And I said to her that for a lady or a girl there is no love so good and beautiful as that of a clerk. I have put it to the test, for clerks are wise, noble and of great consideration. You know indeed that this is true. And Florence immediately contradicted this, and said that a clerk is worth very little compared with a courteous knight. Now we submit ourselves to your way of thinking. It is now for you to judge truly as to which love, whether of the tonsured clerk or the honoured knight, should rightly be valued more.'

Then the God of Love replied, 'You shall know that very soon now.' He had his court assemble quickly. When they were all come, dukes, counts, and valiant knights, then birds were the suitors and spoke on their behalf. When all were gathered, the god asked them which love was more to be valued – that of the courteous and knowledgeable clerk or of the brave knight. 'You should conceal nothing and, by the faith you owe me, you should tell me the truth of it, without sparing the truth at all.'

[355] The sparrow-hawk jumped to its feet, 'My lord king, know indeed that I shall tell you the whole truth of it. I have been throughout the world where love is honoured and held dear, and I never found a lover to compare with the brave and worthy knight. I have learned all the laws made about love, and I never found a clerk so learned that he was a preferable lover to a knight. I will not lie about the one or the other.'

'No,' said the lark, 'you are lying about this. For you will never see a man of sense or intelligence, knight or other worthy person, that did not learn what he knows from a clerk in the first place. If anybody contradicts that the clerk should be preferred, here I am, ready to prove it on my body in battle.'

The parrot, who was never slow to act well, rose up and knelt and said to the king, 'Fair, sweet lord, listen to me, for by my faith, the lark lies. Nothing will dissuade me from fighting the lark.' The lark gave his glove to the king in pledge of what he had undertaken. Then the two bold birds were armed. When they were finely armed in their fashion, they chose a fair field beside a slope in a valley surrounded with running water. They assembled full of ill-will, and promptly came out fighting, biting hard with their beaks, striking with their wings as if with swords, so viciously that many feathers flew in the wind over a whole acre. But the lark jumped highest, and the parrot took him in this attack and threw him down to the earth, then took him by the throat without respite – his argument had helped him very little. He bit so fiercely at his eyebrow that he nearly pierced his brain. The lark begged for mercy then. 'From now I yield myself recreant, and will say whatever will cause my life to be saved.' The parrot granted this, and there is mockery from the birds at the assembly.

[415] When Blancheflour saw that the lark was vanquished, she fainted, and then suddenly died in the sight of the king and his company. Then Florence made her departure: right is on her side, as is and will be the honour of the love of knights, who follow the high road of love. And may God give us joy!

Wanastre made this in English, and Brykhulle translated this writing into French. Honour, beauty, bounty and worthiness be to true lovers, and may he have joy who loves the best! Amen.

Melior et Ydoine

Here you will discover whether it is better to love a gentle clerk or a knight.

Whoever wishes to hear and see adventures cannot always remain at his rest and ease, but must go into strange lands to learn the ways of strange people. He who goes furthest will see most and know most adventures. I know this well because I have put it to the test. In my youth I went away into a number of lands to hear of adventures to keep in memory.

In the season of May, those long days, the birds sing and the flowers grow, and one morning I got up, mounted my horse, and went towards a city which is called Lincoln. I heard some birds singing in their language in a wood. The day was beautiful and the weather bright, and I began to think of the adventures that had happened to me and that I had seen. While I was thinking about this, I left the main road and started on a path, riding quickly through a wood.

[30] Now listen to what happened: when I came back from my thoughts, I began to look around and I did not know where I was, or in what direction I should go, but I remained in these thoughts until I came to a manor which was set among those woods. In all my life I don't think I ever saw one so beautiful, or so beautifully situated.

I got down from my horse and looked high and low, but I could not find a way in and did not know where to go. Then I heard the very delightful sound of noble ladies singing of affairs of love, of feeling and of courtesy. I tied up my horse and went nearer to the garden, and I sat under the hedge of the garden to listen to their discussion. The lady who was most honoured and praised began to speak and discuss with another lady.

'My lady,' she said, 'I will tell you something I have thought. I would be all for loving if I could find a faithful lover, but I do not know which it is better to love: gentle clerk or knight. I beg you to tell me about this.'

'My lady,' the other said, 'I will do so gladly. Worthy knights are very worthy to be loved, for they know how to speak correctly and make courteous gifts. Of clerks I don't wish to speak, for I have no desire to love them.'

[71] A lady smilingly replied, 'By the faith I owe the Almighty, I have often heard tell that clerks are worthy of love, but I don't know the truth of it, for I have never put it to the test. But now I should like to know before I leave this garden. What do you say, my young ladies, who know all the issues of love?'

A young girl then answered, called Ydoine of Clermont, 'My lady,' she said, 'I will tell you the truth, in good faith. There is no man in this life so worthy to have a lover as a knight of great price, for knights very well know how to love without dissimulation and insincerity. Clerks are too inconstant and too light-hearted. If they begin to love today, tomorrow they want to forget it. Don't talk to me about clerks! Whoever loves a clerk is mad.'

[97] A well-educated young girl, called Melior by everybody, jumped forward quickly, like a woman full of animosity, 'As God help me, dear friend, you are wrong to have spoken ill of clerks here and blamed them before my lady. According to what you say, it now seems that you despise them. This is neither sense nor courtesy, if you love chivalry. You ought not to criticize the clerks, for they are to be praised above all people. Beneath heaven there is nothing so sweet as the love of clerks – that you should know. The love of clerks is a select, superior thing. Just as the rose is nobler than any other flower, so the love of a clerk is nobler, finer, indeed, than that of any other type of person.'

Ydoine said, 'It cannot be that the love of clerk or priest could be so sweet or so agreeable as the love of a valiant knight. Knights are nobly arrayed on their heads and bodies, as is fitting for their order. Clerks are tonsured and shaved on top, sheepish and silly. If they have to talk of love they show themselves up as foolish.'

[131] Melior replied courteously, 'By the faith I owe to God Almighty, I do not wish to argue, or speak ill, or cast aspersions on knights. It is the simplicity of clerks which you call foolishness. Clerks are not gossips, nor are they base or reckless. If they are in love with some esteemed lady or girl, they are not silly or cowardly, God help me. In the chamber they are gay with the fair one, and in hall as simple as a young girl. People of such worth are truly worthy to have love.'

Ydoine replied, 'By St Denis, if I love a knight of price, he will go to the tournaments and perform acts of prowess for love and win praise and worth. And when he leaves the tournament, I assure you, he will send me a fine horse, a noble falcon, or a hawk, which he has won for love of me among knights of great price. And if you love a clerk or priest, however great a master he may be, he will never do anything else for your love than say his psalter in church before the alter and turn over the pages – that is the deed of prowess that he will do!'

[167] Then Melior answered, 'If I love a worthy clerk he will give me beautiful jewels, golden rings and buckles, rich apparel, furs, silken girdles, valuable palfreys, gems and pearls and beautiful tokens of love, and everything I wished to ask for. And he will have no bad wounds to his head or body. When I am holding my dear lover between my arms in my bed, I shall be able to finger his shoulders, his arms and his sides, and I shall find them as sound and healthy as an apple. It is better to love such a man than a cowardly knight who will be beaten each day at the tournament in hopes of winning. May such a profession be cursed! When he returns from the tourney, he will give you a palfrey or a charger that he has won, but consider what it has cost! When he goes to a tournament he needs to take money from his people to buy horses, and when they do not have any more to give, he must sell or mortgage lands, or tenements, or fine manors, to spend on this fighting. I don't esteem this sort of valour at all. When he comes back from the tournament, beaten and nastily crushed and trampled, he has to be treated by being covered with muck – he will scarcely have a very sweet mouth. Then, when he is lying in bed in your arms, he will complain all night long of his wound and his pain. God bless me, fair friend, but whatever you say about praise and renown, I would rather love the gentle clerks!'

[209] Ydoine answered clearly, 'There is no sort of person so worthy of love as the gentle knights, for if they are in love with an esteemed lady or girl they

can come often without people's gossip, for it is fitting for knights to haunt the company of noble ladies – this they can do often without people's gossip. And if a clerk openly loves a lady or a noble maiden, the whole country will speak of it, and she will be shamed forever. Thus she will lose her love and will have no further wish to love. Whoever gives her love to a clerk is mixing with great wrong. Even if I were a spiteful step-mother to a girl, I would not wish her to love a clerk.'

Melior answered, 'You are speaking slanderously when you accuse clerks of deception, for they are true and fine lovers – there are none so worthy in the world. They are not false or deceitful like proud knights who have many roles at investigations and assizes; they take money very eagerly, and often put wrong to rights. A gentle clerk would never do it for all the gold in Syria.'

Ydoine said, 'Let's stop arguing, and I should like to ask you one thing: which is whether you would be willing to submit this to judgement?'

[249] Melior replied courteously, 'Fair friend, I consent. The judgement can be without delay, for we have a wise judge who will not consider wrongly.' Ydoine said, 'You speak wisely. From the birds of this wood I shall choose one for myself, and you another, by St Richer.' Melior replied, 'Now choose yours, I beg you.' Ydoine said, 'I wish to have the thrush, which sings so clear and which is brought up in the chamber and knows about love, I assure you.' Melior said, 'You speak well. Now I will choose mine. I wish to have the nightingale, which is brought up in a lofty school, often in a curtained chamber, and of its nature knows about pure love. The turtle-dove will be our judge – this office is fitting for him, and he will give judgement for us. Friend, do you agree with this?' Ydoine said, 'I consent. The birds will come now, for they are about the garden and have heard our dispute.'

The thrush quickly spoke, 'I have indeed heard how you have been at odds. Melior, you will be proved wrong, for everybody well knows that a knight should have the prize in loving over all those living.' Then the nightingale answered, 'I declare that gentle clerks should have the prize in love, for they hate all baseness, and if anybody gainsays this, I will prove it on my body in this place without delay.'

[291] The turtle-dove came in here, 'Now listen – whoever wishes to have judgement, it is first necessary that it should be accepted by both sides and the judgement listened to. You know that this is the law, and I tell you in good faith that I will give you judgement. Young ladies, listen to me. You should certainly know, you wise young ladies, that I well know the practices and business of knights. I will not lie to please you. I say that knights are very worthy of love, but I will tell you something about them. Commonly, wherever they go, in every country, they wish to love and court various ladies. And when they are all together, these knights of great price, they begin to talk, and each likes to boast to the other about his lady love, and reveal all their personal affairs. And I will tell you something else as well: however beautiful the love that they have, they also wish to have common women as well. This is their way and their custom, and in this they act very basely. But if clerks love, then they love very purely and with a faithful and whole heart. If clerks love ladies of rank so that nobody knows by whom they are loved, then clerks will suffer death rather than reveal their love. And I will tell you something else: all our good comes from clerks – all the sense in our life, grace and courtesy, worthiness and love and intimacy: it is all written by clerks. Because of this I tell you openly that I here give you

the judgement that the clerks should have the prize in fine loving and friendship.'

[339] Ydoine jumped up quickly, 'I reject the judgement, for it will be proved by battle that you have judged falsely.' Melior replied, 'I consent. The battle will take place without delay, for I have my ally all ready, who will be the victor, if it please God.'

Melior brought the nightingale and had armed it well, clothed in a hauberk of fleur-de-lis. She gave him a most valuable shield of rose-petals and a lance of sycamore: his gonfanon was of a violet and his doublet of a sword-lily. His helmet was made of oakleaves – there was none finer in any realm. Now the nightingale is well armed, and the thrush is armed as well, with lance of rose and gonfanon, hauberk of thistle-leaf, shield of briar-leaf, doublet of leaf of wild-rose, and the device on the shield was of fern. The thrush boasted a great deal about jousting well: the bird had a helmet of another flower, and was sure he would be the victor.

Now they lead the birds into the jousting place, and at first the thrush struck the nightingale through the shield: his lance shattered except for a small bit, but he is not wounded because he is so well-armed. The nightingale hit back with his sharp lance, which went through the body of the thrush, and the bird then cried: 'Mercy, mercy! I am overcome.' The nightingale replied, 'Do you concede?' The thrush cried out aloud, 'I grant that gentle clerks should have the prize, the advantage, the lordship in love. Curses on him who gainsays it!'

[389] Ydoine sees her champion lying dead on the sand, and begins to cry in a loud voice, 'Alas, alas, I am betrayed!' and then fell down in a faint, and the lady cried out. The damsels gathered round and carried her into the hall. I do not know what happened afterwards, for I came away from there and mounted my horse, and went straight to the inn. If I had slept at such a time, I would not have seen such a happening. Better to love is the clerk than the haughty knight.

Here finishes whether it is better to love a gentle clerk or a knight.

La Messe des Oisiaus
et li Plais des Chanonesses et des Grises Nonains

Jean de Condé

The text is translated from *La Messe des Oiseaux et Le Dit des Jacobins et des Fremeneurs*, ed. J. Ribard (Geneva, 1970). For a study of the poet, cf. J. Ribard, *Un Ménestrel du XIVe siècle: Jean de Condé* (Geneva, 1969). Jean de Condé, son of the trouvère Baudouin de Condé, was a 'ménestrel attitré' to Count Guillaume I ('Le Bon') of Hainault, and lived from around 1275–80 until 1345 (Ribard edn., p. ix).

While thinking of the sweet joy with which a lover cheers himself in his hope, I went to bed one May evening, quite free from sorrow and care. I then went straight off to sleep, and I dreamed that I was in a forest, in the most lovely wooded country to be found from here to Ireland, on a fine knoll with a pine tree with great spreading branches.

The birds were not silent, but were singing throughout the forest, for they sensed the day approaching, when it began to lighten just after dawn, a little before the sun rose. Nobody ever saw so many birds in his life, and it seemed that they were trying to outdo each other. Whoever searched through all the world would never find so many all together. I certainly thought that they were assembled there by some arrangement. With their song they completely stole my heart and ravished me with joy.

And afterwards I saw a parrot approaching, who was a very fine talker and who came flying to the pine tree. As soon as he had arrived, every bird grew quiet, as quiet as if Mass were being sung. The parrot was the messenger of the goddess of love, who was to come there, and three days earlier she had sent such a message by him.

'Listen to my words,' he said, 'all birds great and small, who are come here to this place by the command of my lady, who wounds many hearts throughout the world. I entreat and inform all of you that you should make such celebration as is fitting in order to receive my lady, for she will come with a great company of people, and she will wish to lodge and stay in this country for the whole of today and tomorrow. She may well be able to stay longer, but I do not know. However, what I have told you is true.'

[51] And when the birds heard this, it seemed that they rejoiced such that this new joy was out of all comparison with their earlier happiness. Each of the birds strove with his voice so much that their joy seemed to me a hundred times greater than they had had, and they organized themselves into different groups of singers, each in his type. It would have been useless to seek for greater

happiness, for it could not be found, and it seemed more like that of life eternal than earthly joy.

The Lady Venus was not far off from there, approaching with so great a company that the number could not be told. It seemed to resemble a veritable paradise – it would be too much to try and convey the joy of those who were coming with her. But one could hear everything imaginable to make the heart rejoice by way of instruments sweet to hear, songs, motets, part-songs, and a number of other diversions. They came straight into the place where I was. A lofty throne was prepared, so rich and of such fine workmanship that it seemed more like divine handiwork, and that such work could not be had from mortal hand. No one ever saw a more splendid throne, and there the goddess Venus was seated to dispense justice. Those who were in her service came there to adore her and, as much as they were able, to do her honour.

The sun was risen on high, and the weather was bright and fine with a sweet and gentle breeze. The meadow was clothed once more anew with green grass and many different flowers, white, yellow, red, and deep blue. There were many and various trees in full leaf, and there was an abundance of blossom. Truly, the place was splendid, for there were numbers of sweet clear springs that never dried up, flowing gently over fine gravel.

[104] There was many a new complaint by those who were in love, who made complaints to the lady. But she deferred everything, and told and promised them that there would not be any complaints, nor would justice be done, until after they had dined, and so the pleas were cut short.

Venus summoned the nightingale and commanded him in a loud voice that he should sing Mass in her presence, and that the other birds who were the most attractive and gifted in singing should accompany him. The nightingale gets ready immediately, as one who made no objection to the command, and said his *Confiteor*. And after that, without more ado, the various species of larks began the *Introit* in a loud voice, and then three other birds came forward and they all sang together. To whoever heard them it certainly seemed that he had never on any occasion heard any thing which so lifted his spirits. And after that, everybody sang together in full voice the *Kyrie* with clear and lovely voices. The singing was very splendid, for everybody tried his utmost, and put everything he had into his singing. When the *Kyrie* was finished, the noble-hearted nightingale began the *Gloria in excelsis* with the words very well articulated, and the other birds with great devotion accompanied him in a loud voice.

But there was a bird amongst them who greatly displeased the nightingale and, in everybody's hearing, he ordered him to be quiet. It was the cuckoo, that bird of highly dubious parentage, who has slandered so many a man. Whether he liked it or not, the cuckoo had to leave off singing, for the other birds chased after him and threatened him fiercely, so that he fled away in terror.

[150] When the *Gloria* was recited through to the end, the wise nightingale turned towards the congregation and said the *Dominus Vobiscum*. The birds are not lazy in answering, and the response was made by more than a thousand voices, for everyone seeks to sing it. The priest said the Collect, and the thrush – who had been chosen to do it – straightway afterwards read the Epistle in the most elevated way that he could. He was greatly esteemed for it by many lovers: there was no one there who did not praise him for it.

Afterwards the various larks, for whom singing never palls, began the Alleluia, for the Gradual was not being sung at that time. They kept very strictly in time, and, as far as I could determine, more than five hundred companions sang with them. When they finished this alleluia, four birds sang another. One of the birds was the goldfinch and another was the linnet. The finch also joined in with them, and the fourth member was the wag-tail. It was a fine thing to hear such a choir for they sang with the four voices, and each was striving to surpass his fellows in singing beautifully and strongly.

Then one lark and then another began the sequence, and all the other birds joined in, singing high or low or somewhere in between. The music there was ten times greater than I can tell you. The blackbird read the Gospel, and neither in the country nor in the town have I ever heard a chant more melodious, more agreeable or graceful. The nightingale afterwards began the *Credo*, so hard was he striving to carry out everything as it should be. All the other birds sang together well and willingly, and then afterwards they sang the Offertory. Venus instructed the parrot that she wished him to preach briefly, and through him to pardon those who were faithful lovers. He replied, 'My lady, I will do your bidding.'

[203] He then began his sermon: 'Noble lovers, you who hope for joy in love know that you must strive to have in your heart four virtues of very great price, by which a lover can be instructed and come to perfection. Now please try to maintain them. The first is obedience, and the second is patience. The third can never be concealed and is called loyalty, and the fourth is hope, which maintains the lover in the perseverance to pursue his thought. I want to pursue my original purpose without digression, and I will first speak about obedience. In the service of his lady, the lover must always give himself over to following in everything what he is able to discover and observe to please his lady in word and deed. To this end he must offer up his soul and body. Afterwards he must happily suffer all the griefs, pains and evils, the woes, the vexations and labours that he feels through the force of loving. He must not complain or lament about it elsewhere than to his own lady for whom love thus directs him. And if wicked and ill-bred slanderers slander him and vent their malice, it is better for him to suffer in silence, and neither say nor do anything which might lead to some sign of temper which in turn, if it were followed up, could harm him as much as the others.

'Then he must be loyal, for this kingly quality is the distinguishing mark of love. And he who does not love loyally is wrongly called a lover. But he rightly deserves the name of lover who wishes to keep secret his liaison and honour his lady, nor for a moment wants to change his love for one more lovely or more wealthy, but wishes to spend his time in her service. Such is as a lover should be, who properly performs his duties in love.

[253] 'The lover must bide his time joyfully and strive to be in joy and, in the hope of attaining his ends, he must labour in word and deed joyfully and gaily, and maintain himself with elegance. Through this virtue of Hope, Love makes its dwelling place in the heart, and all Love's griefs are borne away and Love's sorrows are comforted. In loving there is no fault to be criticized that cannot be blamed on lack of one of these four virtues. The lover who is invested with them has certainly not missed his reward.

'Now I wish to grant pardon to you all. For those to whom joy is granted and sent by my lady, their joy my lady increases, and she diminishes by half the sorrow of those who are trying hard with a good will to be more worthy and to find the path towards joy by the sweet hope that she sends them. May those who have been faint-hearted lovers come to repent and wish to amend, and my lady will receive with alacrity all those who surrender themselves to her gladly and beg for mercy for their misdeeds, for she well knows the contents of their hearts, and according to their penitence she recompenses them richly. All you lovers who are here, sue for mercy to my lady on your knees for all the wrongs that you have done against her in thought, word, and deed, in your comings in and your goings out, in wretched covetousness and every other piece of bad behaviour. Ask for absolution for these from your heart with good intent.'

[297] All the lovers who were there knelt down and beat their breasts. There was not a sound there at that moment. And while they were like that, the cuckoo – who had fled away silenced into the forest – thought that he would revenge himself by slandering the lovers and all the birds who were gathered there in silence after the sermon. He came flying over them then beating his wings furiously. 'Cuckoo! Cuckolds!' he cried, 'You're all cuckolds! Cuckoos!' He infuriated many a lover's heart by flinging such an insult at them, and a great murmuring went up. A sparrow-hawk chased after him, but the cuckoo hid himself in the hollow of a tree, for he was shamed and humiliated if he were seen in daylight.

The nightingale, who much enjoyed his role as officiating priest, then entered on the Secret, and afterwards in a firm, clear voice began the Preface, and he sang it with so strong a voice that he lost nothing of it. Afterwards the birds who were there rejoicing sang '*Sanctus, Sanctus.*' Then the priest with great devotion made the Elevation of a red rose, that supremely delightful flower which surpasses all other flowers in beauty, fragrance, and grace, and which was so pleasing to look at that nobody allowed his attention to wander anywhere else as long as he could see it. The priest well knew how to set the flower down again gracefully, when all the lovers who were able to see it had done so. He then sang the Our Father and led the office up until when the *Agnus Dei* was sung. It was the wish of the priest that the dove should bear round the Pax, or kiss of peace, and many a lover was comforted by the green branch which he carried in his bill and from which came great sweetness.

[345] From the rose the priest took three petals with which he served himself, and yet the rose nevertheless remained one and entire. If a sick man, who had lain for a long time in a litter, had received some of the sweet fragrance that came forth from the rose, he would have been completely cured, and a deluded and misguided man brought back to the true way. The courtly priest drank the wine and water from a goblet, and did everything that he should do. Then all the birds sang the Postcommunion with great gladness and in a clear voice. The noble nightingale, very much wanting to sing well, recited the last collect, and then the blackbird promptly said *Ite Missa est.* The other birds were not slow off the mark, but responded with *Deo Gratias.* The priest gave the Benediction – it was the end of the Mass – and in a low voice he recited the Gospel, which should not be forgotten. When the glorious service – which was so graceful – was over, all those who were in love and all the birds complained to the goddess about the cuckoo.

They say they will really massacre him if they can get hold of him – they are very distressed at what he has done to them. Venus says, 'Let this rest: you cannot gain any honour from it – he is descended from bad blood, he is bad by his very nature. If he does evil, he acts according to his nature, and he usually does so. When his own mother, from whom he comes in the first place, finds the nest of another bird, she eats the eggs and lays there an egg of her own. And when the other bird finds it – as has often been tested – she sits on it in the nest and hatches it, and brings up the chick and cherishes it as if it were her own. But in this the fostering she provides rebounds bitterly upon herself, for the bird that she has raised ends up by eating his foster mother. How could he then ever do good, that wretched bird of evil lineage, when he so wickedly rewards the good deed of her who gives him life and brings him up? If you consider his deed you can learn something from it and draw a cautionary example from the evil-doers and evil talkers, the betrayers, who do nothing except seek out false tricks and japes to do you harm. May their accursed eyes burst and their tongues stick, which they know so well how to use in uttering insults and indecency, for they are full of great wickedness, which originates and wells up from their evil hearts. One must stop one's ears against them every time they are heard making some tasteless joke that one cannot completely counteract. It is as well simply to ignore them, for as one often hears said: "The more one stirs muck the more it stinks." – From this you can learn something.'

[417] And so the complaint rested there, for it was the time to have dinner. On the green grass the cloths were spread, and the company of people seated themselves, each in the place that best pleased him, if he could. There were gathered there all sorts of folk in their hundreds and thousands, both high-born and low, both clerks and laity. And the ladies and young maidens were much regarded in the company – all of them were beautiful according to the testimony of their friends. The throne of Venus was set right in the middle of those who were seated there, so that from all sides they could see her. At her will she commanded service. Each did not have what he asked, for it was fitting that what the lady wished should be served.

The first course was one of looks, and there were quite generous helpings of this course to go round, for those who could not have any of the looks stole them when they saw their time and opportunity, and that is what happened to me, for I had to steal them – all the looks that I had on that occasion – since I was forbidden to have them. The next course was of sweet smiles, fashioned and nurtured in great love, but some people failed to get any of this course and did not steal any. I missed getting any of that course and I still regret it, but to some people the lady was very prodigal with the course, for they had as much as they could ask for. I noticed there a most courtly butler who served with such courtesy that nobody was refused. He was carrying all the time a great goblet, full of a drink so sweet that one could drink of it as freely as one wished, for it was so delightful that whoever put it to his lips did not think he had had his fill. I drank enough of that potion, as the cup-bearer very often came towards me, for he liked to see me drink. And I, who did not know how to watch myself, drank so much of it that I was completely drunk; and yet I was still not free of that drink, for the more deep draughts I drank of it, the greater thirst I had. And most of the company drank just like me, and they were as drunk as I was. Those who were occupied in serving set an *entremets* in front of us. It consisted of sighs and laments. I was quite full up with this dish already, for I had as much of it as I wished to have. I let myself be taken unawares by a marvellously strong drink, and I began to crave it. It happens this way with' hard drinkers: they had to take some more of this *entremets* because of the strong drink, and the steward brought them the drink after the food. Whoever asked for drink had it immediately without any argument. Some there were who collapsed and fell asleep on the ground. Others worked themselves up so, that they seemed filled to brimming with folly, and the mad behaviour of those who were drunk was seen in that place.

[494] Afterwards a course was served, and sent round to some of the company. It was a dish of roasted railleries, served with jealousy sauce, but this was not a much esteemed dish, for it had been on the fire too long and for this reason had a nasty taste. I tasted a little but realized it would not savour very well if I had some of this dish, and that made me refuse it. But the butler was near at hand, and I then took so deep a gulp that I could not speak a word whether in Teutonic tongue or Romance, so hot and on fire did I feel then, and likewise did most of the others, for they took more than I did of this worst and most sorrowful of courses.

Of a more sweet tasting dish I saw great helpings in abundance being served. This was a dish of prayers soused in tears. It was an expensive dish, and there was not enough for all the tables. Of a very rich and costly *entremets* I watched great bowls being served and carried before the ladies to give comfort to their lovers from their anguished and tormented love. This gracious course consisted of fair answerings, of sweet grantings. Ah, Lord! how precious it was! Some ladies there were who were generous in distributing it unreservedly to their lovers.

But there were a number of them who kept the bowls in front of them quite full, so mean and ungenerous they were, for they kept back that nourishment, and did not give any of it to anybody. Before one noble maiden who had a full bowl of it I went with my hands together in supplication, to beg that she would be pleased to grant me a share of that dish with which she was so amply provided. I received some of the sweet answerings from her, and much cheered myself with that, but I did not receive any of the grantings at all. I often said to her, 'Sweetest love, how can you be so hard to me? I don't know how your heart can endure that I die from hunger in your presence. When you have the means to satisfy me so well, it's sinful! Most of the assembly are all too well served before the ladies who are here and who have granted them some of this course. But I do not know what you can be seeking to gain when you see me here suffering such hunger, and you do not wish to help me.'

[556] Then I saw the butler coming, carrying his goblet completely full, and he directly gave it me to drink, but I did not care to drink only a little of it, and completely emptied the goblet. I sprawled on the ground, neither hearing nor understanding anything more than if I had been dead. Love's drink was too much for me: I could not guard myself against it. I got myself noticed by many of those who were there, but I didn't care about that. The drunkard is not embarrassed by anything he does while drunk. My face was all on fire. The goddess was well disposed to me and esteemed him who had got me drunk, for he knew his job well.

He had given me more than a *sestier* as they measure it in Biaumont: they have sought everywhere by hill and dale all the hard drinkers, and from them they have taken their measure of what is a draught. In that realm nobody was ashamed of getting drunk, for king and duke and prince and count, great prelate, bishop and abbot, can there be made fun of, just like ordinary people. The most drunken are held most dear by the lady, and what made me drink deeply was that she took pleasure in those who made themselves drunk. And I had such a heaviness in my head that I could not hear or see anything, nor could I hold myself up.

A young servant was ordered to come over to me, called Memory. He woke me, and I jumped up, composing myself in front of her who had been so careful in keeping her dish full. I looked at her four times more gladly than before. Afterwards, the servants served a dish to appease the gourmands – it consisted of hugs and kisses, of which many a lover obtained as many as he could ask for – and there were also many who failed to get any unless they stole them. I set about very intently to see if I could steal a kiss quietly from the fair one, but I did not know how to conduct my business sufficiently stealthily and silently in order to be able to succeed. And she was so incensed with me about it that I trembled and shook all over. She wanted to go far away from me. I stole an embrace from her and begged her: 'Mercy, for God's sake, fair sweetheart, stay here, for I promise you truly, if I cannot have a kiss by your will I will not try again today, but will await your good will.'

[621] In order to stimulate the thirst, a further *entremets* was served, consisting of fair jests and beautiful games. Anywhere else such a generous cup-bearer would be considered outrageous, for he did not wish anybody to be idle or behindhand in drinking. If one barrel could be emptied, then he would immediately produce another, and do as much as he could that one should be intoxicated. He who drank less was less esteemed and honoured by the lady. I pledge to you here with both hands that I was not among those who drank less, let everybody be sure of that! By the generous steward called Desire I was served with very great alacrity. The servants then hastened to remove the covers immediately. Four minstrels played a new *estampie* before the lady on their vielles. Then joy was renewed there once again, and many minstrels practised their art with a will.

[647] When those pleasures were over, those who had business with Venus gathered before her, for they saw that it was the time and opportunity for it. A canoness rose to her feet before the goddess, surrounded by a great crowd in white surplices. Very soon the park was full of them, for they had a great company. The knights who were escorting them had soon made a path for them through the press. Many people said that their company was very noble, and everyone prepared to do them honour and bring them forward. Then they arrived before the goddess, and after that the first canoness began. She was used to speaking, and was considered very wise in the law of love, while she knew enough of its practice. She spoke thus:

'My lady, you know that I and the other ladies who are here – who have served you for many a day and wish to go on serving you without slackening – have come to complain to you about the grey nuns who wish to surpass us, and are striving as much as they can to draw our lovers away from us. They are very often out to thwart us, for they are getting their clutches on whatever comes their way; and they behave in such a fashion that when any man leaves one of them he well believes that he has part of her heart. And in this way, by their false tricks they have drawn our lovers away to themselves – those lovers who used to do service to us in order to deserve the bliss of love, and who, to that effect, used to organize diversions, Round Tables, and jousts. But now they have changed their practice, for those who ask the grey nuns for their love find very little resistance from them, so that they can make conquests of them with very little trouble. It is this that we are complaining about here. My lady, give justice to us. We ask you that they should not practise love in this way, and moreover, that they renounce what they have undertaken against us. May the rule of chastity of their order be taken up again – for they certainly need it – and may it never happen again that they attract our lovers to themselves, but may they draw back from their presumption, and leave us the right to love, in which they should not claim any share. My lady, in this we petition for judgement without delay.'

[705] The speech was well understood, and the goddess replied immediately, 'I do not by any means refuse you justice, but I tell you that I wish to hear from the nuns and, according to what I hear, I am ready to let justice be done.'

A grey nun prepares herself to reply against the complaint – she has many companions with her. She hurries before the goddess and begins in these terms: 'Oh, courteous, noble, and perfect lady, whose power never ends, in whose service, in refinement of feeling, we wish to remain until the end, for from you we await very great joy – we have heard everything that the canonesses have said here by way of opposition to us in love and in the rights belonging to it.

'We call Nature to witness that we are able to love as well as them. Do not doubt for a moment that we have ladies amongst us as young, as handsome, as delightful and as amorous at heart as they do. It is true that they are more proud of their attire than we are, but in everything concerning the heart that we are able to do to gratify you, our will is certainly not slow. They say that we are taking their lovers away from them: we wish to prove our innocence in this by the truth of reason. To tell the truth, they are losing their lovers by their pride, their haughtiness, while we are winning them by being kind and sweet. We do not ask them for love, but we know how to respond very graciously to them, and give them a hint of our wishes, so that they hold themselves rewarded and come back to us by their own free will. We please them so well, that we do not need any other control over them. If the knights are leaving the canonesses, how does that concern us? If the truth be told, their acquaintance is a pricy thing. There isn't anyone who courts them for a long time who escapes without getting his fingers burned, and they have played with false dice with some who have loved them dearly, and have eventually declared themselves weary of their lovers just when the latter thought they were going to gain mercy. The more one puts into it, the more one loses. And he gains their love who takes little trouble about it. They want to go too far when they want to forbid us to love. We cannot see the justice in it, when we have hearts and wills ready to serve love on every occasion. If we are forbidden it, it wouldn't be right.'

[771] When the canonesses heard the nuns, they were not at all pleased. They were moved with great anger and had no inclination to laugh, for they were seized with burning indignation. Enormously disdainful were they of those grey nuns who had dared to set themselves up as rivals to those who had been so long renowned for their successes. The canonesses were not slow to reply:

'My lady, you have just heard something so outrageous as to outpass description. These nuns certainly have a fury in their hearts which makes them try to rival us. Certainly, their role in this life compares very badly with ours in terms of courtliness, of attire, of elegance and wealth, of beauty, and indeed, of everything. I do not know how they can be so audacious as to dare to believe this for a single hour, and that such insolent presumption should remain in their impudent hearts. Let them take themselves off far away from us, and quit their follies. How can they be so bold as to acknowledge that they love, and claim rights in love comparable to those of ourselves, who have always kept up the usages of love? Their flesh – which has been brought up in coarse woollen habits – is not at all of such a station that it should be comparable to ours. He who did not know how to choose the better side would be greatly misled and very much at fault.

[805] 'My ladies, you impudent and foolish grey nuns, you have been guilty of a great outrage: many men have had very easy dealings with your love. They have had a very prompt response, and have not very often been made to suffer pain – very soon have they been let off their initial period of "penance" by you. You cheapen love when you bestow its blessings in this way. For the more the lover who wants to follow and hold to the path of love with his whole heart is made to burn with love and also to languish in love, so much the more does he strive to be more worthy. But you neglect this, and many desire your over-easy acquaintance who would never put themselves out or suffer pain in order to have your love, if they did not know your light hearts. Do you think in these conditions that men of honour, knights or great lords, would entertain designs on you? Because they are kept waiting very little time, you draw them to your love and far away from us. Take your converts and your monks and give them generous alms: share out your charity among them. Them we gladly relinquish to you. And leave the gentlemen in peace for us, who are gentlewomen, descended from people of quality. Direct yourselves in love towards people who are in religious orders, as you are yourselves. Knights and respectable canons leave alone for us: let abbots and cloistered monks be for you; then your coats will really be cut according to your cloth! They don't care for such folk at Andenne, Moustiers, or Niviele, and I can tell you they don't know anything about them at Mauberge or Mons! We quit-claim them all to you: love them at your will, and in return relinquish our lovers to us. For you cannot keep up such practices, which do not suit a nun who has taken her vows. Love such people – it is perfectly acceptable to us – and enjoy yourselves with them, provided that you know your proper bounds.'

[859] When the nuns hear these words, do you think they were pleased? Not a bit of it. Everybody readily knows that whoever hears himself criticized and insulted becomes annoyed about it: all this is clear enough. The nuns' spokeswoman replied, 'My lady canonesses, you have just hurled some very rude and unmannerly words against us. You haven't advanced your cause very much by that, for everybody knows that one lowers oneself by scorning and finding fault with other people. And you unjustly despise us – may my lady pardon you for it! And I can tell you we would certainly know how to give as good as we got from you, but we do not wish to quarrel or start a fight. For we dare to expect justice, and we would have you know that if it came to violence or a slanging match we should be derided by many people, and we should all be the less well thought of. That's why this present dispute should be settled by a judgement, and that it should be a most equitable one. We agree to this because we feel the justice of our case, and justice often is made apparent to all. From the heart stems all action; from the heart comes goodness and nobility, and also ill-will and weakness; from the heart is Love served without fail; no service of the body is worth anything, unless the heart is at one with it, and whoever

knows what is right, there is nothing but attraction in love. This is easy to recognize, for a man feels as great a love for a poor young girl with neither rich clothes nor wealth, as he does for a duchess. The good of Love and of Nature does not go at all according to nobility of birth, as Scripture very well bears witness. The poor man will never be loved among the rich and leisured. He who devotes his heart to the service of Love ought to be received, if he wishes ardently to obey in word and deed and with all his being. Love does not depend on wealth, or accomplishments, or pride of rank. Love brings together high and low and makes one united state out of them. The poor would be shamed, if Love acted otherwise in this and rejected the poor. We Cisterican nuns in our grey habits are not suited to your fur-lined cloaks nor to your rich adornments; there is no comparison at all. But in the heart, where the essential spirit resides which keeps the commandments of Love – there we wish to compete with you, and participate in the riches of Love, if we can win the grace of that. It seems to us that we are perfectly worthy to have a benefice in love, since nothing is found lacking in us for this office – and curse him who refuses us! We pray that my lady give a right judgement so that it is known whether we are in the right or wrong in love, and whether we have spoken justly.'

[939] There was then great dissension in that place, for everybody was very determined on his point of view. One argued with the other for the party he supported. Many an unseemly, ill-suited and ill-considered word was uttered, and there would have been a fight, but then the goddess arose and threatened them sternly; and thus they quietened down then and no longer disputed or made a din. Each one awaited the verdict. Venus commanded everyone to be silent, called the parties to her, and spoke out clearly in everybody's hearing:

'You who have asked me to give judgement, listen to my speech. I have – after God and Nature – dominion over every creature that is born, male or female, suckled at the breast or nourished in any other way. I have my dominion over everybody, in accordance with what is granted to me by Nature, who is at one with me. For she is the primary active principle on earth after God, who is above everything, the beginning and end of all. It is He who established and created Nature and accorded to her her power, and I was created by Nature, who has established my authority. When her power unites with mine and they accord well together, then without the aid of the Sovereign Creator no man can find means to protect himself against us by whatever strength or wit that he has. Nature and I cause love in all animals that have a sensible soul, in beasts, in birds, in fishes of the seas, the rushing rivers and the standing waters. Without love they cannot bear fruit, and so they love when they wish to engender their offspring. Such love has its season and its hour: it does not reside in them without interruption.

[987] 'But the love between man and woman is something else, it is the summit, the essence; nothing is comparable to this, because men and women have rational souls. Because of this, it is right and reasonable that love amongst humankind should be stronger than that in any other creature in the world. In man it is so strong and sure when it is well rooted, that it can never be ended as long as life be in the body. For in the case of man the will is doubly strong because the soul joins forces – the soul which through the five senses has experienced the strength of love like the body. Body and soul gain the man's complete assent so that – thanks to them – the heart, kindled with a perfect desire, surrenders itself to me, and I, Venus, perceiving very well its desire,

receive it to myself straightaway. All to whom Nature gives life, all human kind, Jews, Saracens, Christians, every other people in the world – I receive them all and reject none. Whoever takes up this service and comes under my dominion, religion is not regarded at all, nor great youth nor great age, nor great poverty, nor great wealth. I receive everybody, both high and low; I never put up any objection at all. And Nature works in such a way that many a time she makes as handsome a job of work of the son of a poor man as of the son of the Emperor of Rome; and a king dies as cruelly painful a death, and sometimes even more painful, than the poorest man in the world. For from the one and the same matter both the great and the humble derive their form – this is the way of Nature.

'And thus I receive equally all those who present their hearts to me and who consent to serve me, for service stems from the heart. And because of this I enkindle everybody with a flame. For he loves who wishes to love, and he can exercise his choice at will. I humble the most exalted and make them leave pride and presumption and take a lowly place, and thus the humble and lowly can have hopes. And so those who surrender themselves up to serve me and give me their hearts, them I make equal. For the great would be too cruel and unmerciful towards the lowly if my influence did not promote mercy. I soften the greatest kings, I humble the proud, make the brave tremble, and give heart to the most cowardly.

[1049] 'You who wear white surplices, your deeds, your practices, your appearance, your thoughts and wills, your hearts so willing to serve me – all these I prize highly. And I tell you certainly that I will give you a share in my good things: I will never deny them to you. You ought certainly to be first and sovereign of all orders in nobility and worthiness, and so you have been many a day. It is true that beautiful attire and elegance bring desire to many a heart and put it in the way of love: by means of such things people undertake to serve me. You have served me for a very long time and I too, as you well know, have distributed my great benefits to you. I know your worthy desire to serve. I beg you then that you go on wishing to follow this path with your whole heart. Keep up your custom in this and hold to me truly, so that I will always consider you as friends.

[1074] 'But you should know that I have no wish at all to banish the nuns from my court, or deprive them of my delights. There would be no reason for that. They serve me discreetly, with such complete willingness, with hearts so desirous of love, and with such great desire, that they please me too much. It is true that they are in more constricted circumstances than many other women, and about this they complain and lament. But when they manage to reach such of my favours as I have given them, their hearts are more given up to receiving joyfully those benefits, and they pay their dues better, than many other women do. Whoever they do wrong when they love, in truth they do no wrong at all towards me. Why should I reject them for that? It would be against Nature, when Nature urges all creatures of the world to love. It is true that in dress you are more elegant, and you are nobler and more distinguished, but in truth, those with shaven heads put in just as good a day's service as those like you with long hair. The peacock is an elegant bird and has a beautiful resplendent plumage and fine feathers, but the flesh is more valuable than the plumage. It is truly said that one can see a peasant with a daughter as beautiful in a threadbare tunic as a crowned queen adorned magnificently according to her station.

Nobody has any right by inherited rank to the goods which Nature distributes and nor to mine either. In many places it happens that the poor man is rejected, although he may be worthy of love and intelligent, while the rich man – base at heart, contemptible and stupid – is accepted. Because of the lust for riches, true gentility often loses out and love is overlooked, because the poor man is left to one side and the rich lover is taken. Such love – where there is no love save love of having – should be called by its proper name of covetousness. It's open for all to see in many places: I call the truth to witness. If you are listening to what I am saying to you, you can see that the Grey Nuns are able to love. I do not wish to reproach them at all for what they have been reproached about. I want them to keep to their manner of life, and always maintain the customs that they have begun.

[1142] 'Just now you quarrelled, and from this undoubtedly evil can spring. Now I wish that the disputes should stop and that the truth be understood. If the sufficient amount of merchandise for a day's sales is brought to market, it is all sold: whoever likes the goods has them, if he can agree with the vendor. You have often heard it said that our bread cannot remain without a taker: one wants white, another wants black. And every type of drink is drunk: whoever wants to drink wine and doesn't have the money for it – and that may grieve him – will have to drink beer if he can get it, or even water. Everybody does not have his choice in what he wants and desires and must do without as best he can and take what he can have. And one often sees it happen this way with women, for whoever could arrive at the point where he wanted to be would choose the loveliest and best, and go where he thought to find the best. Some rely on me to the extent that henceforward they will not change any further their initial choice, nor care about their advantage, but will remain true to their first affection and never give a further thought elsewhere. There are some who have gone to seek adventure through many lands; they have seen hundreds and thousands more beautiful women than they know how to tell you about, but yet love cannot take over their hearts. In the end, one is found, whatever she be, fair or dark, and he will have seen many more beautiful than she; with her his heart and eyes are taken, so that he will never have rest again, and thus he comes to his destination.

[1185] 'You who wear the white surplices, refrain from quarrelling any more with the grey nuns. If they have served with good hearts, they have not at all deserved that I should banish them from my court, although you began to love previously. But maintain yourselves according to the customs which are and have been current, and keep good hold on your lovers. Be sweet and affection-ate, and always constant in your thoughts. It pleases me very much that men great and less should entertain and honour you. If somebody prefers to love a grey nun, do not sorrow over it, for one cannot give rules and regulations to one's desire: that would be very difficult to do. It's well known you are of greater rank and more noble, but this is of no consequence. Complaints and recriminations are of no use at all. The only thing that has any force in love is that which gives pleasure – the pleasure principle. When hope coincides, it is folly to resist. So I beg you to quiet yourselves and make your peace with the nuns; and if any insulting words have been uttered on either side, then let it be called quits. Thus I give my judgement.' Nobody contradicted it. Both sides accepted the judgement, and thus the hearing of pleas is brought to an end.

[1219] You have heard some light and delightful remarks, and some things well wrapped up and disguised. Much good can be learned from them if one can extract the moral, for the greater part have a spiritual application, though they seem frivolous. I will explain part of them to you before leaving, for it would be too much to gloss everything. Whoever wishes to provide explanations after me will be able to understand many things for himself.

And so, in order to fulfil my promise to you, I will begin at the Mass sung so clearly by the nightingale, who had such delight in his song that he forgot all other cares. Take note of this thing, because it is symbolic of the priest, who must be wise and devout, and, when he is about the service of God, must so attend to the office that he should not think of anything else. If the priest well considers what he has to perform – how by word the bread becomes flesh, and then the wine becomes blood – he should be of pious conduct, pure in heart and conscience. In some, wisdom is lacking, for whoever holds with bad habits cannot be taken to be wise: he who knows what is good and does not do it, does much greater wrong than a fool.

[1253] Now the birds who were making merry there and singing with the nightingale, they are the clerics who should help in the service of God at church. To be worthy of that service most high, they should lead the most holy of lives, and wholly give themselves over to preserving purity of mind and body: they are often urged to do this. Now attend to their case, as to whether each one does as he should. Not so. A certain number of them go off the tracks, as some people well know. I wish to refrain from discussing it, for everybody will have to carry his burden according to what he does. According to the works and deeds that each man does in life, according to these will God judge him.

As for the cuckoo that was chased away – this you know is symbolic of those who sin in so many ways against Holy Church that they are condemned. This is symbolic of the slanderers and backbiters, who are always to be seen constantly seeking after evil in word and deed. Thus a double moral can be drawn here.

Whoever attends to the four virtues in the sermon and well considers them, can draw a very good and succinct moral. Obedience teaches us to obey without swerving those commandments of the law which Holy Church instils. Patience consents to suffer the afflictions, the trials, the evils and the tribulations of this world and its cruelties. Fidelity next teaches us that we should do justice to everyone, just as in the holy Gospel we find the Evangelist says: 'We must love our neighbour as ourself.' For God commanded it when a Jew asked him what were the greatest commandments of the law. Next, he who is a lover of God must have Hope in that joy beyond, where God will receive His lovers in joy. He must hope for that both day and night, and accordingly persevere in keeping up good works. He who can maintain these virtues in himself will necessarily possess all the others. This would be easy enough to prove, but I want to keep my tale short, and so I will speak of another thing.

[1316] By the sacrament of the rose, one can easily understand what the words would signify: the bread consecrated on the altar undergoes such a miracle through God that it is utterly His Body, whoever bears witness to this true account. I have expounded the dogma of transubstantiation by means of the image of the rose, which is more prized than any other flower for its loveliness, its fragrance, its gracefulness and its colour. But really, the rose is not at all comparable, for the sacrament surpasses any earthly thing more than a hundred fold, for it is the heavenly handiwork of the most high Godhead and of the Holy Trinity, and is the Body of God indeed. It is only modestly fitting for me that I shouldn't put more into my poem than suits me, or falls within my competence. I am not of such dignity that I should talk of such great theological matters: what I say at this time is enough for you. By the sacrament the sick are made whole, and souls that have strayed are brought back to the right path. When the sinner returns to good, recognizes his sin, and (having undertaken his penance) receives the holy sacrament in great faith and repentance, then he is cured of his spiritual sickness.

[1350] The great joy and the melody of the happy birds' songs signify to us the sweet songs of gracious Holy Church, of God and of the glorious saints, and of Mary, Queen of Heaven. None is so wretched, nor so preoccupied with grief, if he determines to attend to this song, that his pain will not be stopped and his sadness abandoned.

I do not want to talk to you any more of the Mass and the sacrament, nor do I wish to interpret the whole feast in theological terms: there would be too much to say. But just as Venus was intent to have drink passed around in order to intoxicate the lovers, and as she praised those whom she saw grow more drunken, just so are those of greater price to God who are most inflamed with His grace, and who have the most intense longing to serve Him to the end. Such grace comes from the Holy Spirit. But now, as for the looks and laughter, the complaints and sighs, and all the other courses described above, let them be interpreted by others.

If one comes back to the words of the White Surplices to the Grey Habits, and the judgement of Venus, then that judgement must be taken as founded on the laws of Love and of Nature. According to Holy Scripture, God plainly shows us such a thing. By way of evidence, the Gospel records in one passage a dispute between the disciples in the presence of their Lord Jesus Christ as to which among them should be considered the greatest. St Luke describes it. Jesus said to them: 'Whoever wishes to be the highest and the greatest shall be he who serves all the others, and who by his humility deserves that he be considered the greatest.' Nobody is reckoned great by God, be he of high or humble birth, unless he is reckoned by the good he has done. The soul of a duke or a count no more wins His esteem than that of a poor man who begs for his bread, unless that esteem is gained by good deeds, just as you have heard from Nature and Love, because of the recriminations of the quarrelling ladies who have issued complaints against each other.

[1409] Whoever disposes himself to serve God, whenever it be, whether early or late, God receives him among those who love Him, and he is numbered among those who work in the Vineyard, where the same payment is received by those who started work last as by those who started work first. The Gospel relates how those who began work at the hour of compline (when the work was almost all finished) partook in the payment, and even though the work was nearly completed they received the same payment as those who had begun work in the morning. He who gives himself to God and wishes to serve Him in his heart in order to deserve His great glory – if he dies in this thought his soul will be saved from Hell, and we ought to believe truly that he will gain that high payment which is the glory of Paradise. And we should remember that in this God bestows on us a grace surpassing all others, for whoever dies sincerely repenting of the evil he has done in his life receives an absolute pardon from God, and God without delay opens to him the path that leads straight to

Paradise, provided he has performed his penance. And thus are His labourers paid by the Lord, who loves us with a true love and is full of mercy.

[1448] Now the Judgement of Venus made above accords very well with the Gospel, for just as at every hour labourers come to the Lord's vineyard, just so Love maintains young and old, high and low: none are excluded. And do you know how those who have submitted their hearts to love are paid? They are paid with pleasure. For he who loves, and who declares himself a courtly lover, is so much pleased by the object of his love that nothing else pleases him. Such are the customary wages of love, with which each is paid. Thus the complaint of the canonesses, and the wicked words, and the judgement, can be applied symbolically to those who tend the vineyard. Those who have started to labour on the land in the morning and kept it up until nightfall will complain greatly. Because they have worked more – and since daybreak – they will say that they ought to have more wages than the others. The Lord says: 'I am doing you no wrong: when you came to work I took you on by an agreement, for a fixed sum of money. If I later take on other people, and if it is my wish to be as good to them, then you can't ask for anything more, because I paid you well in the first place.'

[1485] Those of you who heard the judgement can understand the connection: how Venus receives everyone in whom she recognizes the desire, and how arbitration was achieved in the case. Whoever calls the words to mind can hear many things in them to make the heart light, for if you reflect on them there is much food for thought there. For this reason Jean de Condé has fashioned his poem in such a way that it can please both the wise and the foolish: the wise can draw the moral and the fools can be entertained. For sometimes grace must be hidden from possession by all, and there is nobody, however knowing, who must not sometimes find a way to win the approval of fools. This is not to say he should consent to follow the path of their ways, but whoever knows how to adapt so that he can enjoy himself and linger among fools, he must also be well placed to mix and get on with those who are endowed with good sense. In this *dit* that I have rehearsed to you, very great good can be learned by fools, for – as one finds it written – he who always holds with foolishness is committed to a bad road. It is because of this that the sinner must acknowledge his Saviour, for if during life or at death he does not repent of his sins nor wish to renounce evil, then he is damned, as we must believe.

[1527] You canonesses and nuns who quarrelled just now, you take delight in folly and fill your hearts with many vain things. Too much has Venus deceived you when you fell into her snares, for Love – of which Venus is the mistress – is utterly contrary to your souls and mixed up with damnation, even if Nature may draw you on. Nobody who ought to be serving God should be serving Love or doing it homage, for it seeks only damage and eternal damnation for the soul. There is a reasoned love which can be upheld by all who wish to marry – to them this is available. It was given to Adam and Eve by God when He created them. The marriage bond is confirmed by Holy Church and is so tied that it cannot be untied until death shall untie it. He who wishes to love in any other way acts wickedly and madly against God. Above all, people in Holy Church – if they do not wish to change their estate – must not enter into the peril of love: they must devote their whole hearts to God. To canonesses, to canons, to priests, to monks, to nuns, to all people of religion, I say – and I don't know if it will annoy them – that they should have no sort of reputation, if it is not for the true love, that of God which lasts forever, and wherein is no sin or uncleanness. And every other worldly love should be banished far from their hearts, for love of the world is never anything more than a dream: it lasts as little time as a passing puff of wind. But as Holy Scripture reminds us, the love of God has no end: it is so pure and refined that it can never be ended. Now let us pray to God with a pure heart that He enflame our hearts perfectly with the true and eternal love. Here my tale comes to an end.

Le Songe Saint Valentin
Oton de Grandson

Le Songe is translated here from the text in *Oton de Grandson, sa vie et ses poésies*, ed. A. Piaget (Lausanne, 1941), which also contains a full account of the life of the Savoyard knight whom Chaucer describes as 'flour of hem that make in Fraunce' when concluding his own *Complaint of Venus*, freely translated from three of Grandson's balades. The initial letters of the six opening lines of *Le Songe* form an acrostic on the name ISABEL, but her identity is uncertain. For Grandson's great contemporary reputation as a brave and loyal knight and a servant of love, cf. H. Braddy, *Chaucer and the French Poet Graunson* (Baton Rouge, 1947), ch. 1. Froissart speaks well of him as a diplomat and a brave knight. Grandson (born *c*.1340) visited the principal courts of Europe, and enjoyed an international fame beyond France and Savoy. He was captured when with the Earl of Pembroke's expedition in 1372 and held prisoner in Spain. Accused of involvement in the murder of the Count of Savoy, he died in a duel fought to establish his innocence in 1397.

On the influence of Chaucer on some of Grandson's other works, and on the *Songe Vert*, cf. J. I. Wimsatt, *Chaucer and the French Love Poets* (Chapel Hill, 1968), ch. 8.

*I*t is very delightful to *think*,
*S*hould it be only in order to while
*A*way sometime an hour in the day,
*B*ecause thought greatly rests the body,
*E*ases it greatly with real repose,
*L*ulls and soothes the heart with musing.

A man may think both day and night, and it may give him pleasure or pain. It cannot be known whether he is thinking wisdom or folly until he lays it bare himself by word or deed. It is a great comfort to the heart that when a man is heavyhearted or weary, and wishes to take his rest, he may think on such thoughts and plans that he will fall asleep with those thoughts. And while sleeping he will dream something wonderful or trying for him, just as I did on the morning of St Valentine's Day.

I had not been able to sleep that night for my heart had troubled me with various thoughts which were not all passed away. It so happened that I fell asleep on a bed where I was. And it seemed to me as I slept that I had left a ruby ring and a diamond ring in an orchard the day before, and had to go to look for them on this morning.

But when I came near to the orchard where I thought to find my rings, I saw within a number of birds of all lands: black and white, wild and tame, young one-year-old birds of prey, birds in moult, falcons who have scarcely left the nest, birds that live among the branches, birds of the forest, of the fields, of the river-banks, birds who live near to houses or in dove-cots. Large and small, all were there. And sea-birds of various types had come there. There they were separating off into pairs. Each bird chose a mate in that place where they could see each other clearly; the male and female birds embraced with their wings and preened themselves. The gentle male birds kept the sweet female birds company, one beside the other, and they spread their wings out in the sunshine. Those who could sing wanted to practise their skills. The nightingale and the thrush kept quiet with great difficulty and made themselves heard above all others. The turtle-doves kissed each other. Each one of them did in his own way what seemed good to him. And they very well knew how to take their pleasure, whether it was in looks or in kissing, or in all that one knew would please the other. To them it seemed appropriate that each one was content, for they had sufficiency and great abundance of all these good things.

Amongst them all an eagle was president, dispensing justice and right to everybody, according to the day and the season. The eagle had her mate beside her. This pairing off there was very fine, for all were in two's. I was highly pleased with the sight of them and their delight which I could see, and from this great pleasure it seemed to me in my heart that I understood their language, which comforted me very much. And my joy was such that I forgot my rings in order to listen to the birds and hear what they were saying.

I understood that it was their custom every year at this time that each of them should choose as a mate the one that he liked best of his own rank. And then they live together, equal in heart and love, until the end of the year. And when the season is over, whoever wishes may change his mate and choose another. But certainly, whether it be any type of falcon, gerfalcon, sparrow-hawk or kite, they who first break the friendship do something false. I am telling the truth about this, but now I want to get back to my dream.

As I slept, it seemed to me that I saw among the others a bird sitting in a pine-tree which seemed to be a peregrine falcon: in its wings, its head, its body, in its feet, its beak and plumage, in its eyes, and in its length, fullness and size, it very much resembled the falcon. I noticed particularly that the bird kept watch all on its own, without any string tying him and without chaplet. But he had around his feet fine bells and beautiful jesses. The eagle noticed him, for she was very observant, and made him come before her in order to keep up the tradition. And she said to him without more delay, 'Why do you come in this way to look on at our doings and our council, if you do not wish to choose a mate as the others do who are assembled here round about?'

'My lady eagle,' he said, 'have mercy, for the love of God. Be assured indeed that I have chosen so well, so beautifully, so perfectly, that I have no wish to choose another and I cannot have her whom I have chosen. My position is humble, although I am one of the gentle birds, and I am not so strange that I would wish to change. To me change is neither handsome nor noble. I was before set apart from people and, if I can, I will be still. I am sad that my affairs have miscarried, but my desire was unfortunate. If you want to know about my life, then you should certainly know that I have been, for more than a winter and a summer, in the keeping of a gentleman. – There is no necessity for me to give his name, but he trained me well and keeps many very fine birds: terclets and every sort of falcon, trained to fly and to hunt and to respond to instruction. They all fly very high and well when they wish to and the weather is good.

'There is one amongst these falcons which is not at all like the rest, but is as different as the sun is different from the moon. This bird has the luck to be loved and held dear above all others. She is so beautiful and flies so well that everybody wishes her well. She is confident in all her deeds and flies the highest. Yet notwithstanding the great height she reaches, she would never make a wrong move, so much does she know about the art of beating wings. She achieves more than two dozen other birds would do, whether in hunting the heron or other river birds. She always puts her whole heart into what she does. But she has no interest in killing – instead she holds everything in subjection. For it is her noble nature always to fly highest. There would never be a day so hot that she would want to go diving, so noble is her nature. There is no need to talk of her excellence in flying – there is no bird that can last better than her, as long as the world endures. There is no need to urge her on with cries for she is always right up towards the high clouds. No bird – mallard or kestrel – escapes from her, whether by strength of wing, or by flying into the wind, for she intercepts them from above or below. And she is then so courteous to them that she does not wish to do them any harm, but takes them alive. She flies well in the evening and better in the morning, and does very well in summer, and even better in winter. Change of weather does not affect her. She surpasses all others, and is not slow in doing good, for she is so noble and virtuous, that good, beautiful, gracious bird. It certainly shows that she is of good birth, for nobody is more good-natured, more gentle, or better-mannered. And she has the most beautiful plumage that any bird could have. It is a delight merely to look at it, whether at home or in the fields. There is no bird more knowing and more graceful. I never saw so sweet a look in any bird, as God preserve me, nor one who was so elegant and neat everywhere it went. And if anybody wished to train or feed her, she knew what was due to her better than her master.

'I would never have finished telling you of her excellence and beauty if I had two whole years, but I will gladly tell you how I have used my time. You will please excuse me for not seeking a mate here. I ask another thing of you. You should know indeed that this bird that people consider so beautiful, so good and so gentle, is the one I have chosen above all, although she does not know it. For I would commit a great crime, great folly, great outrage against a bird of her rank, if I asked for her for my mate. I am not of the sort that should do it. Yet nurture cannot appease my nature, nor restrain the great desire I have that she would choose me – and on the other hand, I have great fear that she would not be my mate if she were able to notice me.

'By doing my duty and avoiding all dangers in the hope of finding comfort, I have taken heart a little, and my heart stays by her and never leaves her day or night, and I would not wish to choose any other place for it. I shall never choose another. For her I will give up my liberty and all the delights of the forest. I will put myself in service, whether perched on the fist or immewed, without ever being released. It does not matter to me what means I use, provided that I often see her. For I do not have a feather ruffled when I am in her company. I am in perfect delight while looking at her face. Nothing could pain me in watching her. I am so happy when this happens that I no longer remember my woe.

'And if I could have known how I have suffered, and do suffer night and day since I left her, be assured that I would not have left her for anything. I had never in my life before felt what sorrow it is to go away from someone one loves with one's whole heart. I have now so experienced it that I have had many an evil day. And I know indeed that love from afar is certain to yield sorrow. It is death to fall in love when you would stay away for a long time without coming back to the one you love. You must often think yourself wretched if you do not have a heart of iron or steel. For it is one of the torments of hell, without rest and without end. I know it truly from the personal experience of my feelings. In brief, and to tell the truth, it is certainly the worst of all evils. And for that reason I shall return as shortly as I can. Now I have told you all about myself, and I do not wish to be among you anymore.'

Then he cried in a loud voice, 'I commend you to God, and now I am going away.' He took wing and flew away. And the eagle, who spoke first, said when she had heard him that he had given a very good account of his situation, and that the bird who was leaving them behaved very loyally. They spoke no more of this case, but all of a sudden took wing. It seemed to me that each one joined his mate as they flew through the country.

And when they left I – somewhat disturbed and having slept part of the day – woke up and turned on my bed, lying there with very little pleasure. For the birds that I dreamed of, who have both sorrow and joy in love, made me understand as I dreamed that people do very little wrong if they wish to love. They are wrongly blamed for it, and rightly, they would not be blamed at all. The birds chose according to their desire, and people choose to love where their pleasure directs them. There is often disagreement, for what pleases one does not please another. Each one seeks what he thinks is good. But when there is agreement nobody lives so happily as do these lovers, so delightful are their joys.

Love makes people join together in pairs, and nothing is to be compared with it. Love is a natural thing, but it is not so faithfully and lawfully served among birds and beasts, who have no sense in their heads, have no fear or shame, and take no account of resistance, but live without understanding. The love of humans is otherwise. Human beings have the clear and faithful sense to know the good from the bad, and they know the good way to keep that good which God gives them. And if they must suffer sorrow, they also know how to hide it and bear it with humility. It is a great pity when people have sorrows. I wish so many good things to those people who spend their time in loving, and a tear often comes to my eye for their grief and sorrow. Indeed, when the memory of their pain runs through me, my heart almost breaks with the woes they must suffer.

As I was thinking all this, then it seemed to me that, out of pity for them, I felt part of the sorrow and woe that these lovers have, when they love from the bottom of their heart and are far away on journeys or in the wars, and have great fear in their hearts because of anxiety over staying away so long, or because of anything that distresses them. Whether the times allow them to return, Fortune is against them when they wish to draw near that place where their heart draws them. Fear slays them that they do not know what will become of them when they come back, any more than did the bird that was so constant and faithful. Such people have very little comfort if hope does not sustain them.

I am not now concerned any more with the birds, but the sorrows of human lovers upset me, although I am not one of those who have a lover. I am not a lover and never was, and I don't wish to meddle with other people's profession. For I would be thought very foolish if I bore such an office, where I do not know how to sing or read except by hearsay. But notwithstanding my own great simplicity, so much is wounded by love that I have pity on all lovers, be they English or German, from France or from Savoy, and I pray to God that he guide and comfort them in their need, especially those who are far away from where their heart is set, for this makes many people sad and pensive.

And I beg the God of Love that he be pleased to know of their complaints and hear their tears and laments, and the looks with which they are filled. And may the ladies' hearts be made to remember their lovers, and good news be sent between them, and may they return quickly and everything turn out well for them. And when the lovers have come back, may they be considered so faithful that no slanderers or envious people may trouble them, but rather may they have in abundance the gracious reward of love, to have perfect delight, everyday more and more in honour and the favour of ladies, and to the pleasure of all ladies who are inclined to love. And let them never be blamed for this. And may all those who call themselves lovers have joy of those they love, according to the state of their service, preserving all rights and freedom, and all the points of loyalty promised before. May it never please the God of Love that a loyal heart should lose its place through any new interloper – that would be most unfitting.

I cannot help lovers anymore, except only by wishing, as I would do for myself if I were in the snares of love where many people have been caught, who have there learned how to love with a pure heart. Here is the end of my dream.

III

*Sources and Analogues of
'The House of Fame'*

Le Dit de la Panthère d'Amours

Nicole de Margival

Nothing is known of Nicole de Margival, apart from his authorship of a short poem on the vices and virtues and of *La Panthère* (probably *c.*1300), in which the lady is represented by the panther, with the qualities attributed to that creature by the bestiaries. The account of the house of Fortune offers an analogue for Chaucer's *House of Fame*. These selections are translated from the edition by H. A. Todd, SATF (Paris, 1883).

To his beautiful, good and wise lady, noble in heart and in lineage, he who dares not write her sweet name – in order to give no opportunities to gossips – instead of salutation sends her his heart and all his thoughts, together with this work that he has put into rhyme especially for her. But although he has done it principally for her, still he does not dare send it directly to her, for he does not wish to start envious people off thinking evil thoughts, but rather wishes to guard against them, if he can. And indeed, he does not know if she would receive it. So I am sending it around to a number of places, to her friends of both sexes, and more generally to all those who love well and faithfully. For somebody may show it to her for whom it was begun and brought to an end, and when she sees or hears it she will clearly be able to recognize that it has been composed for love of her, because, from the subject that is treated in it, she will clearly be able to see that it is written precisely for her. Nobody else will know it, or have the power to notice it. I beg her that she receive favourably what I have undertaken to do for her. And now the subject matter begins, and begins in this way:

I have heard since childhood that dreams are sometimes a very good indication of truth, and for this reason I have put into words a dream that I dreamed not long ago.

[47] One night at harvest time, I was in bed at Soissons and extremely pensive – it was the eve of the Assumption of Our Lady – and, by my soul, I was thinking that I was far from my own country and could not return there soon. That night it seemed to me that I was carried away by birds and borne into a forest which was then – and still is if it is like I thought it was when I was dreaming – full of very various animals of different colours, green, yellow, various blues, golden-yellow, fawn and violet, white and black, red, brown, and all sorts of others. Many fierce beasts were there, lions, leopards and other animals storming through the wood, and the thickets echoed with wild boars. There were bears, and unicorns and other horned beasts, stags, and various

deer, and wild goats grazing the undergrowth. And there were rabbits and hares, wolves and foxes, and hedgehogs with their sharp coats, together with other animals that I cannot put a name to, or cannot remember because I saw so many. While I was involved with all this, I looked a little towards my right, and there I saw an animal appear at the entrance of a valley which was closed off with nettles, brambles and big thorns, because of which all the animals around were very frightened to go into that valley.

[91] Whoever wanted to describe the form of that beast would need to take great care, yet would still fall short of describing its beauty, so much there was to say about it. I marvelled at one thing very much when I looked at this animal, for she was unlike any other creature in colour. She received a great deal from them, without doing them any harm. I looked hard through the wood, but I saw no animal welcoming her, yet they did not seem to hate her, for they drew as near to her as they could, turning their steps towards her and approaching her very gladly for the love of her sweet breath, which was extremely pure and good. For the breath that issued from her cured them from all ills, and for this reason they all followed her in a body, all except for the dragon, because he would die as soon as he felt the breath which brought the others to health. For he was so full of such poison that he could not feel anything in the world, and so when he knew the panther was coming he went away at a great pace into deserted places. All the animals were better for the sweetness they found in her breath: each was improved by it and should speak well of it. Such a creature should be blessed, through whom each creature that sees her wishes to do well. And when the panther had done its work, it went to its own place without doing anything against the animals. And when they saw this they immediately left that place and went elsewhere, just as fortune scattered them.

[145] When the creatures had left the place and gone elsewhere, I then remained all on my own, and was deep in melancholy thoughts as to how I could find somebody who would interpret the meaning of what I had seen. I had hardly waited a moment when I heard within the wood something which made me very happy, for I heard such great melody that the like was never heard. I heard new notes being played on citoles and vielles; I heard dances and airs from Poitou, and Saracen horns. There were all sorts of drums, and trumpets, bagpipes, psalteries and pipes, and their playing delighted me very much. There were all sorts of instruments, and those who brought them were singing in full voice. Those who were skilled in it sang songs very delightfully and with great joy sang motets and *conduis*, not as if it were any effort, but as if they had left behind every care and every thing that could do them harm. It is a very good master who knows how to instruct his people to conduct such a joyous festivity as this.

Afterwards, when I had heard all the joy, which I listened to very willingly and should certainly pursue, I was then taken with a great desire to see those who so well knew how to keep up such happiness. I lay down a little while on the grass to listen for the direction from which I heard voices, in order to go straight there.

[189] I went quickly, without delay, towards the wood, and saw approaching the company I had so much wanted to see, proceeding with great delight. All who arrived there were very fine, both great and small. When I saw them, I had such great joy that I could scarcely express it. I went up to a young person amongst them, for I had great desire to know if I could obtain from one of them

the true interpretation [of what I had seen. . . .]. And I heard a soft voice and prized it highly. It seemed to me that it said that they were of great rank, for each one was clothed with samite, or with cloth of Tartary, or with gold cloth of great value, and trimmed with fine fur. They all went along two by two in a dance. Some danced, some jousted, and others went along singing. I certainly saw that a more beautiful company was never heard, nor one more festive.

Amongst the others I saw approaching a man who well knew how to bear himself like a noble man, and from here to Constantinople there was none more handsome than him, I think. And because of this I delighted to take in his fine figure. There was nothing about him that was not perfect: he was big, straight and tall to perfection, with blond, curly hair, and a fair, gentle face. He had a gracious expression and a clear, rosy complexion. As I looked at him, I marvelled at where such a creature came from. In his hand he held a sceptre, which was very beautiful and fine, and on his head he had a crown of gold and precious stones, very delightful to look upon. His comely hair shone like gold, and he had a robe of flowered silk, not at all rough or sharp, but as good as could be made; pearls of the Orient were worked on it in the form of animals and birds. Very handsome was the young lord and his cloak was very splendid, nobly embroidered all around with gold thread and beautifully set with sapphires and many fine stones, and emeralds green as ivy. With all his splendid, embroidered clothes he was mounted on a charger, of which the bit and the stirrups were all of heavy gold. The saddle-bow of the saddle in which he was seated was of such lovely ivory that you would scarcely believe it. Bridle and harness, what shall I say of them? All were of silk. The panniers were of samite, such as suited the saddle, and nowhere could one find a finer horse. To lead him, so that no one could do him any harm, there were three knights around him, one at right and left, and the other by his foot leading the lord by the reins. The birds too sang sweetly and loudly as if God Himself were there.

[287] Afterwards, in the fair company of ladies and maidens, knights and squires, and clerks, there were the delights and sports of the season, for it is right that people of all conditions who are in good company should lead a good life and aim to pursue all that is loyal, for there was no ill-will in them. After I had seen how they conducted themselves, because I wished to talk to them, I put myself in their way so that they saw me clearly. Then I first greeted him who was their lord . . . and he immediately returned my greeting and said to me: 'God save you, friend! Who are you? and who has brought you here?' And I, who had no wish to lie, recounted to him my whole adventure. I told him all I had seen, as best I could. I told him all I knew of the animals I had seen, and how all the creatures followed one of them for the sweetness that was wont to issue from it, and how they went away when this mild creature returned to her own haunts.

When I had told my tale and he out of his great goodness had very courteously listened to it, he then called me very gently and said, 'If I thought, and was certain, that you would wish to deserve my favour and serve me with an obedient heart, I would arrange for you to know the truth about what you are asking, and if you still ask me and would do homage to me I shall make you wise about this.' [336]

[337–1951: The God of Love explains that the animal is a panther and represents the dreamer's loved one – the fragrant breath is her words, and the dragon is the envious enemy of love. A number of episodes illustrate the dreamer's timidity: his horse bolts to where the panther is sleeping, but the dreamer dares not say anything to her; Venus gives the dreamer a poem and ring to give to his lady, but he dreams she rejects both poem and ring. Eventually, the God of Love declares the lover can rely only on Fortune. He sets off for Fortune's castle accompanied by Esperance, Dous Penser, and Dous Souvenir].

[1952] Then I departed from that place and from the God of Love, and we set off on our way, I and the three I was taking with me, whom the God, through his courtesy gave to me to keep me company. We went along for so many days, by mountains and by valleys, until in quite a short time we came straight to the house of Fortune, full of chances. The house is very perilous, for it stands entirely on ice whatever the weather. But on one side it is very beautiful, noble and furnished with all good things. On the other side it is in such a bad state that there is no hospitality, and it is all ruined and deserted, so shattered and bare that if it blows with rain or wind nobody can escape feeling it there, for the rain and wind come in on all sides. At the entrance of this house was Blind Fortune to receive the travellers. For indeed, you should know that everybody has to put up there, for there is no hostel nearby where one can stay, whether nobleman or shepherd. There are two sergeants in the house who do not make use of right, but use their will, and each has plenty of folk. One of the two has the name of Good Fortune (*Eürs*) and the other is called Misfortune (*Meseürs*). Eürs guards the part which is most beautiful and best furnished, and that is called Prosperity. The other part is called Adversity, which is dirty and ugly, and in this Meseürs dwells. The one always makes war upon the other, and takes and plunders what he can. Such is their usual custom, but it is necessary for Fortune to give them the authority. For when Fortune is angered, Meseürs can take from Eürs, and he does not dare prevent it. And when Fortune is appeased, then Eürs has the authority, sets himself up in great state, and keeps Meseürs in distress.

[2008] When we came to the door, Fortune – who spares nobody – was at that moment in a rage and had us put by Meseürs into the region of Adversity, where I was very uncertain and had to suffer before enough time had gone by that I could leave. And I would have suffered still more, but Souvenir and Esperance and Dous Penser greatly comforted and relieved me. For when they saw me in misfortune they said, 'Be assured: Eürs will help you yet.'

I was in torment for a long time there and never had any relief. Neither through prayer nor through promise could I put myself out of this misfortune, this burning torture. One day it happened by chance that Grace, a sensible lady, was riding through that region and with her a damsel called Bone Volenté, who would not be able to neglect any good thing. She sent word to Fortune that she would be staying at her house.

When Bone Volenté came there, it so happened that Fortune was in a good mood, who before had been enraged. Shortly afterwards Grace arrived, and there was nobody who did not make much of Grace and her people. Fortune herself conducted her into Prosperity with Eürs, who was in a position of great authority for he can do everything he wishes when Fortune is without ill-will. And when he saw himself in power, he wanted without delay to go to Adversity and do Meseürs down. As he was going, he saw Souvenir beside me and asked him softly: 'Tell me, friend, without delay, what has brought you here and whom are you seeking?'

[2060] Souvenir said, 'Know then, for sure, that Fortune – who sees nothing – put me and my company here when she was annoyed, and we have been here winter and summer, forbidden to leave. The others that you see here are a very pure and faithful lover – as firm as a diamond – and Dous Penser and Esperance. We are here out of fellowship and to seek for mercy, because we are held to him, and cannot fail him whoever wishes to attack him. I have told you the truth, and I beg you by your goodness and by your great courtesy that you will lead me and my company out of Adversity and take care of this lover, for he is faithful and true.'

Eürs replied, 'I will gladly accept your request and, you may be sure, lead you into Prosperity. I have also come to harm Meseürs, because he takes delight in harming me when he has the power to do it.' Then Eürs led us out. When we came into the place of Prosperity, before Grace, Eürs so advised Grace that she retained me in her service. Bone Volenté begged her to, and for that reason she granted it more quickly. At that moment, indeed, Fortune was in Prosperity where there is much delightful accommodation. Pity came and lodged there, bringing her dear daughter Mercy with her, and she brought the gentle panther which is so beautiful, pure and radiant that she lights up all the places where she goes.

[2108] When they had arrived, they were very well received, and warmly welcomed by all who were in Prosperity. But when I saw the panther come, I did not know how to contain myself and showed my feelings. Then Esperance comforted me and said, 'Take heart, and do your utmost. And since Pity has come, you will have what you desire, if you win the support of Grace, so that she asks on your behalf that you be granted Mercy.' Then I begged my lady Grace so much that, without further delay, she begged Pity about my need. And all who were there with Grace begged her. Then Pity said, 'It seems to me that you are such a noble company, of such high rank, that you would not know how to do anything amiss, and would make no request to me which was not good and honest. And because of this, I do not disagree, if the panther is agreeable to it. But I want you to know that without her agreement, I do not agree to do this. For without that, I do not ask my dear daughter Mercy to grant the request of any man alive, whether for entreaty or for reward. But I will do so much for your love, that I will gladly entreat her, and you also will beg her, and cause Eürs to plead, and gentle Bone Volenté, who is present to do all good things. And you should know that we shall certainly not fail if Bone Volenté begs her.'

[2150] Then without delay they started between them to beg the panther that she should receive me in such great love that she should grant me Mercy. When the panther saw that everybody entreated her, then she softened a little towards me and said, 'Since Pity wishes it, who is my mother, I would not refuse it, but rather I desire it and would always do so. When Bone Volenté begs me, Eürs, Grace and her company, whom nobody should refuse, then I would not know how to excuse myself. For I believe they would not entreat for anybody, if they did not know that he was worthy of what they asked. For this reason I dare not refuse them. At this you should have no sorrow, for at your will, in all good and all honour, without any ill thought or dishonour, I grant you utterly myself and Mercy.' Then I said, 'And I thank you, sweet lady, as much as I can, for I have never had any other thought, since I first saw you, than of loving you wholly, and that my love might please you, sweet, gentle panther. For this, I give up to you both heart and body, for you have by your granting given me such perfect joy that I could not have any greater.' There is no man that ever had such great joy as I had then, and it was very near to dawn. Then, without waiting, the guard, who was very near to my ear, signalled the break of day on his horn, and I awoke.

[2190] When I found myself awake, I felt very pained with what I had experienced in my sleep as I dreamed. And I began to go back over my whole dream, and when I had considered my dream, I found nothing in it which was untrue, except that I could never find mercy, however much I might put my heart to the test by labouring faithfully. But in hope of success, I shall labour faithfully everyday. . . . [2202].

[2203–2665: The poet eventually determines to go to his lady with a roundel expressing his love, and he imagines a kindly answer. He ends with expressions of humility; he hopes mistakes in his poem will be corrected indulgently, and includes an anagram of his name].

Le Temple d'Honneur

Jean Froissart

The text translated here is that in *Dits et Débats*, ed. A. Fourrier (Geneva, 1979), which contains a full introduction to the poem (p. 22ff.). Fourrier supports an early date for the work ('Les manuscrits', p. 7ff.), perhaps just after *Le Paradys d'Amours*, and suggests the poem could have been written for the marriage in May 1363 of Humphrey de Bohun (b. 1342) and Joan of Arundel.

Here follows a poem of morality which is called The Temple of Honour.

I think and believe, and have been told (and constantly observed) that there is never a day that dawns, whether one is travelling or staying put, whether one is enjoying oneself in one way or another, that one does not hear tell of something new that has happened somewhere or other – if one witnesses it oneself it is all the more credible, better observed and more agreeable. Something happened to me this year which has not been very widely known until now – and for that I thank my own feelings, which have preserved it and held it back, held close and in prison, until I have reason to speak and come up with it again. Now it has come back to me again, for my pleasure requires it, which willingly forges on ahead. And this makes me communicate it, and so I dare to reveal it.

I was in a company made up of fine people, and whoever knew of anything new related it there to great delight. I there remembered a dream which came to me this year in my sleep, and I began to relate it and everybody to listen very happily and gladly. I had not related a third of it, when something prevented our continuing and I had to stop. But before I left, I was very pleasantly begged that within a short time I would have it set down (and I would be rewarded) so that it could be read.

I granted their request, and racked my brains so thoroughly that with my own hands I wrote my dream, neither more nor less, in the form that you see. And I want you to prepare yourself for reading it and attend properly to what the material may mean, for the novelty of the subject may naturally stimulate the heart and, if the attention is divided, then the act of reading urges it to be more perceptive and receptive to novelties.

[63] It seemed to me, according to the vision I am relating, that I was in a forest where I did not stop wandering high and low, and took great delight in looking at the trees – as many oak trees as myrtle bushes – and the delightful,

shady places. I went up and down a great deal, and then I saw a man approaching on horse-back. I drew towards him, for I could see he was fresh and handsome in appearance and of good birth, and I much wanted to ask for directions. And he, who did not notice my approach, came towards me, and when he met me, he saluted me and I also greeted him in carefree fashion. And in greeting him I said, 'Friend, chance has brought me into this wood, and you have ridden into it, so you will know how one enters and leaves it.' And he very nicely said to me, 'You'd best come with me, and then you are unlikely to lose your way.' I gladly agreed. Then in my vision it seemed to me that the two of us rode together along the paths.

[99] Whilst I rode with him I was often eager to talk and, with this in mind, I urged him to tell me his business, where he was going and what he had to do. He replied, 'You're welcome to know. Whoever you may be, in my company you cannot help witnessing a noble and flawless festival, which is to be held today in a temple very near here.'

I said, 'Friend, do be kind enough to tell me which people are holding this celebration? For if it please God, I would be reluctant to miss it.' And I think he replied to me, 'Today, as I have been informed, Honour is marrying a son of his called Desire – in him he has a fine young man of great nobility and good renown, and is giving him for a wife Plaisance, daughter of Courtesy the wise. Messages have been sent out to assemble a great gathering, for everybody strives to celebrate this occasion, and there you will see Honour and his company making a great and elegant display in very noble and powerful fashion. Honour will give a famous sermon as the heart of the day's proceedings, which will be good to hear, and delight all young hearts and those who gladly hear tell of arms and praise that profession. For Honour has the custom, which I consider very wise, that when one of his children marries, in the name of him and his spouse he makes a speech of great consolation, and very profitable to hear for those who wish to attend. And that you shall gladly hear. Believe me, this path leads us straight there if we follow it.'

[150] 'My friend,' I said, 'this is very much to my liking. Now ride on, and I'll follow.' Then it seemed to me that near there we left the shady forest, but he took a grassy path that skirted the wood. We went along the edge of the forest until, on the summit of a delightful hill, I saw the place I mentioned, which seemed to me a very beautiful temple, finely built and covered with slates. I don't want to say too much about it, for it was made exactly as one would wish, in a beautiful place. We each went forward until we came directly to where I saw the temple. We dismounted and left our horses, and then hand in hand we entered the temple which was open, for the door was unbarred and thrown wide. Without any prohibition or gainsaying we went into the temple, I tell you.

[183] If the temple was fine and beautiful to see outside, inside it was beautiful beyond expression, pure and spotless without shadow, well-glazed and well-arranged. I was very much absorbed in looking all around – the memory of it pleases me still. The entrance was adorned with very fine tapestry and, towards the altar, extensive cloth of gold. And there, right in front of the altar was set a chair which all could see, for it was raised up high. You ought to know that this chair was extremely sumptuous. My companion then pointed out to me Honour, who was right at the head of the company. Afterwards he showed me something that pleased me, for I saw seven steps and each step had

a man: on the first he named Counsel (*Avis*) to me; and on the second Boldness (*Hardement*); thirdly, Enterprise (*Emprise*) was there; on the fourth step was Moderation (*Atemprance*) in very noble and good order; on the fifth was Justice (*Justice*) which stayed there well and handsomely; on the sixth was Loyalty (*Loyautés*) which is worth more than three kingdoms; on the seventh, highest step was Generosity (*Largeche*) which is worth so much and nearest to Honour. . . . [*The poet here goes on to describe the couple who are to be wed.*]

[255]. . . Before her the bride had seven ladies, and I looked at them carefully: each one was placed on a step. On the lowest step, beside the bride and groom was she who is called Manner (*Maniere*), and she was not pale or greying but had a very fresh and pleasant expression – I think she was a king's daughter. And on the second step nearby followed Humility (*Humilité*); Candour (*Francise*) was on the third step, whom I much admired; on the fourth was Courtesy (*Courtoisie*), full of goodness; and on the fifth step was Charity (*Carité*), involved with Pity (*Pité*) who was on the sixth step, and on the highest, seventh step was Faith (*Fois*) . . .

[The sermon of Honour to the bride and groom now follows. Honour first addresses the groom and explains how he is to progress upwards through the steps of the seven qualities, which Honour successively describes and recommends. Afterwards, Honour similarly addresses the bride Plaisance, and recommends her progress through the seven steps linked with her: interpreting, illustrating and commending each quality. The poet thanks his guide who brought him to the temple, and thinks he has seen the bride and groom elsewhere. 'Then I awoke, for it was day'].

IV

*Sources and Analogues of
the Prologue to
'The Legend of Good Women'*

Le Jugement dou Roy de Navarre
Guillaume de Machaut

As its subject makes clear, Machaut's *Jugement dou Roy de Navarre* (1349) was written as a sequel to the *Behaingne*, and in it the poet represents himself as blamed by women for the judgement given against the lady in the earlier poem. When he loses the argument, the punishment of producing certain specific poetic compositions is imposed upon him. Parallels can be seen here between Machaut's handling of 'Guillaume' and the representation of the poet's position in the Prologue to the *Legend of Good Women*, where the translator of the *Romaunt of the Rose* and author of *Troilus and Criseyde* is given the 'penance' of writing the *Legend*. (There is also some parallel between the accounts of the narrators' melancholy in the Prologue to *Navarre* [109–12] and in the *Book of the Duchess* [23–9].) The text of *Navarre* is translated from the *Œuvres*, ed. E. Hoepffner, SATF (Paris, 1908–21).

(*The introductory phase of the poem* [1–458] *represents the poet shut up in his chamber for many months out of fear of the Plague and brooding on contemporary failings and shortcomings*). [459] I was confined in this way for a long time, like a caged hawk, until one day, to my delight, I caught the sound of bagpipes, trumpets, cymbals, and other instruments. Then I went to a window and enquired what it could be, and one of my friends who heard me immediately told me that the survivors of the plague were getting married and having weddings and parties, for the epidemic of pestilence was over, and people were no longer dying. And when I saw them enjoying themselves as happily and cheerfully as if they had not lost anything, I was certainly not downcast, but straightway resumed my former manner, and let the air blow on my eyes and face. That air was so soft and clear that it called on me to leave the prison where I had been for the season. Then I put all fear behind me and mounted Grisart, my gently ambling palfrey. I rode quickly into the fields to enjoy myself in that sweetness which comes from peace and delight, when the heart takes its pleasure without thought of argument or disagreement but cares only for what is honourable.

I too was concerned for honour in what I was doing. If I could, I very much wanted to take some hares by surprise, and so catch them. Now some might ask whether it is an honourable pastime to hunt hares. To this I would reply that it is an honourable and delightful thing. It is an activity of noble reputation and esteem, a graceful undertaking which it is honourable to begin and carry on. It is very agreeable to do, and the honour lies in doing it perfectly. I so devoted myself to perfecting my technique that I thought of nothing else. And the good hunting dogs I had so increased my pleasure, that I could not tire of seeing them run across the fields, or of the melodious birdsong, or of the lovely air of that season that gently bathed my whole body. It is certainly likely that if people rode by I would not notice if they greeted me because I was so preoccupied. Thus an adventure befell me, which was a little frightening for me, but soon turned out well, as I will straightaway go on to tell you. I shall not lie at all about it.

[541] Whilst I was so enjoying myself there that all sorrow and depression were forgotten, a lady of great nobility, finely and richly adorned, arrived there with a handsome retinue. But I did not see them at all, because I was away from the road and wholly engrossed in my hunt. The lady saw me first before anyone else, but gave no sign of this to her escort. Then she called a squire and said to him, 'Do you see that man amusing himself over there? Go to him, and report back soon to me on who he is.' The squire did not fail to come quickly and greet me, but I didn't change what I was doing and said, 'Welcome, sir.' He then returned as fast as he could to the lady: 'My lady,' he said, 'by the faith I owe my soul, it is Guillaume de Machaut, and you should know that he is so engrossed in his hunt he cares for nothing else but his dogs and himself.' When the lady heard these words she appeared deeply happy – not on my account, I am not saying that at all. It was for a certain other reason that was then occupying her will. Her aim was to give pleasure and comfort to herself and plunge me into melancholy. I was not wanting in this, for I was mocked, derided and attacked by her as if I had committed a great crime against her.

[597] When the squire told her about me, the lady said aloud, 'Now let's just see how handsome and pleasant Guillaume is. It seems to me that he should be aware of all honourable pleasure. At night he stays awake studying, and then by day he exerts himself in such labour as tends towards honour. Thus he goes about all the time giving his body pleasure through behaving well, and this maintains a man in worthiness. But I shall briefly take away a great part of his delight. I shall twit him – I've long wanted to do so – and I am going to fulfil my wish.

'Now go back to him and tell him as briefly as you can that he should come here immediately. Tell him bluntly that there are to be no excuses, and that it is my command.' 'My lady, at your command,' said the squire, 'I will tell him just as you say, as soon as I can: I am ready.' Then the squire rode over until he came up to me, and called to me as he galloped up close. As soon as I heard his voice I immediately went towards him, for he was an old acquaintance. And he, looking very happy, greeted me in the name of God the Father, and His dear gentle Mother; and I briefly and courteously returned the greeting. Then I asked him for that most welcome news to me: whether my lady is well and happy, without any disturbance or annoyance? 'Guillaume, have no doubt about anything: for my lady is in every way well and happy and untroubled. Indeed, you will be able to find out soon enough according to what you will hear me tell you. It is indeed so that she sends for you – it is not exactly a command, but you can be sure it is her intention that without excuses you should cheerfully come to her. She believes faithfully that you will come.'

[671] After this speech I replied, 'I tell you that I am not a third or a quarter my lady's, but I am hers with my whole strength, unreservedly. If my lady sends for me it would be madness to think I would wish to refuse. But I would

rather like to ask you – so that there should be no misunderstanding – how far away my lady is from here?' 'Guillaume, my answer is, that it is under three days' journey.' I said, 'Let us go without delay and ride night and day to accomplish what my lady wishes. Nothing can more fill me with happiness than to do her pleasure.' 'Guillaume, I well understand your answer, and I want to give you a little encouragement. Just look over this open country a little beyond this farm land. There is my lady with her mounted retinue, waiting for you – you may be sure of it. Now don't let your heart be seized with fear about going too far, for you will be able to talk to her.'

[707]With these words I turned my head and looked to where he was saying. And when I saw how things were – that my journey was shortened – I wasn't at all irritated, but instead was very happy about it, and began to laugh and then said to him, 'Fair friend, you played at putting me to the test, when you gave me to believe that my lady was far away. I am delighted to discover the truth – that you were fibbing, and my lady is very near. I will go to her: now follow me or stay here, as you please.'

'Guillaume, don't rush – you will get there at the right time for the matters in hand. It would be a good thing if you had a little knowledge of how to conduct an argument and become your own advocate, for you will certainly be liable to be taken by surprise if you do not know how to defend yourself.' We amused ourselves in discussing such matters, and talked as we rode along, until we approached the lady's company. Then I went forward, and when I saw her noble figure, endowed with honour, with grace, with knowledge, in sign of my great reverence I wanted to get down from my horse, but she straightway forbade me, saying graciously, 'Hold on, Guillaume, do not dismount, by any means. You can talk to me on horseback.' When I heard this I complied, and offered her the fairest greeting I knew and as I ought to, as I had learned how to pay respect to people of such rank. And she too knew very well how to carry off perfectly all there was to be done, and replied amicably, while preserving honour and propriety. Then she said to me very formally:

La Dame: 'Guillaume, you have become amazingly strange. You would not have come here, if it weren't for my message. I think that you have become too prudent or too slow, uncaring and ill-willed, or have slackened off in your pleasures, or you esteem ladies much too little. When I was riding I took the way to the right and was looking to the left. I clearly saw you riding, whistling and calling to your hare-hunting dogs. I could hear what you were doing just as I could see it. And this makes me certainly believe, Guillaume, that you saw us, and so why, when you heard our horses riding past and whinnying, did you not deign to come until I sent for you? For this reason I give you such thanks for coming as I must.' [786]

Guillaume: Then I said to her, 'For God's sake, my lady, do not say that. Saving your honour, I reply – by the faith I owe to Our Lord – that I saw or heard nothing, I was so delighted with my hunt, which occupied my thoughts, and which I wanted to bring to an end. I was quite carried away. My lady, I would not willingly do anything to displease you, and what would I gain from such a slight lack of respect? I know very well that I would be the worse for it. You ought to excuse me.'

La Dame: 'Guillaume, I don't want to tease any more about this – in my heart I believe you. But on the other hand, another accusation is growing against you considerably which needs some explanation. I shall cause many things to be against you unless you concede your fault. Guillaume, listen to me: you have wronged ladies, and accused them of things you will see that you are unable to support.' With these strange words she adopted towards me a sharp, cruel, and fierce manner, with signs of great ill-will, to make my heart sorrowful and throw all my thoughts into fear, care and doubt. She put me in great pain with this, for she knew that I esteemed her so much that I would greatly fear her anger. When I heard these words I indeed was afraid, not because of any offence I had committed but because of gossips, who sometimes through falseness and envy do harm to good people who lead good lives. But I was sure that never in my life had I wronged any ladies whatsoever. And I replied advisedly:

Guillaume: 'My lady, you have made a speech in which you show my great dishonour, but the case is not put in proper form. To make a true judgement, you ought to tell me how I have offended, and bring in evidence all the reasons. At the moment, it is all held secretly in your own mind, and if it is not disclosed to me I would not know how to respond to it. Now kindly specify the cause of your complaint. And if you will do this, you will follow the true path of justice. If not, you ought to allow me to go free and acquitted of this wrong that you charge me with. In this I shall wait for justice.' [861]

La Dame: 'Guillaume, you ought to know that henceforth you will not get any more from me. The matter is like this: you know it as well as I do, for you wrote it in one of your books. Look then in your own books. I know very well that you are not drunk when you write your works of love. You know very well, when you write them, if you are doing well or committing wrongs, for they are written with great effort. If you like, you will not have any more from me for the present. You can be sure this is my intention.'

Guillaume: 'My lady, what are you saying? You seem to know much more than you have said. I have for my part certainly written various works of very diverse types, which do not resemble each other. If I wanted to look all through all of them in detail, from beginning to end, it would take too long, and I would like to save myself from that. And moreover, I could not find what you are asking if you do not expand on your words. It is for this reason, my lady, that I do not wish to read my books, not to contradict you. But your invisible thought cannot come to my knowledge unless your heart is unlocked by the key that arranges things, and I am informed by the words of your mouth. When you have told me, I would gladly be blamed and corrected. My lady, please now judge, according to your opinion, whether I am wrong.'

La Dame: 'Guillaume, since it is like this, I agree and concede the point. But your offence against ladies, which is so very great, would need a very harsh reparation. Now kindly listen to what I'm going to say, for I am very strongly moved. And when I have told you, I shall rebuke you so that you will be much blamed and covered with shame towards the ladies.

[929] 'A question was raised some time ago in a very fine poem, very beautifully and courteously done, but afterwards very badly managed. The first premise was that a most worthy lady, with very amiable trust, was to love a faithful lover, so that she would always be a faithful beloved to him. And he, while preserving courtesy, would always love her, and do all in his power to cherish and honour her. And the better to love her, he would maintain all nobility, honour, courtesy and largesse. He was a handsome man, celebrated for his figure, his limbs, his face, perfectly graceful, and very well proven in

deeds of arms, and he was like nobody else in committing his life and being to pursue jousts and tournaments and all amorous diversions. Thus they loved each other, and would always keep the courteous points of loyalty in right and truth. Then it befell them that whether through violence or nature, the lover died. And she, when she knew of this, remained grieving and distracted, a faithful lady without her lover. For her heart would remain enflamed with love, and the death of the lover makes her more steadfast. I won't say more of it, but will add the other side of the picture to this. Now listen, Guillaume, to what I say.

[975] 'Another mild lover, just as worthy as the one I've described, as much in grace as in goodness and all other qualities, and true to honour, is also to love a lady, with nothing but worthy and honourable thoughts. He causes her to know this, and when she knows the truth she receives him gladly, happily grants him her love unreservedly. I don't want to prolong this. He will love her faithfully and trust her firmly, for he thinks he has gained her lifelong love. But it will turn out quite differently. When he will be in his greatest joy with her and confident that he is loved in return, she will play a trick on him, in which he will discover broken faith and disloyalty towards him, not to be denied. It is no surprise that this should afflict him. But it is not equal to the sorrow of that love which is cut short by death. Guillaume, if you have listened to me, you should easily enough be able to recognize your wrongdoing, in order to lessen your dishonour. You have said and written and given it as your considered, definitive judgement, that he has much greater sorrow and suffering who finds his lady untrue to him, than the very sweet, dear lady who will have her lover close to her heart, and then will know him to be irretrievably dead. And how dare you say it, or write it in your books? It is true that you have done it, and in this you have grievously sinned. I advise you so to act that you efface this judgement and quickly revoke it. Guillaume, to prove your worthiness you could well maintain exactly the contrary. For the contrary is right in all amorous places.' [1038]

Guillaume: 'My lady, by the faith I owe Holy Church, in which all my trust is placed, I would not do it for anything. I will not go back on what I have said: I will maintain the judgement that I wrote. But whoever would like to come forward to maintain the opposite – I would very gladly obey whatever I ought to obey. For I am not so strong nor so wise that I may not be beaten. But if I can, I shall win; if I cannot, I must bear it. I don't wish to say anything else. And nonetheless, my sweet lady, in order that you are not annoyed with me, we will do something openly, not secretly, that your calm may be preserved and my honour sustained. For it would be to my great shame, according to your own account, if I denied the judgement. We will have a powerful judge, of most sufficient renown, a wise and discreet man. To him will be recounted all the secrets of the affair that concerns you and me. Let us now agree to do this. But you will make the choice of whom you wish. You will not hear me gainsay it, for I am agreeable to your will. It will be splendid to hear the arguments repeated, and the parties arguing subtly with fine arguments to gain the judgement.'

La Dame: (At these words the lady began to laugh, and in laughing to say) 'Guillaume, I am quite agreeable to what you suggest, and moreover, for better or worse, I nominate and choose the man who is known as King of the Navarrese. He is a prince who loves honour and hates all dishonour, wise, loyal and truthful, and reasonable in all his acts. He is so knowledgeable and worthy that, to tell the truth, I could not choose any one better. The task will be agreeable to him for he is much inclined to love, and wise, courteous and well-taught. He loves the honour, and the worthiness of arms, of love, and of ladies. He is a king by whom no dishonourable man would ever be supported. He is quite without all unworthiness and furnished with all nobility. I could not say too much about his excellences if I always spoke about them from now on . . .' [1114].

[1115–4212: The poet and the lady now proceed to the castle of the King of Navarre, where the case is argued, at considerable length with various exempla, between the lady and her allegorical attendants and the poet. The lady argues that the loss of the dead lover is the greater sorrow and that the lady suffers more, but the poet persists in his view. Eventually the king gives judgement for the lady and against the poet, and sentences Guillaume for his punishment to write a lay, a chanson, and a balade.]

Le Dit de la Marguerite
Guillaume de Machaut

Machaut's *dit* is translated from the text included in the Appendix to *Jean Froissart: Dits et Débats*, ed. A. Fourrier (Geneva, 1979). For a full study, cf. J. I. Wimsatt, *The Marguerite Poetry of Guillaume de Machaut* (Chapel Hill, 1970). The references to overseas and to Cyprus suggest the poem's association with Pierre de Lusignan, King of Cyprus (cf. Wimsatt, p. 42).

Here begins the *dit* of the Marguerite.

I love a flower which opens and inclines towards the sun during the day while the sun traverses the heavens, and when it is set, underneath its curtain of dark night, she closes up before the day comes to an end. Her petals are of a pink colour above, and underneath whiter than ermine in pure whiteness. The stem is greener than green where the flower is properly set, and the seed-head is yellow by nature, its root surpassing and putting in the shade all other sweetness. And it holds my heart in such joy that its pure sweetness cures in me the woes of love.

Now let us look at this sweet flower: it seems to me she surpasses all others in worth, and has surpassed all in sweetness, nor can any be compared with her in colour. She is richly endowed with fragrance and adorned with verdure to give comfort. Her great sweetness cures the ills of love, and her golden centre can raise the dead to life, for she cured me from beyond the sea of my sorrow. And I should certainly serve and honour her and put heart, body and thought in her, and love and cherish her above all with a pure love.

That she opens and inclines towards the sun means that there is no pride in her, and that she is humble and courteously welcoming. And, without lying, every time that I gather her with my hand and can look at her at my will and lift her to my mouth, to my eye, and kiss, touch, smell, and feel, and gently enjoy her beauty and sweetness, then I wish for nothing more. For all the flowers that man could have could not so delight my heart, or cause such joy to enter me, as I receive from her, so that nobody should be surprised if I wish to think of this flower and always strive to remain near to her, sweetly reserved as she is. One could not wish for any other flower that a lover should so much praise and esteem, and indeed, everybody is made happy by seeing her. Whoever holds her can have no ill, and whoever smells her, Love moves him without delay to love her from his heart without deception. For my own part, I say that, with a will disposed to love, I have given myself to her with my whole heart.

Since my eye first saw her and I gently smelled her fragrance, I was so taken in love that, by my faith, I instantly became her servant and utterly gave up to her my heart to do her sweet bidding. Now it is so that I see her very little, but I do not cease loving her because of that, nor believe that she loves another. For truly – because I serve her with heart, body and life – Love, her heart and mine are so involved that they form but one heart, so much do they love each other, these three.

And if I am far distant from this flower, Memory is always nearby, and Dous Penser is friend and companion to me, who represents this flower to me. Then it seems to me that I am certain that I see her and hold her in my hands, and that I feel her sweet smell which is present to me from afar, and that I see her beautiful countenance and colour which move me to love. Through this I am full of the good things that Love gives to lovers, and, when the wind blows from her sweet country, all the time that it blows upon me I feel better because of it.

It seems an amazing thing to me that from so far away, by means of loving thought, I see this delightful and graceful flower. And it seems to me that she has such powers that in the world there is nothing so dangerous that should frighten a lover, for whoever is furnished with this flower cannot be killed. He should not fear pain or death, but his spirit should lead a joyful life. It is the balm that grows in paradise, with which everybody is comforted and cured.

Very happy was the hour in which I became her lover; and when through her such great happiness comes to me, every time that I remember her, it will increase a hundred thousand times, if it happens that I see her – and this is something I must do, for it is the flower that keeps me alive, it is the stock which holds up my honour. And what shall I say of it? As God preserve me, I should be worth very little and would never attain high honour, if I did not love her with a true heart. It is fitting that I serve, love, fear and believe her, and that I am hers quite unreservedly and should not give my heart, which loves and fears her, to any other.

But if it please God and if I can, I shall be such as will do her pleasure and will, and will always love her faithfully without going back. I shall protect her peace, her well-being, her honour; I shall spread the praise of her everywhere to the utmost of my power, and will do anything I can to her advantage. And if I cannot very often be near her, that should not displease her, for I shall serve her loyally everywhere without mistake.

For in truth, it is my greatest pleasure to serve her who is my hope, and to think of her sweet appearance which is etched in my heart by her words, her deeds, her simple expression, so that from beyond the sea I see it in my presence, when my thoughts are privately turned that way and I am all alone. But it grieves and troubles me a little that I am afraid that I have had too little time to serve her, and that she has been too little honoured by me, who have her in my thoughts more than anything.

Now God give me grace, strength, and life to serve her, without any unworthy thought, and give her the heart not to forget me or do me wrong. And what have I said about this pretty flower? I do not fear that she will ever change, but I am certain that she will be a true lover to me until death, and will remain so if I die. And if I am alive all my comfort and resort will be in this flower which I carry near to my heart, because I do not doubt for a moment that it is the true port of my honour.

It is the sun that gleams, it is the moon that makes the night clear, it is the star which guides me across the sea, it is the ship, strong, secure, and full of delight, it is the steersman who guides me, it is the oar which cleaves the sound of the sea, it is the strong mast that never bends because of the wind, it is the sail which billows on my boat and propels it in all weathers, it is the food on which I live, it is the sweet and lovely water that refreshes and revives me and is always pure, clear and fresh.

Everything that I have in this world, of renown, of well-being, of peace, of honour and of success, comes from her whom I have always in my memory. It does me so much good that no song nor story anywhere could make me believe that I could give up her love. I take too much delight in this flower which I have chosen as my favourite above all others, for when I am in Cyprus or in Egypt my heart very gently dwells in her, and I hope for joy from this flower, for if she seems little she is rich in honour and worthy of merit. In French she is called *marguerite* or daisy – this is a true thing.

Here ends the *dit* of the marguerite.

Machaut's *Dit de la Fleur de Lis et de la Marguerite* also contains a description of the daisy in similar terms, and is connected with the other Marguerite poems translated here. The poem has been edited by J. I. Wimsatt in *The Marguerite Poetry of Guillaume de Machaut* (Chapel Hill, 1970). Wimsatt would feel the poem influenced Chaucer 'though no single parallel offers conclusive proof of it' (p. 34).

The poet declares his intention to honour the *fleur de lis* and the *marguerite* and first discourses on the beauties and properties of the lily. After this he comments that the lily is a masculine flower and the daisy is feminine (conceivably alluding to a French royal marriage, although the lily's qualities are compared to those of a lady).

Now the poet celebrates the daisy ('C'est une fleur moult gracieuse,/ Mout tresbele, et mout vertueuse./ Tant a bonté, tant a valour,/ Qu'an mon gré n'est plus bele flour,' 187–90). He tells how there are four colours: green, white, red, and yellow, and comments on the flower's 'stem greener than grass'. He continues (213ff.): 'She has a circlet of petals so white that there is nobody who sees her who does not rejoice, for the whiteness signifies joy. On her head she has a crown with which Nature has crowned her as lady, mistress and queen of sweetness and fine beauty. The crown is all red, which unites well with the white. . . . But the reddish tinge signifies bashfulness and fearfulness. . . . She has a seedhead all yellow, which is so delightful and pure that it seems to be gilded, so has Nature created it. But it is a marvellous thing, for when the daisy has closed her petals then she has her treasure with her – this is her seedhead which seems like pure gold. And I believe she does this so that her golden centre should not be ravished or stolen away. Moreover, unless it will annoy you, I shall tell you what she does at night time: she closes up her petals so tight that nothing can enter in there. . . . And thus by night she covers herself up, and in the morning she reveals herself. Then indeed I gladly behold her, for she adores the sun, and all day, wherever he goes, she does not cease to bow towards him. And it seems she has some awareness of the sun and his power . . .' (256).

The poet now digresses on the other forms of the word *marguerite*: it can mean a precious stone that ornaments lords and ladies; Marguerite is also a saint in heaven; and Marguerite is a frequent lady's name. The flower is said to have healing qualities just as his lady does.

The poet concludes that he has compared his lady to the lily, and also has made a garment for her from the marguerite, with which she can adorn herself to advantage (385–8). The poet declares he will never forsake the marguerite while he lives, and he has committed his life to her, for through the marguerite he can have hope, joy, peace . . . 'souffissance' . . . etc.

Le Dit de la Marguerite
Jean Froissart

Froissart's *dit* is translated from the text in *Dits et Débats*, ed. A. Fourrier (Geneva, 1979).

Here follows an amorous treatise that is called the *dit* of the marguerite.

I ought not to hold back from praising, prizing and honouring the flower of flowers, for she is much to be commended. It is the consound, or daisy – thus I wish to name her. And whoever wishes to give her her own name, it cannot be removed or taken away, for she has a name in French, it is quite clear – the *marguerite* – which one can discover all the time. She is so delightful and beautiful to look at that I can never see her too much. I would like to remain with her always to take in properly her virtues. It seems to me that she has no equal and Nature wishes to work as she pleases.

She is small, white and red, and customarily dwells in all green places – elsewhere she does not like. She likes just as much the little meadow of a hermit, provided she can grow there without opposition, as she does the beautiful gardens of Egypt. The sweet sight of her does me tremendous good, and because of this is imprinted so clearly in my heart that night and day in my thoughts I recite the great virtues of which she is composed, and say in this way: 'Blessed be the hour when I chose such a flower for my own, which is called the sovereign of goodness and of beauty. And, if Fortune does not spoil things for me, I am hoping for so great a recompense that no gardener, however knowledgeable and wise, working to put trees, flowers and fruit in the garden for his delight, ever had the equal of the joy truly that I shall have, if chance allows it to me.'

Thinking of this has kept up my hopes for a long time. And the little flower grows in one place where it is fostered by such a gentle environment that no cold or heat, rain, hail, or wind, can do it harm; there is no planet or sky which is not ready at her command. A bright sun fosters and lights her himself.

And this flower which is so sweet and pure, lovely in her growing and benign in looks, has a custom and a worthy virtue that I hold very dear when I consider it: for as the sun passes on his way from rising until he goes down, the daisy bows towards him, as she who wishes to bear witness to his goodness and his instruction. For the sun which perfects her in beauty, forms in nature the vault and curtain of her world, defends her against all foggy drizzle, and enhances her hues of white and red. These are the sure tokens why the flower bows towards the sun.

149

I have chosen very well when I took such a little flower to my heart, which first appeared out of the ground without either seed or sower. A young girl loved her lover so much – this was Hero, who suffered so many woes for the true love of Cephei that the fair creature poured out her tears on the green grass where her lover had been buried, and she wept, lamented and groaned so much that the earth gathered up the tears. It had pity and opened up to the tears, and Jupiter – who felt for this love – fostered them through the power of Phoebus, and converted them all into beautiful flowers of the very same type as she is that I love with pure intent, and will always love for as long as I live.

But if I could happen on the luck that Mercury once had, then no creature was ever happier than I would be, I swear it to you. Mercury, as the text says, first found the beautiful flower that I love beyond measure, for while leading his flock to pasture he came across the tomb of Cephei that I mentioned, and he noticed there in the enclosure the sweet flower I care about so much. He was rightly amazed, for in January – when because of winter all flowers are dead – this flower appeared white and red, and showed the brightness of her colour. Then he said to himself, 'Now I have my desire!' He went to gather the flower for a chaplet – he very much wished to keep it – and was going to entrust it to Lires, and beg her to bear it without delay to Ceres, who did not think him worthy of her love. If she took it favourably, he would hold his life more dear. The messenger immediately did as asked and came to present the chaplet to Ceres. She took it with a heart light and whole, and said, 'I certainly ought to thank him who delights to send me a gift that makes me happy, and I really should reward his courtesy, and wish that he be told from me that he will never love without return.'

This answer was heard with great joy when Lires faithfully reported it, no more, no less. The flower then had a pretty power, for she caused somebody to have a lover who before was quite unsuccessful. Could it ever be like this in my life? I do not know, indeed. Nevertheless, I put my trust in good hope to help me. But I am certain that the lovely flower I call the daisy will always be cherished in my heart. She is worth it and I love her above all. And I am guided in true love by Mercury, who was full of all good qualities, for he loved her so much that every evening and morning, whatever season it was – Christmas or All Saints – a chaplet was borne for the love of his lady Ceres.

I have a comparable view, for the beautiful colour of the flower so pleases me that I think no human being, no rough and unworthy person, should touch it with his hands and nails. And if I have had the luck to find it first, I don't make any mention of it in joy or sorrow, because I am afraid to lose it. I wish to put myself in a certain place lamenting night and day, and thus say: 'May it please the God of Love that I may see safe in a tower or garden the gracious flower, and that there is no man or woman in the tower that can come across that place, and may it be in some out-of-the-way place – I don't care where!' In this wish my thought was of everything that is honourable, but to wish gave me pleasure, to look at my leisure at her white and red colour, set on the green sward. If I lived in this way, I think no man should seek for a better, when I so love and desire the flower that I have no other desire than to have it, to watch it at leisure close in the evening and open in the morning, and follow the sun all day and open out its petals in the sunlight. It seems to me that such virtue should be welcomed, and indeed, so I do: in that lies all my pleasure. I think that as I gaze attentively at the flower during the day nothing but good can happen to me. And for the love of one alone for whom I long – of whom I can only take pleasure in the looks (it is little enough, but I must suffer) – I wish to honour and serve them all henceforward.

And I declare by the little flower, when I come into the places where many of them grow, all for the love of her, I shall gather one or two laughingly and will say, remembering her great goodness, 'Here is the flower that keeps me in happiness and makes me feel as much good as I need. For the more I see her, the better seem to me her sweet look and delightful manner. For in each petal, I assure you, the flower carries a piercing dart, through which I am so wounded by looking at her that there is no limb in my body where it has not spread. But I beg the power of the God of Love to cure me.'

Here ends the *dit de la margheritte*.

Le Lay de Franchise
Eustache Deschamps

The text of the *Lay* is translated from the *Œuvres complètes*, ed. le marquis de Queux de Saint-Hilaire and G. Raynaud, SATF, 11 vols. (Paris, 1878–1903), Vol. II, pp. 203–14. It can probably be dated to 1385, for Raynaud comments that in 1385 at the Château de Beauté-sur-Marne at Vincennes, 'à l'occasion du 1er mai, il prend thème d'une fête où l'on voit figurer le roi au milieu de dames et de jeunes seigneurs parés de vert, pour adresser à Charles VI son *Lai de franchise* et lui conseiller d'aviser au mal présent, la convoitise qui règne partout, et de se garder d'aimer trop la bonne chère, penchant funeste à la santé' (Vol. XI, p. 46). The sixteen year old king described in the lay is evidently Charles VI (born December 1368), and Deschamps alludes to his famous youthful victory at the Battle of Rosebech (November 1382). On 1 May 1385 Charles VI would have been sixteen, and from historical sources it is known that the king spent that day at the Château de Beauté. For a full account, and for the suggestion that the 'tresdouce fleur' of the poem is Marguerite de Bourgogne, cf. J. L. Lowes, 'The Prologue to the *Legend of Good Women* as Related to the French *Marguerite* Poems . . .' *PMLA*, 19 (1904), 593–683. It is known that Marguerite de Bourgogne visited the Château at that time, and the closing lines of Deschamps' *Lay* seem to refer to her departure.

Because habit is a great thing when one takes it and pursues it from infancy, it is very difficult to leave it, for perseverance always makes somebody think of that thing of which he has sweet memories. And for this reason I want to come to my subject: it is that in the sweet time that advances all flowers, trees and bushes, and the earth seeks to become all green and spread its flowers, there came to me the recollection of the month of May, when many people in France have the custom of going in this sweet season to gather the may.

On the first day of this delightful month, which is the true hope of lovers, in order to maintain the custom of the day, which I have honoured and reverenced ever since I was truly aware of it, I wished to offer up and sacrifice my heart and body, all dressed in green, to the gentle month which prospers gentle hearts to delight in love with their ladies, who this day will listen to their complaints. Then I put myself in order and set off to go to the wood, where many a lover rushes for his love and seeks his joy.

I set out from my lodging at day-break, seized with amorous sorrow, and took my way through open country thinking of the beauty of the very sweet flower, who in goodness, in sweetness, in honour, and in all good, is the sovereign flower. She has a stem of green, a seed-head of pure gold, and white and red are her colours. The green stalk represents constancy, the white conveys her lasting purity, and the red shows her bashfulness and fearfulness. The golden seed shows her great worthiness and how she is at all times pure.

But she also has great natural vigour, for to the sun when he gives out his brightness she opens her flower, she is so humble and kindly; and as the sun moves round during the day she bows towards him. And in the evening when the sun goes down, she closes her petals so that none can harm her, showing that she is true and sure and wishes to show her finery in daylight. But in darkness she keeps herself so tightly closed that no slander or other base thing can ever find a place to lodge there. Because of this, she has the grace and love of all, for she is the earthly goddess of flowers.

[53] And it certainly seems that everybody holds her dear, for I see no man who does not seek her and does not wish to bear her or have her. I see her painted and depicted in many ways – in fine cloth of gold, on walls, and on glass. And she can be seen on many clothes, and all the time seen on vessels and artefacts, as she who is the true light, the shining stone of precious knowledge, through whose power all those who are sick and languishing can receive health. There is no flower that can compare with her. For her fragrance is not haughty or fierce, and she would not know how to deceive any man.

Thinking in this way, I came across a heath to a great park of trees and ferns which was secured with marvellous strength: there was a great tower at the first gate, moats, a strong, stone castle and a very rich manor. A great lord was the owner of all this. And in the middle was a gate and a sumptuously ornamented bridge. But there was never such a tower as the one there, in design, height, and strength, and I don't know who could have conceived it. For it was not of ancient workmanship, and he who made it was powerful and wise. But it was not absolutely finished in all points. On the pillars many images had been carved, and there were very many rich windows. Each tower resembled an abbey, and would not fear any assault or siege. And the main tower was set on a wooded knoll. The top of the tower where the look-out gives his call is very much higher than the branching woods round about.

I turned my pilgrimage towards a pool, but as I passed I saw out on the grass a very noble company of youths all dressed in green, and there were other people of high rank who were carrying bill-hooks as tools to work with, and were beginning to cut down the foliage. I passed by so that they did not see me, and hid myself in a bush to observe the life of these people, and to hear the sweet music of the nightingales crying in the garden: 'Occi, occy.' I saw many wild creatures pass by and many flocks of birds.

[105] All sorts of song birds were singing there, various finches and linnets, larks, goldfinches, pigeons, ring-doves, turtle-doves, blackbirds, magpies, and jays, and all other birds, even the cuckoo, whose song is not pretty, the quail as well, the pheasant and the partridge. The sound of their singing in that place was very great, and the festivities that they made there. The birds were making their nests there, and the rabbits were nibbling in the meadows. Stags and deer could be seen there, and all the delights of the forest.

Through this wood came ladies and young men who were singing new songs because of the sweetness of that beautiful season, gathering flowers and leaves with which they were making garlands and chaplets. And all were clothed in green. The day itself was an earthly paradise, for many made wooden pipes and flageolets which they played continually, and others recited poems of love and spoke of honour and faithful love, with which every true heart must be taken.

That morning there was such a very sweet dew in the wood that it was delightful to see, for the sun had come out from a slight cloud to light up the dew. One could not mine finer silver than those droplets of water seemed to be. The sun caused them to drip on to the green grass, so that its colour and beauty were all restored.

I heard many secret matters of love, but my memory was a little disturbed by a great noise issuing from a valley where people had come to joust. There was a great assembly on horseback, and amongst them a King, who indeed should be loved, for nowhere is there one more handsome or with gentler manner. Nature could well give him sixteen years of age who – before he was thirteen – won such great renown when he overcame 26,000 men in battle.

[157] He was mounted on a horse in green apparel, accompanied by his brother. Counts and dukes, knights and barons, and ladies were there – which did not surprise me – lofty, noble and most affable in manner, who were making presents of chaplets and boughs. The young lords joyfully spurred on to the joust, and broke their lances on each other with a tumble. There was no great plan about the gathering, instead everybody jousted as he pleased, without sparing anything.

Those who, free from sadness and grief, were further on in the wood heard the cries and the sounds of trumpets, and the echo of the drums and instruments, and very meekly came to salute the King on their knees. The King said aloud: 'Let us sacrifice to May, for none of us must have sleep. Let us offer up hearts, bodies and thoughts, and give good love to one another, and let nothing unworthy be in our sight. It is my wish that we lead a life of complete happiness, and then we will all go together to the castle of Beauté.'

Honour was there; Joy and Solace were there; Valour was in evidence there; the great ancient deeds were spoken of there; some there pleaded the cause of arms; for Love some arguments and questions were moved there, and the benefits were demonstrated that Love gave to those who were his and through him prospered. One person said: 'There is nothing worthy in such love, for today we are all feeble in honour and do nothing but jousting contests, and snarl with envy like dogs.'

[196] There were ladies who said: 'Alas! If Sweet Looks takes one step forward everybody says "He has that lady on a lead, don't you see it?" Thus through a single unguarded look there will be suspicion and bragging. I do not hold with such love: it is this which has overthrown honour and deadened noble hearts. Such love is not strong, and whoever takes it up is wretched.'

Then the flower spoke, and to the agreement of all, wisely declared in fine words that there could not be prowess without love, citing the great example of Troy, and referring also to the Brut, to Juno, the amorous goddess, to Medea who taught the secret means to strong Jason who thereby overcame the bulls, to Hercules who vanquished great hosts, and to Theseus. Covetousness has lost the territory that has been conquered by Enterprize, Love, and Largesse.

And when the King heard these gentle words, he said he would keep these three with Delight, Boldness and Happiness – for without these three Worthiness would never be anywhere in town or castle. Cowardice, the false thief, could seek lodging elsewhere. Let Covetousness be put away, for she wastes and wounds all men and eventually will destroy all princes. So Honour spoke and showed noble hearts how to avoid Idleness.

Thus with the sound of horns and with dancing everybody set off from there towards the castle of Beauté. It was girt on one side by the river Marne, and the garden had splendid moats with many fish in the water. Fine rooms were there, and from the windows could be seen the beautiful mills, meadows and cornfields. From the upper rooms they could see the vineyards, and they greatly praised the rooms and the tower, while they were also delighted with the fountains. They had never before seen or come across a more beautiful place.

[248] And it was very richly decorated, hung with green, adorned with rich hangings; the curtains were of silk and gold, and richly embroidered cushions were on the beds. A lofty canopy covered the whole table where the King was; ladies accompanied him, counts and dukes and all the other lords. They had many courses before they had finished dining, and minstrels heralded all the courses with horns. This feast was conducted with very great joy, and excellent wines were drunk that day.

From my bush I jumped out like an animal, and when I had seen the eating and drinking at the feast, the great state, the food and commotion that was there, the noise and din, I came away and took to my road once again. And as I went along I found, underneath a beech tree in a high place, Marion and Robin drinking from a stream, and they had just a little bread ready to dip in the water, and sang then an honest song with pure and loving heart.

Then Robin said: 'Marion, great feasts are shameful, and he who lays them on is in danger of dying in the end. By my head, I live more happily than do these great lords who have so much vexation, who fear a villain's poison, and live on tenterhooks, on the look-out, evening and morning. My bread is good; nobody needs to clothe me; the water is pure that I want to drink; I fear neither tyrant nor poison; I am master of the wood; I have free will without constraint, and I am richer than king or count.

'For I swear to you that I know of four kings that are dead, and the fifth can everyday be seen unconscious. And what is gained by stuffing one's stomach in this way? The body is often made ill, and he must die. Or otherwise evil men kill him for his possessions. Even the servants die more quickly there through bad ways. I have free will and a good sufficiency, and I don't want to keep up any other state.'

[300] When I had heard Robin's wisdom, and saw his state, and his expression, great fear made my body tremble. For the more I thought it over and over again, the more I discerned high prudence in him, which could sustain my own life securely. And, if I can, I wish to follow that way, for courtly life is too uncertain a state. Now may it please God to reward that flower, and the sweet May, which have warned me through Marion and Robin. Now I pray that, as she goes away, her gentle countenance may receive this lay with favour.

Here ends the Lay de Franchise.

Select Bibliography

TEXTS

Alanus de Insulis: *De Planctu Naturae*, in *Patrologia Latina*, ed. J. P. Migne, Vol. 210.

——,   'The Complaint of Nature by Alain de Lille,' transl. D. M. Moffatt, *Yale Studies*, 36 (1908).

Boccaccio: *Teseida*, ed. A. Limentani, in *Tutte le Opere di Giovanni Boccaccio*, ed. V. Branca, Vol. II (Milan, 1964).

——,   *Chaucer's Boccaccio*, ed. and transl. N. R. Havely (Cambridge, 1980).

Chaucer: *The Works of Geoffrey Chaucer*, ed. F. N. Robinson, 2nd edn (London, 1957).

——,   *The Parlement of Foulys*, ed. D. S. Brewer (London, 1960).

Jean de Condé: *Dits et contes de Baudouin de Condé et de son fils Jean de Condé*, ed. A. Scheler, 3 vols. (Brussels, 1866–7).

——,   *La Messe des Oiseaux et Le Dit des Jacobins et des Fremeneurs*, ed. J. Ribard (Geneva, 1970).

Deschamps: *Œuvres complètes de Eustache Deschamps*, ed. le marquis de Queux de Saint-Hilaire and G. Raynaud, SATF, 11 vols. (Paris, 1878–1903).

Froissart: *Œuvres de Froissart: Poésies*, ed. A. Scheler, 3 vols. (Brussels, 1870–72).

——,   *L'Espinette amoureuse*, ed. A. Fourrier (Paris, 1963).

——,   *La Prison amoureuse*, ed. A. Fourrier (Paris, 1974).

——,   *Le Joli Buisson de Jonece*, ed. A. Fourrier (Geneva, 1975).

——,   *Ballades et rondeaux*, ed. R. S. Baudouin (Geneva, 1978).

——,   *The Lyric Poems of Jehan Froissart*, ed. R. R. McGregor (Chapel Hill, 1978).

——,   *Dits et Débats*, ed. A. Fourrier (Geneva, 1979).

Oton de Grandson: *Oton de Grandson, sa vie et ses poésies*, ed. A. Piaget (Lausanne, 1941).

Machaut: *Œuvres de Guillaume de Machaut*, ed. E. Hoepffner, SATF, 3 vols. (Paris, 1908–21).

——,   *Œuvres*, ed. P. Tarbé (Rheims and Paris, 1849).

——,   *Le Livre du Voir-Dit*, ed. P. Paris (Paris, 1875).

—,   *Poésies lyriques*, ed. V. Chichmaref, 2 vols. (Paris, 1909).

—,   *The Marguerite Poetry*, ed. J. I. Wimsatt (Chapel Hill, 1970).

—,   *La Louange des dames*, ed. N. Wilkins (Edinburgh, 1972).

Nicole de Margival: *Le Dit de la panthère d'amours*, ed. H. A. Todd, SATF (Paris, 1883).

Romance of the Rose: *Le Roman de la rose*, ed. F. Lecoy, CFMA, 3 vols. (Paris, 1965–70).

—,   *The Romance of the Rose*, transl. C. Dahlberg (Princeton, 1971).

Somnium Scipionis: Cicero, *De re publica*, ed. and transl. C. W. Keyes (Loeb Classical Library, 1928).

—,   *Macrobius; Commentary on the Dream of Scipio*, transl. W. H. Stahl (New York, 1952).

Anonymous Works: *Les Débats du Clerc et du Chevalier*, ed. Ch. Oulmont (Paris, 1911).

—,   *De Venus La Deese d'Amor*, ed. W. Foerster (Bonn, 1880).

—,   A. Långfors, '*Dou Vrai Chiment d'Amours*: Une Nouvelle Source de *Venus La Deesse D'Amor*,' *Romania*, 45 (1918–19), 205–19.

—,   *Recueil général des jeux-partis français*, ed. A. Långfors, 2 vols., SATF (Paris, 1926).

—,   *L'Ovide moralisé*, ed. C. de Boer, 5 vols. (Amsterdam, 1915–36).

—,   *De Phyllide et Flora*, in *Carmina Burana*, ed. C. Fischer *et al.* (Munich, 1974).

SECONDARY SOURCES:

Ainsworth, P. F.,   'Style direct et peinture des personnages chez Froissart,' *Romania*, 93 (1972), 498–522.

Allen, J. B.,   *The Friar as Critic: Literary Attitudes in the Later Middle Ages* (Nashville, 1971).

Auerbach, E.,   *Literatursprache und Publikum in der lateinischen Spätantike und im Mittelalter* (Bern, 1958).

Avril, F.,   *Manuscript Painting at the Court of France: the Fourteenth Century (1310–1380)*, (London, 1978).

Baird, J. L. and Kane, J. R.,   *Rossignol: An Edition and Translation.* (Kent State U.P., 1978).

Bastin, J.,   *Froissart; chroniqueur, romancier et poète* (Brussels, 1948).

Batany, J.,   'Paradigmes lexicaux et structures littéraires au moyen âge,' *Revue d'histoire littéraire de la France*, 70 (1970), 819–35.

Baugh, A. C.,   'Chaucer and the *Panthère d'Amours*,' in *Britannica Festschrift für H. M. Flasdieck*, ed. W. Iser and H. Schabram (Heidelberg, 1960), pp. 51–61.

Becker, G.,   'Guillaume de Machaut,' in *Dictionnaire des Lettres françaises: Le Moyen Age* (Paris, 1964), pp. 353–8.

Bennett, J. A. W.,   *The Parlement of Foules: An Interpretation* (Oxford, 1957).

Bennett, J. A. W.,   *Chaucer's Book of Fame* (Oxford, 1968).

Benton, J. F.,   'Clio and Venus: An Historical View of Courtly Love,' in *The Meaning of Courtly love*, ed. F. X. Newman (Albany, 1968), pp. 19–41.

Bevilacqua, M.,   *Introduzione a Macrobio* (Lecce, 1973).

Boer, C. de,   'Guillaume de Machaut et *l'Ovide moralisé'*, *Romania*, 43 (1914), 335–52.

Braddy, H.,   *Chaucer and the French Poet Graunson* (Baton Rouge, 1947).

Brewer, D. S.,   'The Relationship of Chaucer to the English and European Traditions,' in *Chaucer and Chaucerians*, ed. D. S. Brewer (London, 1966).

Brownlee, K.,   'The Poetic Oeuvre of Guillaume de Machaut: the Identity of Discourse and the Discourse of Identity,' in Cosman and Chandler (see below), pp. 219–33.

Calin, W.,   *A Poet at the Fountain: Essays on the Narrative Verse of Guillaume de Machaut* (Kentucky U.P., 1974).

Caplan, H,   *Of Eloquence: Studies in Ancient and Mediaeval Rhetoric* (Ithaca, 1970).

Cartier, N. R.,   'Froissart, Chaucer and Enclimpostair,' *Revue de littérature comparée*, 38 (1964), 18–34.

——,   'Oton de Grandson et sa princesse,' *Romania*, 85 (1964), 1–16.

——,   '*Le Bleu chevalier* de Froissart et *Le Livre de la duchesse* de Chaucer,' *Romania*, 88 (1967), 232–52.

Chailley, J.,   *Histoire musicale du Moyen Age* (Paris, 1950).

——,   'Du cheval de Guillaume de Machaut à Charles II de Navarre,' *Romania*, 94 (1973), 251–8.

Ciurea, D.,   'Jean Froissart et la société franco-anglaise du XIVe siècle,' *Le Moyen Age*, 76, (1970), 275–84.

Clemen, W.,   *Chaucer's Early Poetry* (London, 1963).

Colby, A. M.,   *The Portrait in Twelfth-Century French Literature* (Geneva, 1965).

Colish, M. L.,   *The Mirror of Language: A Study in the Medieval Theory of Knowledge* (New Haven, 1968).

Cosman, M. P. and Chandler, B. (eds.),   *Machaut's World: Science and Art in the Fourteenth Century* (Annals of the New York Academy of Sciences), (New York, 1978).

Curtius, E. R.,   *Europäische Literatur und lateinisches Mittelalter*, 2nd edn (Bern, 1954).

Dahlberg, C.,   'Love and the *Roman de la Rose*,' *Speculum*, 44 (1969), 568–84.

De Bruyne, E.,   *Etudes d'esthétique médiévale*, 3 vols. (Bruges, 1946).

Douce, A.,   *Guillaume de Machaut: Musicien et Poète Rémois* (Rheims, 1948).

Dragonetti, R.,	*La Technique poétique des trouvères dans la chanson courtoise* (Bruges, 1960).
Dronke, P.,	*Medieval Latin and the Rise of European Love-Lyric*, 2 vols. (Oxford, 1965–6).
Economou, G. D.,	*The Goddess Natura in Medieval Literature* (Cambridge, Mass., 1972).
Elwert, W. T.,	*Traité de versification française* (Paris, 1965).
Estrich, R. M.,	'Chaucer's Prologue to the *Legend of Good Women* and Machaut's *Le Jugement dou Roy de Navarre*,' *SP*, 36 (1939), 20–39.
Faral, E.,	*Recherches sur les sources latines des contes et des romans courtois* (Paris, 1913).
Faral, E. (ed.),	*Les Arts poétiques du XIIe et du XIIIe siècle* (Paris, 1924).
Ferrante, J. M. and Economou, G. D. (eds),	*In Pursuit of Perfection: Courtly Love in Medieval Literature* (New York, 1975).
Fleming, J. V.,	*The Roman de la Rose: A Study in Allegory and Iconography* (Princeton, 1969).
Fourrier, A.,	*Le courant réaliste dans le roman courtois en France au Moyen Age* (Paris, 1960).
Fox, J.,	*A Literary History of France: The Middle Ages* (London, 1974).
Frank, G.,	'French Literature in the Fourteenth Century,' in *The Forward Movement of the Fourteenth Century*, ed. F. L. Utley (Columbus, 1961), pp. 61–77.
Frappier, J.,	'Sur un procès fait à l'amour courtois,' *Romania*, 93 (1972), 145–93.
Fyler, J. M.,	*Chaucer and Ovid* (New Haven, 1979).
Gagnepain, B.,	*La Musique française du Moyen Age et de la Renaissance* (Paris, 1961).
Galway, M.,	'Chaucer's Sovereign Lady: A Study of the Prologue to the Legend and Related Poems,' *MLR*, 33 (1938), 145–99.
Goldin, F.,	*The Mirror of Narcissus in the Courtly Love Lyric* (Ithaca, 1967).
Graham, A.,	'Froissart's use of classical allusion in his poems,' *Medium Aevum*, 32 (1963), 24–33.
Grammont, M.,	*Petit traité de versification française* (Paris, 1908).
Green, R. H.,	'Alan of Lille's *De Planctu Naturae*,' *Speculum*, 31 (1956), 649–74.
Gunn, A. M. F.,	*The Mirror of Love* (Lubbock, 1952).
Gybbon-Monypenny, G. B.,	'Guillaume de Machaut's erotic 'autobiography': precedents for the form of the *Voir-Dit*,' in *Studies in Medieval Literature and Languages in Memory of F. Whitehead* (Manchester, 1973).
Hieatt, C. B.,	*The Realism of Dream Visions* (The Hague, 1967).
——,	'*Une Autre Fourme*: Guillaume de Machaut and the Dream Vision Form,' *ChauR*, 14 (1979–80), 97–115.
Jauss, H. R.,	*Le Génèse de la poésie allégorique française au moyen âge (de 1180–1240)*, (Heidelberg, 1962).

Jenkins, T. A.,	'Deschamps' Balade to Chaucer,' *MLN*, 33 (1918), 268–78.
Jung, M. R.,	*Etudes sur le poème allégorique en France au moyen âge*, Romanica helvetica, 82 (Bern, 1971).
Kelly, D.,	*Medieval Imagination: Rhetoric and the Poetry of Courtly Love* (Madison, 1978).
——,	'Rhetoric in French Literature: Topical Invention in Medieval French Literature,' in J. J. Murphy (ed.), *Medieval Eloquence: Studies in the Theory and Practice of Medieval Rhetoric* (Berkeley, 1978), pp. 231–51.
——,	'*Translatio Studii*: Translation, Adaptation and Allegory in Medieval French Literature,' *PQ*, 57 (1978), 287–310.
Kitchel, A.,	'Chaucer and Machaut's *Dit de la Fontaine Amoureuse*,' *Vassar Medieval Studies*, ed. C. F. Fiske (New Haven, 1923), pp. 219–31.
Kittredge, G. L.,	'Chaucer and Froissart,' *Englische Studien*, 26 (1899), 321–36.
——,	'Chauceriana,' *MP*, 7 (1910), 465–83.
——,	'Guillaume de Machaut and *The Book of the Duchess*,' *PMLA*, 30 (1915), 1–24.
Knowlton, E. C.,	'Nature in Old French,' *MP*, 20 (1922–23), 309–29.
Koehler, E.,	'Narcisse, la fontaine d'Amour et Guillaume de Lorris,' in *L'Humanisme médiéval dans les littératures romanes du XIIe au XIVe siècle*, ed. A. Fourrier (Paris, 1964), pp. 147–66.
Langhans, V.,	'Chaucers Book of the Leoun,' *Anglia*, 52 (1928), 113–22.
Langlois, C. V.,	'Jean de Condé, ménestrel et poète français,' *HLF* (Paris, 1921), XXXV, 421–54.
Langlois, E.,	*Origines et sources du Roman de la Rose* (Paris, 1891).
Lazar, M.,	*Amour courtois et fin' amors dans la littérature du XIIe siècle* (Paris, 1964).
Legge, M. D.,	*Anglo-Norman Literature and its Background* (Oxford, 1963).
——,	'La "Courtoisie" en anglo-normand,' in *Orbis Mediaevalis: Mélanges. . . . offerts à R. R. Bezzola* (Bern, 1977).
Lehoux, F.,	*Jean de France, duc de Berri. Sa Vie. Son action politique* (1340–1416), Vols. 1 and 2 (Paris, 1966).
Lepage, Y. G.,	'La dislocation de la vision allégorique dans la *Messe des Oisiaus* de Jean de Condé,' *Romanische Forschungen*, 91 (1979), 43–9.
Levarie, S.,	*Guillaume de Machaut* (New York, 1954).
Lewis, C. S.,	*The Allegory of Love* (Oxford, 1936).
Lossing, M.,	'The Prologue to the *Legend of Good Women* and the *Lai de Franchise*,' *SP*, 39 (1942), 15–35.
Lowes, J. L.,	'The Prologue to the *Legend of Good Women* as

	Related to the French *Marguerite* Poems, and the *Filostrato*,' *PMLA*, 19 (1904), 593–683.
——,	'Chaucer and the *Ovide moralisé*,' *PMLA*, 33 (1918), 302–25.
Mathew, G.,	*The Court of Richard II* (London, 1968).
Machabey, A.,	*Guillaume de Machault, 130?–1377. La Vie et l'Oeuvre musicale*, 2 vols. (Paris, 1955).
McKisack, M.,	*The Fourteenth Century (1307–1399)* (Oxford, 1959).
McLeod, E.,	*The Order of the Rose; The Life and Ideas of Christine de Pizan* (London, 1976).
Meech, S. B.,	'Chaucer and the *Ovide Moralisé*: A Further Study,' *PMLA*, 46 (1931), 182–204.
Meiss, M.,	*French Painting in the Time of Jean de Berry; The Late 14th Century and the Patronage of the Duke*, 2 vols. (London, 1967).
Morawski, J.,	*Proverbes français antérieurs au XVe siècle* (Paris, 1925).
Muscatine, C,	*Chaucer and the French Tradition* (Berkeley, 1957).
Neilson, W. A.,	*Origins and Sources of 'The Court of Love'*, Harvard Studies, 6 (Boston, 1899).
Nitzsche, J. C.,	*The Genius Figure in Antiquity and the Middle Ages* (New York, 1975).
Nolan, B.,	*The Gothic Visionary Perspective* (Princeton, 1977).
Olson, G.,	'Deschamps' *Art de dictier* and Chaucer's Literary Environment,' *Speculum*, 48 (1973), 714–23.
Palmer, J. H.,	'The Historical Context of the *Book of the Duchess*: A Revision,' *ChauR*, 8 (1973–4), 253–61.
Patch, H. R.,	*The Goddess Fortuna in Medieval Literature* (Cambridge, Mass., 1927).
Paterson, L. M.,	*Troubadours and Eloquence* (Oxford, 1975).
Payen, J. C.,	*Le Motif du repentir dans la littérature française médiévale* (Geneva, 1968).
Payne, R. O.,	*The Key of Remembrance: A Study of Chaucer's Poetics* (New Haven, 1963).
Pelen, M. M.,	'Machaut's Court of Love Narratives and Chaucer's *Book of the Duchess*,' *ChauR*, 11 (1976–77), 128–55.
Pickering, F. P.,	*Literature and Art in the Middle Ages* (Glasgow, 1970).
Picoche, J.,	*Le vocabulaire psychologique dans les chroniques de Froissart* (Paris, 1976).
Poirion, D.,	*Le Poète et le Prince: L'évolution du lyrisme courtois de Guillaume de Machaut à Charles d'Orléans* (Paris, 1965).
——,	*Le Moyen Age: II. 1300–1480.* (Paris, 1971).
Preston, R.,	'Chaucer and the *Ballades Notées* of Guillaume de Machaut,' *Speculum*, 26 (1951), 615–23.
Prioult, A.,	'Un poète voyageur: Guillaume de Machaut et la *Reise* de Jean l'Aveugle, roi de Bohême, en 1328–1329,' *Lettres Romanes*, 4 (1950), 3–29.
Reaney, G.,	*Guillaume de Machaut* (London, 1971).

Ribard, J.,   *Un Ménestrel du XIVe siècle: Jean de Condé* (Geneva, 1969).

Robertson, D. W., Jr.,   *A Preface to Chaucer* (Princeton, 1962).

——,   'The Historical Setting of Chaucer's *Book of the Duchess*,' in *Mediaeval Studies in Honor of U. T. Holmes* (Chapel Hill, 1965), pp. 169–95.

Rosenthal, C. L.,   'A Possible Source of Chaucer's *Book of the Duchess – Li Regret de Guillaume* by Jehan de la Mote,' *MLN*, 48 (1933), 511–4.

Rothwell, W.,   'The Teaching of French in Medieval England,' *MLR*, 63 (1968), 37–46.

——,   'The Role of French in Thirteenth Century England,' *BJRL*, 58 (1975), 445–66.

Severs, J. B.,   'The Sources of "The Book of the Duchess",' *MS*, 25 (1963), 355–62.

Seznec, J.,   *The Survival of the Pagan Gods* (New York, 1953).

Shears, F. S.,   *Froissart: Chronicler and Poet* (London, 1930).

Spearing, A. C.,   *Medieval Dream-Poetry* (Cambridge, 1976).

Steadman, J. M.,   ' "Courtly Love" as a Problem of Style,' in *Chaucer und seine Zeit*, ed. A. Esch (Tübingen, 1968), pp. 1–33.

Suggett, H.,   'The Use of French in the Later Middle Ages,' in *Essays in Medieval History*, ed. R. W. Southern (London, 1968), pp. 213–39.

Sypherd, W. O.,   *Studies in Chaucer's Hous of Fame* (London, 1907).

Tavani, G.,   'Il dibattito sul chierico e il cavaliere nella tradizione mediolatina e volgare,' *Romantisches Jahrbuch*, 15 (1964), 51–84.

Thiébaux, M.,   'An Unpublished Allegory of the Hunt of Love: *Li dis dou cerf amoreus*,' *SP*, 62 (1965), 531–45.

Topsfield, L. T.,   *Troubadours and Love* (Cambridge, 1975).

——,   *Chrétien de Troyes* (Cambridge, 1981).

Uitti, K. D.,   'Remarks on Old French Narrative: Courtly Love and Poetic Form (II),' *Romance Philology*, 28 (1974), 190–9.

——,   'From *Clerc* to *Poète*: The Relevance of the *Romance of the Rose* to Machaut's World,' in Cosman and Chandler, pp. 209–16.

Varty, K.,   'Deschamps's *Art de dictier*,' *French Studies*, 19 (1965), 164–7.

Vesce, T. E.,   'Love as Found in Machaut's *Dit dou Lyon*,' *Romance Notes*, 11 (1969), 174–80.

West, C. B.,   *Courtoisie in Anglo-Norman Literature* (Oxford, 1938).

Wetherbee, W. P.,   'The Function of Poetry in the "De planctu Naturae" of Alain de Lille,' *Traditio*, 25 (1969), 87–125.

——,   *Platonism and Poetry in the Twelfth Century: the Literary Influence of the School of Chartres* (Princeton, 1972).

Whiting, B. J.,   'Proverbial Material in the Poems of Baudouin and

Jean de Condé,' *Romanic Review*, 27 (1936), 204–33.

——, 'Froissart as Poet,' *MS*, 8 (1946), 189–216.

Wilkins, N. E., 'Structure of Ballades, Rondeaux and Virelais in Froissart and in Christine de Pisan,' *French Studies*, 23 (1969), 337–48.

——, *Music in the Age of Chaucer* (Cambridge, 1979).

Williams, S. J., 'An Author's Role in Fourteenth-Century Book Production: Guillaume de Machaut's "Livre ou je met toutes mes choses",' *Romania*, 90 (1969), 433–54.

Williams, S. J. M., 'Machaut's Self-Awareness as Author and Producer,' in Cosman and Chandler, pp. 189–97.

Wimsatt, J. I., *Chaucer and the French Love Poets* (Chapel Hill, 1968).

——, *The Marguerite Poetry of Guillaume de Machaut* (Chapel Hill, 1970).

——, 'The Apotheosis of Blanche in the *Book of The Duchess*,' *JEGP*, 66 (1967), 26–44.

——, 'The Sources of Chaucer's "Seys and Alcyone",' *Medium Aevum*, 36 (1967), 231–41.

——, 'The *Dit dou Bleu Chevalier*: Froissart's Imitation of Chaucer,' *MS*, 34 (1972), 388–400.

——, 'Chaucer and French Poetry,' in *Geoffrey Chaucer (Writers and their Background)*, ed. D. Brewer (London, 1974), pp. 109–36.

——, 'Machaut's *Lay de Comfort* and Chaucer's *Book of the Duchess*,' in *Chaucer at Albany*, ed. R. H. Robbins (New York, 1975), pp. 11–26.

——, 'Guillaume de Machaut and Chaucer's Love Lyrics,' *Medium Aevum*, 47 (1978), 66–87.

Winny, J., *Chaucer's Dream-Poems* (London, 1973).

Zumthor, P., *Essai de poétique médiévale* (Paris, 1972).

——, *Langue, texte, énigme* (Paris, 1975).

ADDENDA

Kellogg, A. L. and Cox, R. C. 'Chaucer's St Valentine: A Conjecture,' in A. L. Kellogg, *Chaucer, Langland, Arthur* (New Brunswick, 1972).

Oruch, J. B. 'St Valentine, Chaucer, and Spring in February,' *Speculum*, 56 (1981), 534–65.

Index of Personal Names

'The Book of the Duchess':
An Index of Parallels

[The following list cites those parallels between the *Book of the Duchess* and its French sources and analogues which are indicated in the footnotes to the translations of *Le Jugement dou Roy de Behaingne* (*JRB*), *Le Dit de la Fonteinne Amoureuse* (*FA*), the *Remede de Fortune* (*RF*), *Le Dit dou Lyon* (*DL*), and *Le Paradys d'Amours* (*PA*)].

Book of the Duchess:	*Sources and analogues:*
1–15, 23	*PA*, p. 41
39–43	*RF*, p. 64; *DL*, p. 66
166–9	*PA*, p. 42
242–7	*PA*, p. 42
249ff.	*FA*, p. 33
339–43	*JRB*, p. 3
388–97	*JRB*, p. 17; *DL*, p. 68
397ff.	*JRB*, p. 4; *DL*, p. 66
452–4	*JRB*, p. 4
475–86	*JRB*, p. 6
487ff.	*JRB*, p. 6
502ff.	*JRB*, p. 4
523–8	*JRB*, p. 4
532ff.	*JRB*, p. 5
560–6	*JRB*, p. 5
599ff.	*JRB*, p. 6
600	*RF*, p. 64
620–1	*RF*, p. 63
622	*RF*, p. 63
633–4	*RF*, p. 63
635	*RF*, p. 63
642	*RF*, p. 63
645–9	*JRB*, p. 16
659–60	*RF*, p. 63
673–4	*RF*, p. 63
749–52	*JRB*, p. 7
759–63	*JRB*, p. 7
764–70	*JRB*, p. 5
771–6	*JRB*, p. 7
778	*RF*, p. 59
779–83	*RF*, p. 58
785–90	*RF*, p. 58
793–6	*RF*, p. 58
797–804	*RF*, p. 59
805–13	*JRB*, p. 7
817ff.	*JRB*, p. 7

Book of the Duchess:	Sources and analogues:
833–4	*RF*, p. 60
835–6	*RF*, p. 59
837–41	*RF*, p. 59
848–54	*JRB*, p. 8
855–8	*JRB*, p. 8
859–74	*JRB*, p. 8
895ff.	*JRB*, p. 8
904–5	*JRB*, p. 8
908–12	*JRB*, p. 9
912–3	*JRB*, p. 9
918	*JRB*, p. 11
919ff.	*RF*, p. 61
939–47	*JRB*, p. 9
949–51	*RF*, p. 59
952–60	*JRB*, p. 9
968–74	*RF*, p. 60
1024–33	*DL*, p. 69
1035–41	*JRB*, p. 5
1054ff.	*RF*, p. 60
1088–93	*RF*, p. 59
1095–7	*RF*, p. 60
1101	*RF*, p. 59
1102–7	*RF*, p. 62
1108–11	*RF*, p. 60; *DL*. p. 67
1146–51	*RF*, p. 62
1155–7	*RF*, p. 63
1183–91	*JRB*, p. 10
1192–3	*JRB*, p. 10
1195–8	*JRB*, p. 10
1203ff.	*JRB*, p. 10
1219–20	*JRB*, p. 10
1226–30	*JRB*, p. 12
1236–8	*JRB*, p. 11
1241–4	*JRB*, p. 11
1258–67	*JRB*, p. 11
1269–70	*JRB*, p. 12
1275–8	*JRB*, p. 12
1289–97	*JRB*, p. 6

PACE UNIVERSITY LIBRARY
New York, NY 10038

TO THE BORROWER:
The use of this book is governed by rules
established in the broad interest of the university
community. It is your responsibility to know these
rules. Please inquire at the circulation desk.

JUN.   1985